Why am I still depressed?

Why am I still depressed?

Recognizing and Managing the Ups and Downs of Bipolar II and Soft Bipolar Disorder

Jim Phelps, M.D.

New York   Chicago   San Francisco   Lisbon   London   Madrid   Mexico City
Milan   New Delhi   San Juan   Seoul   Singapore   Sydney   Toronto

The **McGraw·Hill** Companies

Library of Congress Cataloging-in-Publication Data

Phelps, James R., 1953–.
    Why am I still depressed? : recognizing and managing the ups and downs of bipolar II
and soft bipolar disorder / Jim Phelps.
        p.   cm.
    Includes biographical references.
    ISBN 0-07-146237-6
    1. Manic-depressive illness—Popular works.   2. Depression—Popular works.
I. Title.

RC516.P55   2006
616.85'27—dc22   2006000672

    13 14 15 16 17 18 19 20 21 22 23   QFR/QFR 1 5

ISBN-13: 978-0-07-146237-2
ISBN-10:   0-07-146237-6

McGraw-Hill books are available at special quantity discounts to use as premiums and sales
promotions, or for use in corporate training programs. For more information, please write to
the Director of Special Sales, Professional Publishing, McGraw-Hill, Two Penn Plaza, New York,
NY 10121-2298. Or contact your local bookstore.

Every effort has been made to ensure that the information contained in this book is complete
and accurate. However, the ideas, treatments, medications, procedures, and other
suggestions contained in this book are not intended as a substitute for consulting with your
physician. All matters regarding your physical health require medical supervision. Neither the
author not the publisher shall be liable or responsible for any loss, injury, or damage allegedly
arising from any information or suggestion in this book.

This book is printed on acid-free paper.

To Anna-Maria, the fixed foot of my compass

Contents

Foreword

A patient told me the other day: "I don't expect to be happy; I just don't want to be depressed." We should be doing better, and part of the solution, I think, is to move away from simple-minded diagnoses and prescriptions about depression.

There is so much antidepressant use these days that Prozac is literally in the water in detectable amounts, leading to some environmental concerns regarding the effects on fish.[1] Yet the treatment of depression is not as effective as it should be. One is tempted to recall the ironically prescient words of the nineteenth-century physician Oliver Wendell Holmes who said that "if the entire *materia medica*, as now used, could be sunk to the bottom of the sea, it would be all the better for mankind—and all the worse for the fishes."[2] It turns out that antidepressants are not the panacea that many once thought. One reason is that antidepressants are not always antidepressants. In some persons, like those with bipolar illness, they may not work well and in fact can make things worse.

The key issue in diagnosing and treating depression is to know what kind of depression one faces. Is it vanilla—straight, regular, "unipolar" depression—or is it chocolate—depression with mood swings, manic symptoms, "bipolar" depression? And if bipolar, is it standard bipolar disorder—classic manic-depressive illness with extremes of high and low—or is it a variety of the bipolar "spec-

1. http://www.cnn.com/2003/TECH/science/11/14/coolsc.frogs.fish
2. Holmes OW: Medical essays 1842–1882. Boston: Houghton Mifflin, 1891

trum"—recurrent depression with milder highs or other features of bipolar illness?

To understand depression, to treat it, and to recover from it, we really need to understand more about the two varieties and especially the bipolar spectrum. This is not a straightforward topic; a great deal of controversy rages in academe, and it has for decades, a sure sign of our ignorance. We have not understood this disease well: depression in all its varieties. We have not studied and examined the bipolar spectrum concept as well as we should. We do not clearly understand, beyond a reasonable doubt, when to use antidepressants and when not to use them. Yet recognizing our lack of knowledge, and increasing our awareness of these problems, is the first step forward.

In the daily work of clinical practice, this awareness of our limitations paradoxically opens new vistas in the diagnosis and treatment of depression. Not all depression is the same, and not all depression responds to antidepressants. In *Why Am I Still Depressed?* Jim Phelps provides a nuanced and clinically wise rendition of the state of the art. Here he describes the varieties of depression, the concept of the bipolar spectrum, the utility and limitations of antidepressants, the benefits and limits of mood-stabilizing agents, and, perhaps most importantly, how to put it all together. He does all this from the standpoint of a highly informed practicing psychiatrist, someone who observes the academic wars, and then sees what they mean in the daily treatment of patients.

Phelps's book, though clear and concise, does not avoid complexity—a real complexity that corresponds to the reality of unipolar depression and the bipolar spectrum. Yet he sheds light on that complexity in a way that should be helpful to clinicians and enlightening to persons with depression. While books on depression abound, I have not seen a book of this kind. This is not a typical depression book. One might be tempted, in imitation of William James, to call this a book about "the varieties of depressive experience": a pluralistic, practical book about what we really know and what we really do not know, and how to make decisions anyway, in the face of the limitations of our science, in diagnosing and treating depressive illness.

S. Nassir Ghaemi, M.D., M.P.H.
Director, Bipolar Disorder Research Program
Associate Professor of Psychiatry and Public Health
Emory University, Atlanta, Georgia

Acknowledgments

This is surely first-time author syndrome, wanting to thank *everyone*, starting with my superb high school English teacher Mr. Lavin. But I won't drag you all the way from that point! Most of all I must say thanks to my patients, who through their suffering, their intelligence, and their continued effort to get better have helped me turn research and theory into the practices described here.

However, this book wouldn't have existed without the help of my editor at McGraw-Hill, Natasha Graf. It was her idea, actually, to take my website on this topic and expand it into a book. I am very grateful for her idea and her assistance through this process, especially her masterful reorganization of the first section of the book and her gentle reassurances for a newbie.

Dr. Nassir Ghaemi would have written this book, I'm sure, if he had time. You'll find many references to his work here. He has been utterly gracious with his support, including suggestions on what to include, and what to expand—though if I had followed them all, you'd have a bigger book in your hands. There simply is not enough room in a book like this to present everything he or I would like to include. As a result, this book does not do justice to his research or his thinking, but it's a pretty good start, I think.

Dr. Tammas Kelly, a colleague in Fort Collins, Colorado, also could have written this book. He practically did so with all the hours he spent writing comments on how to improve it. Here, too, I wish I could have incorporated them all. Having another clinician think with me about what to include and how to put it has been wonderful. His sense of humor would have livened things up, if I could figure out how to capture it!

Dr. Rick Bingham, another very good friend and a superb scholar, has listened to me go on and on about the material in this book, with great patience and understanding. His invisible input is prevalent throughout. He could (and maybe someday will) write the child and adolescent version. Or maybe we should just spend more time with our families and our kayaks? Thanks, Rick.

Throughout the book are references to mood disorder research. If you find this book helpful, as I certainly hope you will, then let us together thank the mood specialists who produced the science on which this book is based. In many respects I am merely the presenter of their very hard work, and all I've done is translate that work into a practical guide. I hereby apologize to any of them whose works I've quoted incorrectly!

Good Samaritan Hospital in Corvallis, Oregon, and its director of mental health services, Dr. Mike May, provided an environment that allowed all the ideas you'll find here in this book to grow and organize themselves—even when I was creating trouble in the process! This included a great staff, like Dennise, who would go every extra mile; Judy, who could get anything I needed and make me belly laugh in the process; and a clinical team who continue to work extremely hard for our patients. What looked then like wild ideas are now becoming widely accepted, but I know it took some real commitment to put up with my carrying on about bipolar variations all the time. Good Samaritan has also provided two librarians who continue to place in my hands any research I request. Can you imagine what a luxury that is? Thank you, Dorothy O'Brien and Hope Leman.

The pharmaceutical industry has some very bright spots in Brad, Brad, Kristine, Michelle, Troy, Sharon, Tiffany, Darilyn, and others—who understand what I'm trying to convey and continually try to help me with that effort. They have repeatedly, that's repeatedly, made personal efforts well beyond their job requirements!

The volunteer crew at Bipolar World (bipolarworld.net) has supported me while I learned how to write about bipolar disorders, patiently forwarding questions, formatting answers, and maintaining an amazing archive of letters, all simply from the desire to help others. Would that we had more such people in the world. Thank you, Colleen, Allie, and your friends.

Only for the sake of my readers do I stop here and forgo naming many friends and colleagues, such as my dear residency group and my current collaborators, whose interest and enthusiasm have kept me going and writing. Thank you!

Introduction

Another book about depression? Aren't there enough already? And what about bipolar disorder? Aren't we turning these conditions into easy explanations—and turning too quickly to medications with both short- and long-term risks? What happened to the idea of "pulling yourself up by your bootstraps"? There is some merit in these concerns (certainly about the number of books already available!). At the same time, as a psychiatrist I see patients who have tried many different approaches, on their own and often with the help of their primary care doctor. They have tried medication and nonmedication approaches (including herbs, vitamins, and other alternative therapies), each time with little lasting benefit, and sometimes finding themselves getting worse rather than better. From this experience I believe many, many people can benefit from a different way of thinking about depression.

I ask you, as an invitation into this book, to consider the following: do you have *repeated episodes* of depression? Does your condition sometimes seem *more than depression*? Do you sometimes also have anxiety or irritability? Do you sometimes sleep a few hours then find yourself mostly awake the rest of the night? Do you sometimes have thoughts that just won't stop? Combine any of these symptoms with depression, and you *might* have a condition that could be another form or variation of bipolar disorder.

People with bipolar variations often look depressed, sound depressed, and get diagnosed as depressed. They frequently are treated with antidepressants like fluoxetine (Prozac). But antidepressant medications can make some of these people worse, even to the point of thinking about suicide when they never did before.

Of course, very low mood, energy, and motivation, as in official *Major Depression*, can also be a severe condition. Treatment with antidepressant medications is often very helpful for that. So what is this variation where antidepressants can make things worse? Whereas depression alone causes symptoms such as low energy, low mood, and low motivation, this type of bipolar disorder includes all these *and* some additional complicating factors. As I mentioned previously, these factors can be symptoms such as agitation, irritability, difficulty sleeping, or rapid, unstoppable thoughts. They can also include dramatic swings in mood or energy. Sometimes there is a complicated family background of mood and anxiety symptoms, or many relatives with alcohol problems. Sometimes there may be repeated episodes of depression that end on their own or for which antidepressants work temporarily but then stop working. One of the most important markers is depression that keeps coming back. Most people with true Major Depression will have one or two episodes in a lifetime. Having repeated brief episodes, two or three months long or less, is more likely to be a form of bipolar disorder.

Any of these additional symptoms or signs should raise the possibility that you are dealing with something more complicated than Major Depression. However, notice that we're still talking just about depression, plus some other symptoms. We are *not* talking about "going crazy," manic, psychotic, or losing control of your behavior. But we are talking about an extremely common mood problem. Some mood experts think it might be about one-third of all versions of depression.

The good news is that we have well-known treatments, which often can work as well or better than antidepressants for these bipolar variations. The bad news is that there is tremendous confusion about these variations as a diagnosis. The very doctors whom you'll need to see for treatment sometimes can't agree on what you have. If you get the wrong diagnosis, you can get the wrong treatment, which can actually make your symptoms worse. There is so much confusion about this condition that some doctors are starting to worry that it is being *overdiagnosed*, though the evidence suggests it is being significantly *underdiagnosed*. We'll take a serious look at the consequences of overdiagnosis in Chapter 4, just to make sure all risks are examined.

How This Book Can Help You

Part I of this book focuses on the diagnosis of Mood Spectrum problems. After explaining the details of the Mood Spectrum and how to use this model to figure out your diagnosis, the first section concludes with a brief look at current thinking about what causes bipolar disorder, with links to resources that will stay up-to-date as research in this area proceeds—because fortunately the pace of discovery is accelerating! In the rest of the book, you'll find a series of chapters on getting good treatment for your mood condition. You can use the table of contents and hop around to chapters that may be of most use to you, but read the first three chapters as a group: together they explain the concept of the Mood Spectrum. This way of thinking is used throughout the book.

Additional Information and References

Believe it or not, I've tried to keep most of this book relatively simple. Much more could be said about most of the material in here. Some readers will want further information and references. Initially I tried to provide more detail in a set of chapter notes, but by the end of the book, that section was thirty-five pages long! And the book was over a length limit. Rather than cut material from the book, I've moved this section to my website. I apologize for putting this extra information one electronic step away from your hands. But you'll find a bonus when you get there: direct links to further resources! Just enter this address in your Internet browser: psycheducation.org/notes.htm.

You'll find three kinds of additional information there, organized by chapter, so you can jump easily to the section you're reading.

1. Additional thoughts: some details that might interest only a few readers have been provided here. I encourage you to have a look at least once to see what's available.
2. Links: use these to go to other websites that expand on the chapter you're reading.
3. References: you might think that references are only for professionals. But as you read through this book, you'll see my emphasis on evidence. So much health information is available these days that you need a system for evaluating it. One way to protect yourself from being led astray (usually in the direction of making someone richer) is to require that authors show you evidence for their assertions. I'd like you to have access to the references behind the statements made in this book, especially some of the more crucial or controversial ones. I provide a list of citations at the end of the book; however, thanks to the Internet, I can also give you links to the actual journal article (or at least the article summary, called the abstract). Hopefully, you'll find this much easier than chasing references from a list.

Now on to find out if and where you fit on the Mood Spectrum!

Why am I still depressed?

PART I

Do You Have a "Mild" Form of Bipolar Disorder?

CHAPTER 1

Understanding the Mood Spectrum and How It Can Help You

Most mood experts agree that many people have symptoms that represent more than depression, but less than bipolar disorder. But the official rule book of psychiatric diagnosis, the *Diagnostic and Statistical Manual of Mental Disorders* (*DSM*) has no place for these folks. So a new system has been growing alongside the *DSM* approach. Actually, this "new" system is quite old; it just seems new because of how we doctors have been doing diagnosis for the last fifty years. In this emerging way of thinking, diagnoses like depression and bipolar disorder are seen as the ends of a *spectrum* (as seen in Figure 1.1), and people can be found all along this continuum.

As you can see, at one end is *unipolar* depression (which the *DSM* calls Major Depression), and on the other is *bipolar* (which we're going to examine in more detail shortly). But what, you

FIGURE 1.1 The Mood Spectrum

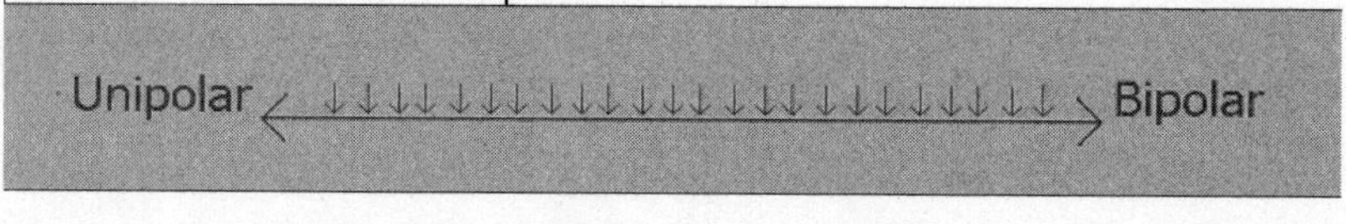

Unipolar ⟵ ↓↓↓↓↓↓↓↓↓↓↓↓↓↓↓↓↓↓↓↓↓↓↓ ⟶ Bipolar

may ask, happened to *manic-depressive*? The condition formerly called *manic-depressive disorder* is the most extreme form of a whole group of mood conditions now referred to as *bipolar disorders*. This condition is characterized by mania, which can include delusions, hallucinations, paranoia, and all sorts of problem behaviors. Whoa, stop right there! This book is not about mania, OK? It is about the rest of the Mood Spectrum, which by definition does not include mania.

Understanding the Middle of the Mood Spectrum

Because most people think of mania when they hear "bipolar disorder," the idea that a person might have something *related* to bipolar disorder, even if so mild as to be nearly at the other end of the spectrum, is frightening. You might react to the idea by saying, "Me? Hey, I know what *manic* means, and I *know* I've never had that." But you may not know about all the other bipolar versions in the middle of the Mood Spectrum. You may only know about the most extreme form of bipolar disorder and not the subtle variations that can look much more like plain depression.

Wow, that's a lot of terms already: *unipolar*, *major depression*, *bipolar*, *manic*, and *bipolar variations*. Does it matter that much what you call it? Oh, definitely, and here's why. Antidepressant medications can make bipolar disorder worse. They can cause people to have a manic episode, including not only the positive, or *euphoric*, version where you feel "on top of the world," very confident, and full of potential, but also the negative, or *dysphoric*, version where you feel agitated and angry, and believe that the people around you are stupid, slow, and pathetic.

Negative version of mania? This may be a new idea for you, but it is not a new idea for psychiatrists, who have long recognized that mania is not always a euphoric experience. Although most people associate the idea of mania with feeling good (much too good, in fact), another version of mania is harsh and unpleasant. This version shares the *acceleration* of the euphoric version, with very rapid thinking, rapid action, and intense, powerful passions.

But there is nothing euphoric about it; in fact, it is quite the opposite and thus the term *dysphoric*. Anger and worry are often very prominent.

Unknown to many people, the negative version is at least as common as the euphoric version. Even less known to most people is that the negative version of mania can occur *at the same time* as depression symptoms, as you'll see in Chapter 2. This *mixed state* is known to carry a high risk of suicide. Most mood experts believe that antidepressants given to someone who has bipolar disorder can cause dysphoric mania and mixed states. This phenomenon is one reason why the U.S. Food and Drug Administration (FDA) recommended that everyone given an antidepressant should be screened for bipolar disorder. As you may have heard, the FDA evaluated reports of people who committed suicide shortly after starting an antidepressant. The FDA concluded that at least some of this risk comes from people who look like they have Major Depression (unipolar), but actually have bipolar disorder and receive antidepressants only to end up in an agitated mixed state. The sidebar presents an example of this state, induced by an antidepressant.

Figuring Out the Real Cause of Her Symptoms: Ruth's Story

Ruth is a thirty-nine-year-old woman with two kids and a very good job. She has always had strong feelings about the way she wants things to be. Indeed, she knows she can get a bit obsessive about keeping things organized. She occasionally would have to go back and check to make sure things were done right, such as checking to make sure the stove had been turned off or the door locked. Her doctor thought she had an obsessive-compulsive pattern of behavior, although this had never bothered her enough to seek treatment.

(continued)

Figuring Out the Real Cause of Her Symptoms: Ruth's Story, *continued*

Then she began to have phases of depression as well. Therefore, hoping to treat both depression and the mild obsessive-compulsive–like behaviors, the doctor prescribed a medication known to work for both conditions, an antidepressant. The change in her mood state that she described to me in a letter began, in her recollection, after the first dose of the antidepressant:

It isn't just hate, it's also a complete lack of caring. I can't seem to get out of it. And, unfortunately, this feeling of hate and indifference makes me completely uninterested in trying to fix it. I hate my life—what it is, what it isn't, and what it is, or isn't, becoming. I hate marriage, feel no interest in having one. I hate being around people, wish I could just be completely alone. The feelings of hurting myself are starting to come more frequently now—but I haven't so far. I never had them until a few months ago . . . I've never felt like I wanted to die before—sometimes only because of my kids—but nonetheless, I wouldn't ever do it. Yet I don't feel anymore like there is any convincing reason why I shouldn't. Why is this happening?

Ruth was referred to me at this point. After reviewing her history, I started her on a mood stabilizer (the medications used to treat bipolar disorder, discussed further in Chapter 8). The medication helped, and fortunately quite quickly. She is now taking a full dose of one mood stabilizer and a low dose of another, and she has been doing very well for three years since the preceding episode.

Though her name and details have been changed to make sure she cannot be identified (as for all patient stories in this book), Ruth's story is an important example of how diagnosis really does matter.

The *DSM* Versus the Mood Spectrum

To understand the importance of a spectrum way of thinking about psychiatric diagnosis, it is important to understand the current, somewhat opposite system of the *DSM*. The spectrum system sees conditions on a continuum, as in Figure 1.1. The *DSM* sees conditions as defined by the presence or absence of specific findings. Consider, for example, the *DSM* criteria for Major Depression, which, believe it or not, I've simplified here:

A. At least one of the following three abnormal moods significantly interfered with the person's life:
   1. Abnormal depressed mood
   2. Abnormal loss of all interests and pleasure
   3. Abnormal irritable mood if person is eighteen or younger
B. At least five of the following symptoms have been present during the same two-week depressed period:
   1. Abnormal depressed mood
   2. Abnormal loss of all interest and pleasure
   3. Appetite or weight disturbance, either:
      * Abnormal weight loss (when not dieting) or decrease in appetite
      * Abnormal weight gain or increase in appetite
   4. Sleep disturbance, either abnormal insomnia or abnormal hypersomnia
   5. Activity disturbance, either abnormal agitation or abnormal slowing
   6. Abnormal fatigue or loss of energy
   7. Abnormal self-reproach or inappropriate guilt
   8. Abnormal poor concentration or indecisiveness
   9. Abnormal morbid thoughts of death (not just fear of dying) or suicide
C. The symptoms are *not* due to a mood–*in*congruent psychosis.

D. There has *never* been a Manic Episode, a Mixed Episode, or a Hypomanic Episode.

E. The symptoms are *not* due to physical illness, alcohol, medication, or street drugs.

F. The symptoms are *not* due to normal bereavement.

As you can see, the *DSM* criteria are not particularly user-friendly. They look oddly precise and yet arbitrary. For example, according to the *DSM* criteria for bipolar disorder, a manic episode must last at least seven days. Well, what should be done if someone's manic episode lasts six and a half days? Is this not bipolar?

However, the *DSM* actually does serve several useful purposes. For one thing, it is an important tool in research settings. Doctors in Pittsburgh, Pennsylvania, can study Major Depression and compare their results with doctors studying Major Depression in Dallas, Texas, and assume that they are studying roughly the same thing. Clinicians like me (who see patients most of the day, most days a week, as opposed to a researcher, who generally sees a lot fewer patients per week) can read their published research and apply the results to a similar set of patients in their own practice.

In addition, the *DSM* categories, such as Major Depression and Bipolar Disorder, can be used as a common language by all who understand its diagnostic rules. This enables doctors and therapists to converse easily using a common set of assumptions about broad diagnostic categories.

Because the *DSM* has value in these ways, we should not ridicule it or throw it out. We just have to recognize its limitations, and recognize that the spectrum model described in this book has some advantages as a way of seeing.

There is a term for this way of thinking about models, such as the *DSM* versus the Mood Spectrum, called *heuristics*. In plain English, it means something like this: Make an educated guess, and see how it works. Try a certain way of thinking or looking at a problem. If using that guess or model seems to lead to better outcomes, keep using it. If not, try another. The next section explains how the Mood Spectrum concept is a useful tool in just this way.

The Mood Spectrum: Just a Different Way of Thinking

In the *DSM* mode of thinking, making an accurate diagnosis requires determining whether the patient with depression symptoms is *unipolar* or *bipolar*, whereas in the Mood Spectrum approach, we clinicians don't ask *what* might be the most accurate label for you. Instead, we ask *where* might your symptoms lie on the Mood Spectrum. The Bipolar Clinic at Harvard's teaching hospital recently began using a system like this, which they call the Bipolarity Index. Instead of saying "yes" or "no" as to whether you might have a bipolar disorder, they try to determine *how much bipolarity you have.* (More about the Bipolarity Index appears in Chapter 3.) But just in case you're starting to feel lost in all the lingo and ways of thinking, remember this. Your diagnosis has two main functions:

1. To help guide you to effective treatment
2. To offer some clues about your future (such as, Will this go away? How bad could it get? Will it come again? or Might my children get it?)

Some people can find themselves in the middle of a debate between doctors about what they have, where neither diagnostic function is occurring. Unfortunately, as you may have experienced, this unipolar-or-bipolar debate can become quite intense. When doctors disagree, the patient can be stuck in the middle, which is never good. If that happens, everyone needs to relax and remember that diagnoses are merely best estimates of reality, not reality itself. Diagnoses are heuristic: they are supposed to help us, not make the process more difficult! Ten years from now, I hope the understanding of mood disorders will have improved so much that our present views will be an embarrassment: "Look how confused we were!"

Using the Mood Spectrum to Diagnose Bipolar Variations

In Figure 1.1, you saw arrows indicating people evenly distributed all the way along a Mood Spectrum. But is this really so? Are there really people at all points along this continuum, or are there natural gaps separating one diagnostic group from another? This very idea was studied by Dr. Franco Benazzi, a mood researcher in Italy who found no such gaps. While this is just a single study, his work suggests that no natural cutoff can be found when trying to distinguish unipolar disorder from bipolar disorder. So there must be a "mixing zone" in the middle where bipolar symptoms have diminished, and finally a point at which they diminish to zero. Thus with a Mood Spectrum way of looking at things, one can have "a little bipolarity." While this might strike you as strange, it's what this very chapter is about—so read on.

Yes, you can have "a little bipolarity," so little that you might not have even wondered if you had manic depression or bipolar disorder. But here's why you *should* wonder: perhaps you have enough bipolarity that antidepressants carry more risk for you than in people who are more unipolar than you. Perhaps you have enough bipolarity that you might do better with the treatment approaches used for people who are more obviously bipolar than you.

Naming and Understanding the Different Types of Bipolar Disorder

As you continue to learn about the Mood Spectrum in this book and from other sources, such as the Internet, you will encounter different labels for bipolar variations. There are two current labels for "a little bipolarity." Chapter 2 looks at one way, called *hypomania*, especially subtle hypomania. Chapter 3 looks at another way that has been called *soft bipolar disorder* and also examines how *bipolar* blends into *normal*. Finally, we'll get to the making of *your* diagnosis in Chapter 4. However, first let's take moment to get these names straight. The official bipolar subtypes are often depicted with a diagram such as Figure 1.2. The boxes below the line depict depression, and the ones above the line depict hypomanic or manic symptoms. The severity of symptoms is shown by the height of the box.

Bipolar I (Mania)

Bipolar I (Mania) is the combination of full manic symptoms (detailed in Chapter 2) as well as full depressive symptoms. When the manic episodes are primarily euphoric, this is often called *classic bipolar disorder*. This version was formerly known as *manic-depressive disorder*; though euphoric mania is what most people think of when they hear the word *bipolar*. But, as you are learning in this book, the reality of bipolar disorder is vastly more diverse and complex.

Bipolar II (Hypomania)

Although the term *hypomania* was informally used for many years, it wasn't until the 1994 edition of the *DSM* that it became an offi-

FIGURE 1.2 Official Bipolar Subtypes

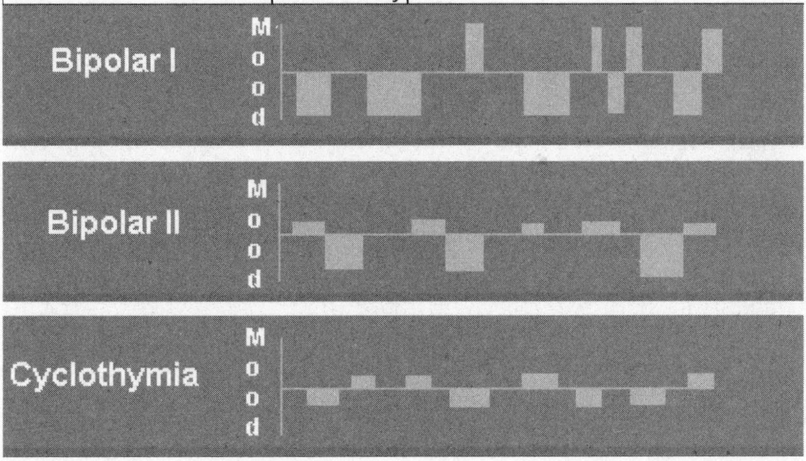

cial term. If you recognize the Greek prefix *hypo* as meaning "under or less than," you can figure out that *hypomania* means "a little mania." That's pretty close: manic symptoms, but less severe and sometimes shorter.

By definition, Bipolar II includes the most common set of symptoms found on the spectrum, namely the combination of hypomania and *full* depressive symptoms. The term Bipolar II is often used to refer to the entire spectrum between Bipolar I and unipolar. However, as you'll read in Chapter 2, hypomania has many variations. Granted, this chapter shows that people can indeed be "a little bipolar" by having just a little hypomania. But *having severe hypomania is not little*. It may be as bad as or worse than having mania itself. The suicide rate in Bipolar II is as high as, and in some studies higher than, in Bipolar I. Watching patients go through the agitation that comes with severe hypomania, one can understand this research finding.

The trick is to remember that manic episodes can be a very negative experience. Roughly half the time that people are manic, the experience is not euphoric, or full of great confidence, joy, hope, and pleasure, but dysphoric, where people experience most sensory input as harsh and unpleasant (lights are too bright, noises are too loud); their thoughts are rapid, intense, and often extremely negative and angry; and they find other people to be too slow, stupid, and irritating. This is also true in hypomania. Many clinicians think that patients like their hypomania and will conceal it, or even fail to recognize it as abnormal. This may be somewhat true for subtle forms of hypomania, but much less so for severe hypomania. People do indeed recognize their agitation, insomnia, and acceleration. When they find something that makes it stop, they are generally very inclined to stick with that solution (managing alcohol or avoiding late night light, as discussed in Chapter 11, or using mood stabilizers, which are discussed in Chapter 8), unless the solution comes with significant problems of its own. Fortunately, clinicians now have many treatment options and can often find one that does not place the patient in this dilemma of choosing between symptoms and side effects.

Cyclothymia

Even though *Cyclothymia* is also an official term in the *DSM*, this diagnosis is rarely used. Because it is characterized by mild depression, in distinction to the full depressions associated with Bipolar II, there may be a natural avoidance of this term by both patients and doctors alike who may hesitate to label such mild symptoms, particularly with a bipolar name.

Bipolar NOS (Not Otherwise Specified)

The *DSM* uses the *NOS* label for conditions that don't meet the criteria of the official labels. Thus there are also Depression NOS, Anxiety NOS, Psychosis NOS, and so forth. Bipolar NOS is supposed to describe patients who have some bipolar features, but do not qualify for a particular bipolar variant recognized by the *DSM*. In practice the *NOS* label sometimes may be used so the practitioner doesn't have to be more specific about exactly which kind of bipolar disorder is involved. In addition, because the very name is rather vague, some doctors—and perhaps patients—think less stigma might be associated with this particular label. Although clinicians are not supposed to do this, I know they sometimes even use Depression NOS for patients with bipolar features that might otherwise be coded Bipolar II, hoping that Depression NOS is the least stigmatizing of all these labels.

Soft Bipolar

The term *Soft Bipolar Spectrum* was introduced in 1987. This is not a *DSM* label, but it has been used to refer to the entire collection of bipolar variations that do not make themselves obvious through mania. As noted earlier, obvious symptoms are more likely to be recognized by multiple observers, creating a *hard* finding that can anchor efforts at diagnosis. By contrast, less obvious symptoms leave clinicians basing a patient's diagnosis on less firm ground, thus the term *soft bipolar*. This term is sometimes used quite generally to refer to any bipolar variant where the data supporting the diagnosis are not hard, or easily recognized and agreed upon.

I hope you're already concluding that making a firm diagnosis of bipolar disorder can be very difficult, and similarly, that firmly ruling out bipolarity may be even more difficult. What is a diagnostician—or you—to do? One defense against this confusion is to learn more about bipolar variations, as presented in the next two chapters.

CHAPTER 2

Can You Be a Little Bipolar? Recognizing Hypomania

This chapter details what hypomania *really* looks like, but let's first clarify the official *DSM* definitions—before muddying the waters with reality! People sometimes forget that the *DSM* definitions are not supposed to represent reality. Rather, they represent ideal types, classic forms that anchor clinical descriptions in accepted terms and help create a system for looking at mental conditions. From there, it is up to clinicians to interpret individual patient's experiences. That is where the Mood Spectrum model can be useful.

In the *DSM* system, the list of symptoms for hypomania is exactly the same as the list for mania. I hate that. Here I am, trying to convince you that you can have "a little bipolarity," and yet I have to show you a list of symptoms that I know in advance are not you! How ironic: the very people I'm writing this book for may not have many of the following symptoms. (As you'll see in Chapter 3, a person may actually have none of these symptoms and still have some bipolarity.) So remember, do not look at the following list and reject the whole story I'm telling you. Read on in this chapter to see what hypomania looks like when it is subtle.

However, let's start with the symptom list, because it is the same for hypomania and mania. Then we'll look at the official differences between the two.

The *DSM* system requires at least three items from the following list, in addition to a mood shift ("elevated, expansive, or irritable") that is clearly different from the person's usual state:

1. Inflated self-esteem or *grandiosity*
2. Decreased need for *sleep* (feels rested after only three hours of sleep)
3. More *talkative* than usual or feels pressure to keep talking
4. Flight of ideas or subjective experience that thoughts are *racing*
5. *Distractibility* (attention is too easily drawn to unimportant or irrelevant external stimuli)
6. Increase in goal-directed *activity* (either socially, at work or school, or sexually) or psychomotor agitation
7. Excessive involvement in pleasurable activities that have a high potential for *painful consequences* (the person engages in unrestrained buying sprees, sexual indiscretions, or foolish business investments).

As you can see, none of these is so unusual as to be clearly abnormal by itself. Indeed, that is the very theme of this chapter: *there is no dividing line* between "normal" and hypomania. This is reflected in Figure 2.1, which shows the gradually increasing symptoms of hypomania across the Mood Spectrum.

FIGURE 2.1 "Mania" Across the Spectrum

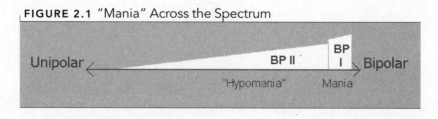

The Difference Between Hypomania and Mania

Two features of hypomania officially distinguish it from mania:

1. It only needs to last four days to be official, whereas mania must last a week.
2. It is not severe enough to cause marked impairment in social or occupational functioning, whereas mania does do just that.

I'm cheating a little here: I left out two features to keep things simpler. The rules of the *DSM* also say that hypomania is not associated with *psychosis*. Therefore, if a person has lost contact with reality, that person by definition has mania. Also, hypomania is not supposed to necessitate *hospitalization*; only mania does that. However, psychosis generally is extremely impairing in social or occupational functioning, and getting hospitalized nowadays is almost by definition a matter of impaired social or occupational functioning. So I didn't cheat much by not including these features.

The time duration (four days versus a week) is thought by many mood experts to be far too long, because in real life hypomanic symptoms can frequently last a much shorter period of time. For example, a version of hypomania (or even mania) lasting less than a day is so well recognized that it even has its own name, *ultradian cycling* (discussed later in this chapter), which has even been associated with a particular gene. In other words, the required time duration for hypomania is not very well respected as a criterion for making the diagnosis; rather, it is frequently ignored, and it does not appear to reflect current research findings.

Thus the primary distinction between hypomania and mania comes down to the phrase "marked impairment in social and occupational functioning." Leaves a bit of room for interpretation, wouldn't you say? If a person is going to work and is so good at it that he or she can operate at half-speed and still get enough work done to keep her boss at least minimally satisfied, is that "impaired occupational functioning"? Like so many other features of bipolarity, this impairment, too, exists on a *spectrum*, from utterly nonfunctional to mildly impaired. Thus when we look closely we find that the *DSM* rules cannot easily be used to make the distinction between hypomania and mania.

We'll look at this ramp of hypomania, including the point on the left side where it disappears, in just a moment. But while we're here, let's get a few more details straight. There is some reason to think that Bipolar II, characterized in the *DSM* system by hypomania, really is different from Bipolar I, characterized by mania. It turns out that whichever version runs in a family tends to continue in that family: Bipolar II parents, if their children are affected, have Bipolar II kids. Bipolar I parents, if their children are affected, have Bipolar I kids (in general, with a few exceptions). This genetic pattern has been referred to as breeding true. Bipolar I is also somewhat more responsive to lithium than other bipolar variations. The latter can benefit from lithium, but not quite with the frequency of Bipolar I. This discontinuity in the Mood Spectrum is shown as a small step-down in Figure 2.1. Note that otherwise, hypomania varies in a smooth, continuous ramp, with no natural cutoff points as it diminishes toward zero.

What Does Hypomania Really Look Like? Identifying Symptoms

Rules, words, diagrams—what does all this look like in real life, in clinical practice? Let's pick several points along this ramp of hypomania and see what a particular person like you might experience, depending on your position on the ramp. This is like drilling into the ground in your backyard and bringing up cores of soil. We'll sample four different "drill cores," or points along the ramp of hypomania—"not present," "mild," "moderate," and "severe"—shown as points A through D in Figure 2.2.

But don't forget—this is a continuous spectrum. Slide over just a bit to the right from point B, and you'll have something that looks slightly more like point C; slide over a bit to the right from point C, and it will look just a bit more like point D, and so forth.

FIGURE 2.2 Drilling into Hypomania and Mania

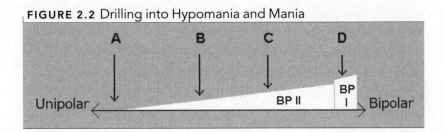

Remember those criteria for hypomania and mania? In Table 2.1, you'll find different "shades" of hypomania. For each criterion, you see an example of what that particular symptom or behavior looks like at four different points along the Bipolar Spec-

TABLE 2.1 The Spectrum of Manic Symptoms

Symptom	A (None)	B (Mild)	C (Moderate)	D (Severe)
Grandiosity	Unchanging view of self	Pleased with accomplishments, abilities, prospects	"Life of the party," charismatic	Unshakable confidence, offending people
Sleep	Unchanging (7–8 hrs.)	5–6 hrs. or awake 1–2 hrs. per night	Fine on 4 hrs.; or frequent wakening	2 hrs. then energetic, or waking and partly asleep, all night
Talkativeness	Like other people	Chatty, lots to say about anything	"Motor mouth," hard to slow down or stop	Uninterruptible, difficult to understand
Racing thoughts	Nothing unusual	Many ideas, good or bad (e.g., creative or negative ideas)	Brilliant or terrible connections, rapid, constant	Fragmented, extremely rapid jumping from idea to idea
Distractibility	Usual level of attention, focus	Sustained attention is decreased, jumpy	Unorganized, much less effective	No focus, gets little done
Increased activity	Usual level, like others, unchanging	More projects and ideas, can be very productive	Increased pace and range of activities, impulsive	Constant, driven, dangerous choices
Painful consequences	Usually avoided	Some choices regrettable, but not irreparable	Spending $100s, increased sex drive, mild risk	Spending sprees ($1,000 and up), unwise sex, drug use, illegalities
Irritability	Like others, controllable	Unfortunate, requiring later apologies	Frequent and surprising, out of control	Hostile, scary, some risk of physical actions

trum. Remember that intermediate forms exist in between these four points.

Let's now look at each of these criteria in more detail, because understanding hypomania in detail is one way to try to place yourself on the Mood Spectrum.

Grandiosity

You might think of grandiosity as an abnormal, puffed-up sense of self. But one of my patients told me, "You know, the opposite of manic is not just depressed. It's lack of confidence." Her remark made me listen more closely to what happens to people's sense of their abilities during mood or energy shifts. *Confidence* seems to be a good term that gets closer to what this feels like for the person actually experiencing it.

However, for your significant others, who are on the receiving end of hypomania and mania, the term *grandiosity* is more useful. When extreme, this feature becomes dangerous, perhaps not by affecting personal safety, but by offending others to the point of lost jobs and ruined relationships. When this is happening, there is no sign on the person's head saying, "Oh, don't worry, I don't really mean to be like this today, I'm just having some pretty extreme hypomania." So bosses and friends won't necessarily assume that "John is just not himself today." Instead they're likely to think John is a jerk and fire him or leave him. Who would choose to put up with this guy who thinks he's so absolutely great and seems to find everyone else too slow and incompetent? (When people see a psychiatrist and happen to be in this phase of bipolar disorder, they may be labeled with *narcissistic personality disorder.*)

Yet when less extreme, this very same symptom can have the opposite effect, drawing people in and impressing them. When most subtle, this grandiosity can be experienced as a brief phase, perhaps one day a month, where you feel ready to participate in groups, feel for a while that you actually have something to offer other people, or feel that some plan you have in mind might just turn out OK. In other words, this feature can look normal yet be experienced as something rare and unusual. Even so, you may not recognize these variations as remotely related to mania. To you, it just feels like you've joined the human race for a day.

Decreased Sleep

By the rule book, this symptom is supposed to be "decreased need for sleep," which indeed is one of the typical features of classic mania and often of hypomania as well. But my patients frequently describe this symptom as an inability to sleep, which they find very distressing. They are very likely to be using some sort of medication, herb, or substance to sleep—that is, to help fall sleep and stay asleep. They usually reply yes when I ask if they find their mind "full of ideas," often for *hours*, while they're trying to fall asleep. In other words, these people are not fine with so little sleep, as a person with classic mania can feel. They feel exhausted and run down, and their insomnia is one of their main targets when they consider treatment.

In classic mania, a person tends to wake very early, such as 4 A.M., feeling rested and ready to go. But the insomnia so common in hypomania has multiple variations:

- Difficulty falling asleep because you can't turn your mind off
- Difficulty staying asleep; most frequently, waking after three to four hours and then having broken, intermittent, "waking" sleep thereafter
- Less commonly, simply waking up early and being unable to fall back asleep

Talkativeness

Sometimes people can recognize this particular symptom in their own behavior. More than one patient has said to me, "I feel like 'Chatty Cathy' today," but often people are unaware of their own talkativeness. They feel an intense need to keep explaining what they are thinking, which is going quite rapidly, so they end up with what psychiatrists refer to as *pressured speech*—where being on the receiving end is like being sprayed with a verbal fire hose.

Psychiatrists can roughly gauge this pressure by noting how difficult it is to interrupt a patient and how often the patient must be interrupted (although this requires a good system for monitoring their *own* behavior as well). Talkativeness is very closely related to racing thoughts, another symptom of hypomania. With extremely fast thought, the ideas come out so rapidly that the person's speech can become difficult to understand. Occasionally people can remember their friends commenting that they found it difficult to understand what was being said in the torrent of words.

When subtle, however, this feature of hypomania can simply be a day when you feel like you actually have some interesting things to say and you want to say them. You might find yourself talking louder or being much funnier than usual, with lots of quick-witted jokes or puns. This might be in contrast to your usual style of being very quiet, having little to say unless spoken to, or feeling at a loss for anything interesting or useful to say, which combines with or is part of the lack-of-self-confidence problem. The result, of course, is shyness—or in current mental health lingo, *social anxiety* (technically, *social phobia*). This anxiety may or may not be a separate condition. Often it improves a bit with effective treatment of mood or energy cycling, but it might require additional treatment to cease to be a limiting factor in a person's life.

Only when I know a patient well can I detect a shift in "number of words per minute," and even then I am usually uncertain whether this symptom represents hypomania. After all, on some days people just feel chattier, right? This is not always a bipolar symptom! In someone with known bipolarity, however, it can be an early subtle marker of an energy shift.

Racing Thoughts

When this symptom is extreme I often hear about it as in the following analogy: a person who loves to read, and always has a book under way, *cannot read at all*. I hear this one frequently. People with extreme racing thoughts find themselves reading the same page over and over until they give up, because what they're reading doesn't stick in their minds. In milder phases they might have three books going and be unable to stick to one and get through it. Their mind keeps going on to other ideas, until they completely lose the starting place. These folks strongly endorse the idea that their thoughts are *fragmenting*.

But when subtle, this feature of hypomania is one of the most desired and exhilarating. You feel highly creative and intensely productive. Ideas come quickly and easily. When extreme, as in mania, this can lead to finding connections in unconnected ideas; think of this as creativity gone completely loose. In milder forms, the connections are still logical, yet also fast and sometimes even brilliant. When tinged with anxiety, however, the thoughts fly from one possible disaster to another, digging up evidence—again, sometimes not well connected—that the feared event could really happen or is happening. Imagine trying to fall asleep when this is going on. During phases of depression, the opposite is also common: my patients tell me that they feel like they're trying to "think through mud."

Racing thoughts are often combined with severe depression. This is one version of a *bipolar mixed state*, where both manic and depressive features are present at the same time (a paradox that is discussed later in this chapter). Any manic-side symptom can combine with depression, but the particular combination of intense and rapid thinking plus a very depressed mood is notable as one of the most dangerous mood states known. You feel like you are being "pummeled" by your own mind, which comes up with nothing but extreme thoughts about how bad a person you are, how worthless you are, how everyone would be better off without you, and so forth. Therefore, racing thoughts are particularly worthy of attention when safety is an issue.

Distractibility

An inability to keep one's attention in one place, distractibility is another way in which racing thoughts are manifest. Patients of mine talk about feeling full of energy, such as staying up late at night cleaning the house, rearranging the contents of drawers, working on old photo albums—all at once! They can have multiple projects going at the same time and find themselves hopping from one to another. One woman described cleaning every room in the house but being unable to complete one before going on to another, leaving each room in the middle of things: rugs taken up, furniture stacked, wash buckets ready but no mop, and so forth.

When milder, this may be experienced more like a kind of daydreaming, with your mind going all over the place on its own. Thus this can look very much like *Attention-Deficit/Hyperactivity Disorder (ADHD)*. In fact, bipolar disorder and ADHD are clearly somehow related—a very complicated area of research. Sometimes the forgetfulness and disorganization will improve with treatment of the other bipolar features, but sometimes even when the bipolar disorder is well treated, severe distractibility can remain. Experts agree, however, on one general principle: when both bipolar and apparent ADHD symptoms are present, *the bipolar symptoms should be treated first.* Many people are quite organized and attentive when their mood is stable, and only find themselves distractible in the context of other symptoms of hypomania. This is obviously an important way of determining whether an apparent ADHD symptom is separate or part of the bipolar condition.

Increased Activity Level

Sometimes the increased activity level is obvious even in my office: patients practically vibrate with energy, they fidget, their knee bounces up and down, and they look like they're ready to leap up and head out the door at any moment. That would be an extreme form of energy and activity.

When this symptom is in the mid-range, you can do a lot and jump from one activity to another as I described earlier without showing much outward sign of increased activity or being aware of it yourself. As you can imagine, activity level is a particularly hard feature to judge as normal or abnormal until it is quite extreme. Increased activity often is only recognizable afterward, when you look back at your own behavior. One patient described buying and reading three books about how to build a laser, as well as buying several hundred dollars' worth of materials. Then all of a sudden, he thought to himself, "Why am I doing this? I'm not interested in lasers." At that point he could look back and recognize that he had been in a hypomanic phase.

When more subtle, this level of activity can just make you look vivacious (literally, "very alive"). It can make you quite attractive to others—while it lasts.

Painful Consequences

Psychiatrists tend to look for some sort of risk behavior and impulsive decision-making as a marker for hypomania or mania. If they don't find something, they conclude the person does not have bipolar disorder, even though some studies indicate these risk behaviors occur in only a minority, perhaps about 25 percent of cases. When present, however, the typical realms of impulsive behavior often have in common a disregard for risk: money, sex, plans, and drugs. The common elements behind these behaviors include an increased interest in *pleasurable activities* and *impulsivity*.

Whereas people with mania can spend thousands of dollars in a short period of time, people with hypomania are less likely to spend that much. (This is a very broad generalization, and the distinction between mania and hypomania is not all that clear.) However, my patients have told me about phases of buying clothes that never get worn, buying a large number of household items and then returning them all the following week, or buying another old car to fix up when there are already two awaiting that same plan. This level of spending is more typical of hypomania. You can imagine what this might look like when it is subtle: how can it be distinguished from just doing some shopping?

Abnormal sexual promiscuity is sometimes easy to recognize. But many of my patients have come in to treatment only after ruining several relationships with their outside sexual activities, finally concluding that they probably were doing this in phases of hypomania. As you can imagine, this kind of story can be interpreted several different ways. Imagine what kind of trouble you might have trying to determine if subtle shifts in sexual activity actually represent a hypomanic shift. However, people often recognize that something is wrong with their level of sexual interest at times; they might use the phrase "sexual addiction" to describe it. For example, an increased interest in pornography is one possible indicator.

Irritability

Technically, irritability is not one of the *DSM* symptom criteria. Rather, irritability itself is one of the possible mood shifts, along with "elevated or expansive." (If you find this confusing, don't worry; it doesn't matter much—it's a *DSM* detail.) But mood shifts are often much harder for patients and doctors to recognize. Family members often can pick these up rather well, but it can be hard for them to describe just what they are noticing, particularly when the change is subtle. One mother said to me about her daughter: "When she wears a hat, you know you're in trouble; she never wears a hat when she's feeling fine." Mom didn't know what the hat meant, in terms of how her daughter was feeling or what she was thinking, but she knew that the hat meant some shift or potential trouble was underway.

On the other hand, when extreme, irritability can be one of the easiest manic symptoms for patients themselves to recognize. For example, you find yourself reacting very angrily to something you know—especially afterward—is quite minor and definitely does not warrant that much energy. One of my patients would know he was in trouble when he would start getting angry at other drivers. Normally he could take the usual dumb things that people do in stride, but when his energy was going up and his sleep was going down, he would find himself yelling at other drivers. Once he was followed all the way home by a police officer, who wanted to check on him and make sure he was OK. He hadn't done anything illegal, but he had attracted an officer's attention. He knew this was too unusual and called me for an appointment.

When less extreme, irritability is not so easy to recognize. Hypomania is often accompanied by an intense certainty that one is right. Anger can feel justified as clearly provoked and not something coming from inside. You can imagine that if you were to become extreme in this way, you could appear paranoid: all bad things are someone else's fault, and their misbehavior seems to be deliberate, focused on harming you. Even my patient who called me after his encounter with the police still felt he was right about the behavior of the other driver and that this was a personal matter.

When Hypomania Is Barely Detectable

Thus hypomania can have many levels and many different combinations of symptoms. Worse yet, however, are the challenges presented when we look at the very small end of the wedge of hypomania (off to the left on the Mood Spectrum). What does hypomania look like when it is just barely detectable? Using our drill cores from Figure 2.2, we can ask what hypomania looks like between points A and B—between "not present" and "mild." Here lies nearly all the controversy about the bipolar disorder diagnosis.

Here's the problem: remember from Chapter 1 that when Dr. Benazzi looked, he could not find a biologic step-down, a real biologic dividing line, between bipolar disorder and unipolar disorder. (This is shown as the smooth tapering of the ramp of hypomania in Figure 2.1.) Imagine there was a dividing point between hypomania and no hypomania at all. Then we could say, "Everyone to the right of this point has bipolar disorder, and everyone to the left of this point does not." But this does not appear to be the case. Instead, in clinical practice we see patients all along a gradual slope of hypomania—*all the way to zero.*

Perhaps this slope actually makes more sense than thinking of bipolar disorder as clearly either there or not there. Bipolar disorder is defined by a collection of symptoms and behaviors. When these are extreme, they are clearly abnormal, but when they are mild, they are part of normal human experience. Irritability, confidence, agitation, great joy, decreased sleep, and a rapid flow of ideas are all common human experiences—unless they are extreme. So besides the *DSM*-driven need to make an illness either clearly there or clearly not there, why should there be an obvious dividing line between normal and abnormal?

This idea of a gradual transition between normal and abnormal is consistent with current thinking about how certain genes might cause bipolar disorder. Briefly, the model says that getting a small dose of some of the bipolar genes leads to creativity, charisma, and willingness to take risks, but a big dose leads to bipolar disorder itself. There appear to be many such genes—at least eight or so. Each could differ in several ways from the genes found in families with no bipolar disorder. If there are at least eight genes (some researchers think there may be many more) with different versions of each, the various combinations could lead to many different personality styles and behaviors. Some combinations might look just a little different from the behaviors of the average person (whoever that is), but not be clearly abnormal. Other combinations might look rather unusual, but not interfere with function to the point where the person needs treatment.

You see? *Abnormal* is an *arbitrary* point along a continuum of styles and behaviors that when extreme are recognized as illness. Well then, where is normal? Good point—we'll get to that in the next chapter. First, let's add another piece to our Mood Spectrum model, one that explains much of the diagnostic confusion about bipolar disorder.

Depression Is a Common Feature

The problem, you see, is that the vast majority of people on the Mood Spectrum—from pure unipolar to clear bipolar—also have *depression*. (There are a few people with bipolar variations whose only mood state swings are manic and who never become depressed. But these are a very small minority.) To add to the confusion, very little distinguishes the symptoms of bipolar depression from the symptoms of unipolar depression. Unusual periods of sleepiness lasting most of the day, accompanied by extremely low motivation and profound fatigue, may mark a more "bipolar" depression. But depression by itself will not identify where a person lies on the Mood Spectrum.

Depression is by far the predominant symptom in bipolar disorder of all kinds, but especially in the middle of the spectrum. This is shown in Figure 2.3. In this study, patients were found to have symptoms about half the time. In Bipolar I, depression accounted for about two-thirds of that symptomatic time. But in Bipolar II, *over 90 percent of time spent ill was due to depression.* Bipolar disorder in the middle of the Mood Spectrum is experienced almost entirely as depression! Manic-side symptoms account for only a very small fraction of the experience.

Thus in the Mood Spectrum model, think of the wedge of hypomania as an iceberg in a sea of depression symptoms. In the middle of the spectrum (official *DSM* Bipolar II), only a small tip of hypomania sticks up above the waves of depression. And far-

FIGURE 2.3 Depression Dominates Mood in Bipolar Disorders

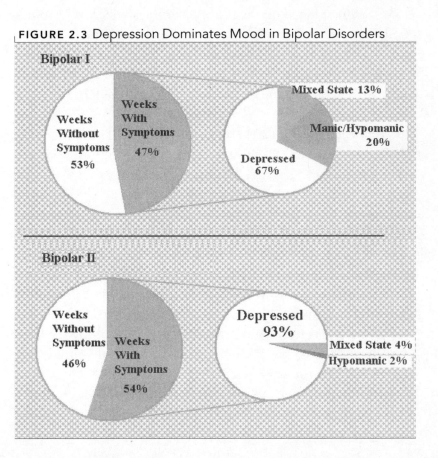

FIGURE 2.4 The Complete Mood Spectrum Model

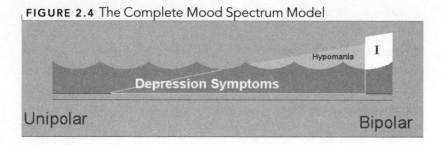

ther down the spectrum toward the unipolar end, it is effectively obscured by the depressive symptoms. To find the vanishing point, where hypomania finally isn't there at all, one has to search *underneath* the sea of depressive symptoms. You may recall that the official distinction between bipolar and unipolar, if one uses a *DSM* system, is based on the presence or the absence of hypomania. However, anyone wishing to establish that hypomania isn't there will have to use a snorkel, as well as a magnifying glass! Thus we arrive at our final version of the spectrum model, shown in Figure 2.4. This is the one I want you to remember.

Dealing with the Diagnostic Confusion

While some doctors think hypomania should be visible to the naked eye, requiring no special searching, others think that to be certain hypomania isn't there requires deliberate effort (like using scuba gear). At present, we have serious diagnostic confusion, as evidenced by a recent national presentation by some of the most respected mood experts in the United States. In a webcast presented by Harvard faculty, with an audience of hundreds of psychiatrists, doctors' different diagnostic approaches emerged while examining a case study of a man with clear symptoms of depression, as well as anger, anxiety, sleep problems, and alcohol use. Even after the Harvard experts had arrived at a unipolar diagnosis, two-thirds of the audience felt the patient was best diagnosed as bipolar.

At minimum, this example shows that even when presented with exactly the same diagnostic information and even when assisted by mood experts offering diagnostic guidance, psychiatrists can end up disagreeing about fundamental mood diagnoses. In Chapter 4 we'll look at how this diagnostic confusion might affect *your* diagnosis. But we have a few more variations on the bipolar theme to explore yet, to solidify an understanding of what we're looking for when it comes to your story. So let's keep on with our tour of "a little bipolarity."

Bipolar III: Antidepressant-Induced Mania or Hypomania

Can antidepressants really cause mania in people who have never previously looked bipolar at all? Indeed, this phenomenon is common enough to have its own name. When mania occurs shortly after an antidepressant is given and the symptoms are so extreme that anyone can see them, then the medication looks like a pretty obvious culprit. Such switching in apparently unipolar patients has been called *Bipolar III*. This term refers to hypomania or mania that is present *only* when an antidepressant is being used; in other words, the patient has never had such symptoms except when taking an antidepressant, and otherwise appears unipolar.

However, establishing whether the antidepressant caused the hypomania or mania is often not so easy, for at least three reasons:

1. Bipolar disorder can begin with several episodes of depression and only later have a manic episode show up—even without any antidepressants involved. So how do we know that an episode of mania or hypomania wasn't just the patient's own illness moving into its next phase? Perhaps it had nothing to do with the antidepressant. Perhaps it was going to happen anyway. There is no way to know this for sure.

2. A switch to hypomania, instead of mania, may be harder to detect. The same difficulty in detecting antidepressant-induced hypomania occurs in detecting hypomania at *any* time. The possibility of subtle hypomania, which is the very problem that leads to all the diagnostic confusion, can

lead to the same confusion when we are trying to establish whether a person has truly become a little hypomanic on an antidepressant. This is one of the reasons why *switch rates*—that is, how often antidepressants actually cause this kind of problem—are still debated.

3. When the switch occurs within days to a few weeks after starting the antidepressant, a possible causal relationship is worth considering. But if the switch occurs months or even years later, causality may be harder to establish. Again, there are other potential explanations. I have two patients where the switch appeared to occur *seven years* later, after an excellent response to the antidepressant.

Bipolar III is not an official *DSM* term. Actually, it is not really a diagnosis. Rather, it describes an event: a person had hypomania or mania when on an antidepressant. This event certainly has implications for the actual diagnosis. In one study, 100 percent of patients who had had this kind of reaction eventually went on to manifest sufficient bipolar symptoms to acquire a bipolar diagnosis. At present mood experts do not clearly agree about how to treat people who have had this kind of reaction. For example, should they take a mood stabilizer to prevent subsequent mood episodes? Or if they later become depressed, should they avoid being treated with any antidepressant at that point?

For now, we should recognize that people with a Bipolar III reaction are much like those with any of the other unipolar depression variations discussed in this chapter: they have depression and also something that makes them look bipolar. At some point, treating them as though they do indeed *have* bipolar disorder may be warranted.

How Brief Can a Bipolar Phase Actually Be?

The *DSM* requires that manic symptoms last at least seven days, and hypomania four days. Less than that is not, by the official rules, mania or hypomania. Uh, what is it then? Well, by now I hope that the spectrum concept comes to mind as a way of handling this less-than-official-but-looks-very-similar problem. If hypomania has intermediate forms in terms of intensity—as we saw with the drill cores—then hypomania probably has intermediate forms in terms of duration as well.

Of course, to admit intermediate duration of symptoms leads quickly to diagnostic chaos: how short can it get and still be hypomania? A day? An hour? A few minutes? Can't some dividing line be drawn somewhere? Ah, this sounds exactly like the problem we were looking at before, doesn't it? Here we are again, having difficulty drawing a line when there is no natural cutoff. Although the *DSM* draws the line at four days, we clinicians recognize much shorter versions. As noted earlier, we even have a name for a version where the hypomania lasts less than twenty-four hours: *ultradian cycling* (not a *DSM* label, but similar—it's Greek!). In this context, *ultra* means more than and *dian* means one day. So *ultradian cycling* means having more than one mood state—hypomania, mania, or depression—in twenty-four hours.

What about symptoms that come and go even more quickly than that? For example, I have patients who clearly have bipolar disorder (that is, they have symptoms that even diagnostic skeptics would accept as bipolar) who have told me of phases of hypomania lasting as little as a few hours. These phases were quite noticeable and quite abnormal for these people. Here again we have reached the limit of a category-based system: is this still bipolar? But using a spectrum-based diagnostic system, we can accept a gradual shift, in this case in duration, until finally we are clearly in the realm of normal human experience. For example, I hope I've made you laugh a few times so far while reading this book. That's not a brief hypomania—that's just laughing. We apparently must accept, based on clinical experience, that the duration of a hypomanic phase can vary from weeks, occasionally months, to days and even hours, so that ultimately we will be unable to distinguish a hypomanic shift from a brief emotion such as happiness or anger.

This is another example of the "uncertainty principle" of bipolar diagnosis: the harder you look, the more uncertain you get.

Imagine trying help a patient nail down whether the emotion of irritability really lasted long enough to justify a diagnosis of hypomania. Is an hour arguing with your spouse sufficient? Most of us would probably think not. How about an hour with no provocation at all, where the anger comes out of nowhere and seems very extreme, such as yelling at the kids for no reason at all? If you have frequent mood swings that also show up in other ways, this example of anger could be interpreted as hypomanic—but one certainly hopes for something more than just this to establish bipolarity. Most psychiatrists would not consider bipolarity with only this example of anger to support it. But what if there was another hint of bipolarity, such as a relative with mood symptoms that sound very bipolar but have no such diagnosis? You can see the problem here.

If we clinicians base our diagnoses on a symptom that can have such different lengths, we would have to admit we are doomed to disagreement. What can a doctor or a patient do to deal with this realm of uncertainty? As you read earlier, turning to a rule-based system to make diagnoses consistent sometimes ends up creating disagreement among doctors. Faced with all this confusion and disagreement, what are you, the patient, supposed to do? First, let's look at one more aspect of bipolar disorder where the Mood Spectrum model may be useful.

Depression and Hypomania at the Same Time: Recognizing Mixed States

The name *bipolar* itself implies something like the North and South Poles, doesn't it? There is depression and there is mania, and they are opposite phenomena. Of course, opposites cannot occur at the same time. But in reality, these apparent opposites do indeed occur at the same time. People can have full manic symptoms and full depressive symptoms *simultaneously*. This combination is one of the most severe and dangerous mood states known. You feel overenergized to the point of agitation, and yet you are terribly depressed. You may feel extremely irritable and extremely hopeless at the same time, giving you an angry, "What's the point, anyway?" attitude. Your mind is usually racing with thoughts, nearly all of them very negative. Perhaps worst of all is a reversed self-confidence, where the grandiosity of mania is instead experienced as a profound lack of self-esteem, to the point where you feel worse than worthless: you are slime, you are a burden to others, and you cannot do anything correctly or of any value.

While depression alone can lead to thinking about suicide, depression in this mixed-state condition often leads to intense suicidal thoughts that seem utterly appropriate. People can really believe that their loved ones will be better off without them. Clearly this is a medical emergency—if it is recognized as a medical condition at all, which unfortunately is not always the case. But current treatments can very rapidly bring the thinking and agitation under control.

Unfortunately, antidepressant medications can bring on these mixed states when used alone in people who may have an unrecognized bipolar disorder, in the opinion of most mood experts, although there is some controversy about this (discussed in Chapter 9). For now, this seems to be another reason for caution in the use of antidepressant medications. Figure 2.5 shows that a more accurate way of thinking of the relationship between mania and depression is to think of them as axes on a graph.

FIGURE 2.5 Bipolar "Mixed States"

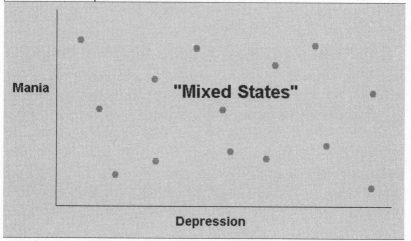

Mixed State—or Adolescence?

All right, so a person can have brief phases of subtle irritability, or overt happiness, or tearful despondence—and even have all of them in a single day. Sound familiar? Surely you've encountered an adolescent somewhere? You too, perhaps, at one time. So, you are wondering, I hope: how does one distinguish normal adolescence from Bipolar Spectrum mixed states?

Once again we face the same problem we've encountered throughout this chapter: there does not appear to be a clear dividing line between the normal phenomenon of adolescence (as abnormal as it may seem to their parents at times) and the diagnosable conditions of the Mood Spectrum. Since I am not specially trained as a child and adolescent psychiatrist, I fear to tread here. As you have seen, diagnostic confusion and disagreement is widespread even if one restricts the question to adults. In children and adolescents, this question becomes even more complicated. I raise it here primarily to illustrate that a spectrum way of thinking may be necessary for thinking about young people's versions of these mood problems, as well as adults'. Interested readers can find excellent resources to help with the diagnostic and treatment dilemmas that arise in the treatment of children at bpkids.org, the website of the Child and Adolescent Bipolar Foundation.

As of 1994, mixed states were officially recognized in the *DSM* rule book, although the criteria require *full* manic symptoms and *full* depressive symptoms to be present for this diagnosis. On the graph in Figure 2.5, a patient who met these criteria would show up as a single point in the upper right-hand corner. However, imagine what happens if we apply our now familiar Mood Spectrum approach to the phenomenon of mixed states. What if more subtle versions of mania could mix with more subtle versions of depression? Just as shown, there would be dots all over. In fact, there could be dots *anywhere*. Some people might only have symptoms in the lower left corner of the graph and would not regard themselves as needing treatment.

Thus through a spectrum lens, we see a multitude of intermediate forms, all of which represent some degree of mixed state. This way of thinking about bipolar symptoms is much closer to clinical reality. In my experience, virtually any mixture is possible, and as I listen to mood experts in their research and their teaching, it seems that many, if not most, accept this more flexible view of bipolar mixed states.

In this chapter we have repeatedly faced the same problem: there are no clear dividing lines. Whether we seek to divide unipolar from bipolar, hypomania from brief mood shifts, mixed states from milder anxiety and depression combinations, or adolescence from a bipolar mixed state, we find no place to divide the pairs without doing so arbitrarily.

The *DSM*, driven in part by research necessity, emphasizes drawing a line somewhere to characterize ideal types that can provide a common language for doctors, therapists, patients, and families. But as you've seen, many patients lie in the fuzzy realm between clear bipolarity and clear unipolarity, and in between brief emotions and long mood episodes. Before I show you how you can use all this information in making your diagnosis, you should know about one more set of Mood Spectrum variations. Sorry, I know you're anxious to get on with things, but remember: your best defense against a diagnostic misunderstanding is for you yourself to understand the many possible variations in bipolar disorder. The next chapter presents one of the trickiest concepts yet: how you can be "a little bipolar" without any hypomania or mania at all.

CHAPTER 3

No Mania or Hypomania? Understanding "Soft" Bipolar Disorder

Say that again? Bipolar *without* mania or hypomania? Aren't these the very definition of bipolarity? The answer is no. Nearly a century ago, when manic-depressive illness was first characterized, other features were also recognized as part of the illness's pattern. These other aspects almost have been lost from view with the *DSM* emphasis on hypomania and mania as the defining characteristics of bipolar disorders.

In psychiatry, for now, diagnoses are simply agreed-upon collections of symptoms and other features, such as family history, that tend to *occur together* repeatedly. They still do not have biological underpinnings, as do many diagnoses in the rest of medicine. They are names applied to patterns. The *DSM* system uses symptoms *alone* to define patterns, but clinicians seeing patients know that other aspects of the illnesses we treat also form part of the pattern.

For example, in most cases bipolar disorder has a pattern of recurrence over time: an episode of depression comes and then goes away, even without treatment, but then it comes back again, or an episode of hypomania comes instead. That episode, too, will go away, even without treatment, but later, without some means of preventing these repeated episodes, another one will occur. This recurrence may take years, but it is very likely to come again.

Another feature is bipolarity in the family history: commonly patients with bipolar disorder have a relative with bipolar disorder, or something that looks rather like it. (If not, we often find instead a dramatically large number of relatives with severe alcohol problems.) An additional feature is the early onset of mood problems, often before age twenty-five.

Looking at the "Soft Signs" of Bipolar Disorder

If Chapter 2 convinced you that hypomania clearly has been a part of your mood experience, you might not need to read this chapter. But if you're still wondering whether bipolarity applies to you, read on, especially if you have any features from the following list:

Onset and Course

1. *Four or more episodes* of significant depression
2. The first episode of depression occurring *before age twenty-five* (Some experts say before age twenty, a few before age eighteen. Overall, it appears that the younger a person is at the time of the first episode, at least down to age fifteen, the more likely that bipolar, not unipolar, disorder later will be the apparent basis for that episode.)
3. Episodes of depression are *brief* (less than three months)
4. Onset of depression within months of giving birth (*postpartum* depression)

Symptoms

1. *Psychosis* (loss of contact with reality) during an episode of depression
2. When person is depressed, *symptoms are atypical*: extremely low energy and activity, excessive sleep (more than ten

hours a day), mood is highly reactive to the actions and reactions of others, and (the weakest sign) appetite more likely is increased than decreased, often with carbohydrate craving

Family and Personality

1. A *first-degree relative* (mother/father, brother/sister, daughter/son) with a diagnosis of bipolar disorder, or individuals with notable mood symptoms of any kind in at least three generations
2. When person is not depressed, slightly higher-than-average mood and energy all the time (called *hyperthymic personality*)

Response to Antidepressants

1. *Hypomania* or mania while taking an antidepressant
2. *Loss of response* to an antidepressant (sometimes called "Prozac poop-out"): it worked well for a while, but depression symptoms came back while person was still taking the medication
3. No long-term success with *three or more antidepressants*

All eleven items have been shown to occur commonly in bipolar disorder—so often, in fact, that we can wonder what their presence might mean in people who have no hypomania or mania at all. The list has been developed through more than twenty years of research on the common characteristics of bipolarity. Some degree of mania or hypomania is, of course, extremely common. But so are these eleven other features that have been referred to as *soft signs* of bipolar disorder. There is a history for the term *soft sign* in the rest of medicine. Doctors often look with some scorn at soft signs, which lack, by comparison, the anyone-can-see-it objectivity of hard signs (an abnormal spot on an x-ray or a blood test result that lies far outside the normal range). Hard signs always trump soft signs. And for now, in the diagnosis of bipolar disorder, hypomania (as long as you don't have to use a snorkel or magnifying glass to find it) is regarded by most physicians as a much "harder" sign than simply having repeated or very brief episodes of depression.

However, as noted in Chapter 1, the Massachusetts General Hospital Bipolar Clinic (affiliated with Harvard University) now uses a *Bipolarity Index* to indicate just how bipolar you are. This system has five categories of information, each worth up to 20 points, for a total scale of 100 points. In the Symptoms category, classic manic symptoms are given 20 points, hypomania is given 10 points, and 5 points are assigned if only soft-sign symptoms have been present, such as postpartum depression. But in their system, the diagnosis of bipolar disorder does not end here. Another 80 points are possible. These are given for the rest of the preceding list of soft signs: family history, age of onset, course of symptoms over time, and what happened when an antidepressant or mood stabilizer was given (response to medications).

Hard signs, soft signs—this might sound like diagnostic philosophy. Yet a major treatment question is based on these distinctions, which illustrates this philosophical issue in real life: who can safely take an antidepressant medication? To understand the complexity of that question, let us press on with a look at several forms of unipolar depression that may represent the intermediate mood conditions that the spectrum concept predicts should exist: mood variations that *look* unipolar, but *act* bipolar—some just a little, some quite a lot.

Known Soft Variations That Look Unipolar and Act Bipolar

Several versions of depression look unipolar in terms of symptoms, but have features of bipolar disorder from the previously mentioned list. These include, by their common names:

- **Recurrent:** depression occurs repeatedly, but does get better for at least brief periods of time.
- **Atypical:** depressive symptoms are unusual—sleeping too much, eating too much (as opposed to the reduced appetite or weight loss of "typical" depression); excessive sleeping (as

opposed to insomnia); extremely low energy; and sensitivity in relationships to even minor signs of rejection.

- **Postpartum:** depression begins within weeks to a few months (some say up to twelve) after having a baby.
- **Psychotic:** depression is accompanied with a loss of contact with reality, including delusional beliefs and hearing voices (and rarely, other forms of hallucinations).

How do these unipolar variations act bipolar? They do so in two ways: in their response to treatment and in their course over time. They often do not respond well to antidepressants. The medication can simply fail to work, or it may work for a while and then stop working. If you have one of these variations, you may react with the same kinds of agitation, insomnia, and even suicidal thinking that people with bipolar disorder experience when given antidepressants. Also, you can get better on the medications doctors routinely use for bipolar disorder—the *mood stabilizers*.

In their long-term course, these unipolar conditions can act bipolar by later *becoming DSM*-diagnosable bipolar disorder. If one watches long enough, many people with soft signs of bipolarity later have recognizable mania or hypomania. One research study, for example, looked at adolescents hospitalized for depression, manifesting the early-onset soft sign of bipolar disorder. Over the next fifteen years, almost half (46 percent) of these young people had mania or hypomania. Figure 3.1 places these unipolar conditions in the big picture diagram you saw in Chapter 2.

The diagram indicates that there is a *Unipolar Spectrum* or *Soft Bipolar Spectrum* spanning a continuum from people who have had only a single episode of depression, to those who have had repeated episodes. In between are people whose symptoms have been associated with some degree of bipolarity: atypical symptoms, psychotic symptoms, or postpartum onset. (What about symptoms associated with other hormonal fluctuations as well, such as premenstrual syndrome [PMS] and perimenopausal mood changes? We'll consider those in later sections in this chapter.)

FIGURE 3.1 The "Soft" Bipolar Spectrum

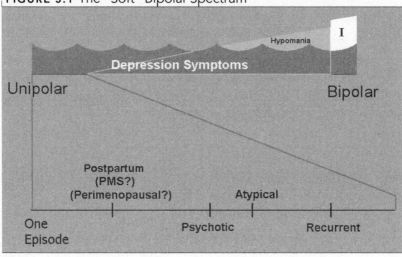

How Well-Accepted Is the Soft Bipolar Spectrum?

This idea of bipolarity without mania or hypomania strikes many doctors as a very radical idea. After all, it flatly contradicts the *DSM* system, since the *DSM requires* hypomania or mania for a bipolar diagnosis. You might be surprised to discover that this idea has been around for more than twenty years and has been described in research and review articles by some of the most respected and widely known mood experts in the world. I myself was surprised. I would have thought their stature and the weight of evidence they present to support this point of view would have led to much greater acceptance of this idea than it now enjoys. These experts include Drs. Hagop Akiskal, Nassir Ghaemi, and Frederick Goodwin. (See my website Notes page for a brief story on each of these experts and the articles on which this chapter is largely based—psycheducation.org/notes.htm.)

One of my primary-care colleagues, on hearing about the breadth of bipolarity when these soft bipolar features are included said, "That's half my practice." He clearly meant to convey his surprise and some degree of disbelief at this concept. If you explain this concept to *your* doctor, especially your primary care

An Observation of One Type of Variation from My Office

Many patients who clearly have cyclic changes in mood never have hypomania—that is the theme of this chapter, right? But in an odd way, some people have a form of hypomania that is rarely recognized as such: they just come up to "normal" once in a while. (Their mood records are reflected in Figure 3.2.) This is an observation of mine, not a research finding; it is not routinely described in the bipolar literature, and I don't know how common this is. Yet I hear this story often.

If people with no mood problems are asked to rate their mood on a scale from 0 to 10, where 10 is the best you ever feel and 0 is the worst, on an average day they will say, "Yeah, I'm feeling all right today, maybe 5 or 6." But many people, perhaps especially those who had very rough childhoods (due to poverty, little time for love from stressed parents, physical or sexual abuse, etc.) live depressed. This is the normal state of affairs for them. On an average day they rate themselves around 3 or 4 on this scale. The *DSM* term for this is *dysthymia*.

Yet some of these people also have cyclic mood shifts for no reason at all that they can recognize, sometimes down to 0 or 1—but also sometimes up. When they go up, which in this particular pattern seems always to be very brief (usually a day, two sometimes and occurring once a month or so), they generally get only as far as a 5 or 6, subjectively. They commonly tell me that when this happens they feel like they've "joined the human race" for a day or two. They can actually enjoy going to a party. They feel like they

FIGURE 3.2 Cycling—into "Normal"

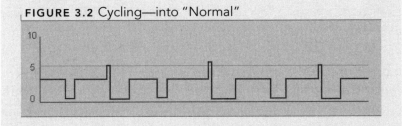

have something to say that others might find interesting. They have fun and they get things done, but not a lot of things and not a lot of fun—and they are not the life of the party. They might spend more money that day, but not hundreds of dollars. They don't take big risks on those days. They are not hypomanic by *DSM* criteria, which is why this variation does not appear in Chapter 2. They just feel far better than they usually do—*for no reason*. And this happens repeatedly as a recognizable pattern. The next day, it's gone again for no reason. I hear this from many patients, who often are surprised that I know about these odd days they have, which they had definitely noticed but did not recognize as bipolar (why would they?).

doctor, you probably need to name the authors cited, making sure their stature and their publications are known or available, because you are likely to get a similar reaction of surprise and disbelief.

Why You Should Know About Soft Bipolarity

Does it make any difference whether a doctor uses a *DSM*-based approach to diagnose depression or a spectrum approach? It definitely might. Remember that antidepressants are known to sometimes make bipolar disorder worse. What if that risk extends even to this Soft Bipolar Spectrum? We have to wonder if some people to whom doctors might give antidepressants might be at greater risk than others. The following case presents this dilemma.

Jane is a woman based on one of my patients. She has multiple features from the soft bipolar list: early onset, recurrence, brief episodes, and postpartum depression. She has a family history of bipolar disorder. She might have a bit of the hyperthymic personality when she is well. Her energy-level shift is consistent with atypical depression. Here's the big question: should she be given an antidepressant?

Jane: A Case That May Challenge the Standard Approaches

Jane Roberts is a thirty-eight-year-old mother of two. She had an episode of depression at age twenty and saw a counselor for it while in college, but only briefly. She can recall perhaps three more episodes since then. One came at age thirty-four after the birth of her second child, the most severe yet. She had just moved to a new town and assumed her social isolation and the stress of the new baby were responsible for that episode. She got better without treatment.

Lately, however, she has been experiencing obvious depression again. Her mood, motivation, and satisfaction with her work are all very low. Her mother had quite severe depressions, and her mother's brother is a very unusual man—brilliant but reclusive and perhaps just a bit paranoid, according to what Jane has heard from her mother about him. Her maternal grandfather had manic-depression.

Her main problem now is lack of energy. She feels exhausted trying to keep up with her kids' needs. She tried to get more exercise but as her mood worsened, she just stopped doing anything extra. She feels like all she wants to do is sleep and does so whenever she can. Her husband is not very understanding of what she's going through. He reminds her that with her usual very bubbly, positive attitude she could easily get a position in the large company for which he works, and this might be what she needs.

She has never been treated with any medications. She thinks she can't really consider a psychotherapy approach because of her child-care constraints, and she is hoping there might be a medication that would help her. A friend of hers had a great response to Prozac (generic: fluoxetine), so she is quite interested in that approach.

Remember that antidepressants can make bipolar disorder worse, bringing on hypomanic or manic symptoms in a large number of patients. Just how many people react this way is debated. Jane has nearly all of the soft bipolar features. If doctors really believed that these identify bipolarity and therefore indicate a potential for a bad reaction to antidepressants, then they might consider giving her a mood stabilizer instead of an antidepressant. Unfortunately, I can tell you that where I practice (in the Pacific Northwest), I have never once seen that done. When patients like Ms. Roberts are treated with a medication, it is almost always an antidepressant.

When Jane came to see me, I explained that because of her family history and other soft signs we should consider, on a theoretical basis, starting with a mood stabilizer. She listened patiently to my explanation that although this approach is not a standard one for patients like her, there is reason to consider it based on a big-picture evaluation of risks. After reading on my website about some of the antidepressant controversies, she understood my concerns. She had also read the safety information about some of our mood stabilizer options, particularly those with antidepressant clout. She accepted the idea of starting with low-dose lithium. But she felt slowed down and dull on that medication. This was the end of our theoretically based restraint. We switched her to fluoxetine, to which she had a very nice response: not rapid and not dramatic, which might also have been worrisome—just a slow, steady improvement back to her usual self. She followed up thereafter through her primary care physician (however, you'll read more about her in Chapter 9, as the story does not end here). When I present her example to psychiatrists as an example of the dilemma we face treating patients with very soft bipolarity, they consistently express surprise that I treated her with lithium. Almost every one of them would have started with the fluoxetine. That is the state of our field at this time.

How Some Doctors Are Changing Their Way of Thinking

Doctors sometimes make jokes about each other being *splitters* or *lumpers*. Splitters like to define multiple variations of a disease process, each with a name, detailing the fine distinctions between them. Lumpers watch them doing this, harrumph loudly, and proclaim, "You treat them all the same way, so why bother with all these micro-definitions?" However, when treatments improve, the splitters may be ready: they will have already sorted out subgroups that might respond better to one approach than another.

As is so often the case with either-or distinctions, perhaps the best approach is to use both perspectives at the same time: to be a lumper when treatment options do not seem to vary across an entire group, but to keep a splitter's eye out for any subgroups who might someday require their own treatment plan when new tools become available.

Jane Roberts's case illustrates that doctors at present are lumpers. All versions of unipolar depression are handled the same way. In current practice, hypomania—present or absent—is the sole determinant of treatment. When doctors cannot find hypomania, then antidepressants are the medication of choice, regardless of how many soft bipolar features the patient might have. After such a patient has had three antidepressants and none of them has worked or perhaps worked only for a while—only then do primary care doctors begin to think about using mood stabilizers (psychiatrists, we could hope, might think about changing their approach earlier).

But the day of the splitter may be coming. Dr. Ghaemi and colleagues continue to study the soft signs. Several recent papers have used the diagnostic framework described here and have shown that it can be used to *guide treatment*. Soon I hope we'll see a *randomized trial* (an ideal research design described in Chapter 7) comparing the effectiveness of antidepressants versus a mood stabilizer with known antidepressant potential in unipolar patients with multiple features of bipolarity.

Hormonally Related Mood Conditions and Soft Bipolarity

Meanwhile, a few more conditions bear mentioning in the context of soft bipolarity. Given that postpartum depression might have a component of bipolarity, could other strongly hormonally

49

related mood conditions also have such a component? To my knowledge this has not been studied, nor have I seen others speculate about it. So I'll offer my own thoughts.

Premenstrual Syndrome (PMS)

You may recall that this book began by talking about depression plus other symptoms—including irritability, sleep disturbance, agitation, and anxiety. Doesn't that sound familiar, in the context of premenstrual symptoms? Perhaps given the apparent similarity between PMS and soft bipolar features, we should wonder whether they are related?

To notice this similarity and not wonder aloud about it could be either cowardice or good judgment. I remember attending the American Psychiatric Association's (APA) annual meeting in San Francisco in 1993, where several groups, including the National Organization for Women, were protesting a decision by the APA to put a new name for severe PMS—they called it *Pre-Menstrual Dysphoric Disorder*—in the 1994 *DSM* rule book. The protesters put forth many clear, well-considered, and understandable concerns about the potential medicalization of PMS, including that this could legitimize the idea of treating a normal condition with medications. This was regarded as a dangerous extension of psychiatric practice, referred to in the protests as "drugging women."

The outcome they were concerned about has since come to pass. PMS, under the official name of PMDD, is now commonly treated with antidepressant medications. I wish we had more data on alternatives like calcium and exercise. These have support from some research studies, but few randomized trials, which are the best kind of evidence. Nevertheless, something very interesting about antidepressants' effects when used for PMDD and PMS: they *often work within twenty-four hours*. This is worth thinking about, especially since one of the common reactions to antidepressants in bipolar disorder is a very rapid response, often much more quickly than in unipolar depression. In bipolar disorder, responses can occur within hours or days instead of weeks, in many cases.

Some may protest even raising the idea of a connection between PMS and bipolarity. After all, little connects the two except similar symptoms and an atypical response to antidepressants. The risk of pathologizing a natural part of human experience is still a concern. But I hope that *thinking* about such a connection is OK—as opposed to putting labels in diagnostic rule books. I'd just like to encourage some wondering about how these conditions might relate.

Perimenopausal Depression

Similarly, mood symptoms often become a problem as women near menopause, often for several years before they finally stop menstruating. *Perimenopausal* mood disturbances often include more than depression: irritability; erratic, often severe sleep disturbance; and a pervasive anxiety are common symptoms in this age range. Consider this chain of connections:

1. Perimenopausal symptoms are more common in women who have had PMS symptoms for years.
2. PMS symptoms are more common in women who have postpartum depression.
3. Postpartum depression is a soft sign of bipolarity.

Or this one,

1. *Seasonal affective disorder* (SAD), or winter blues, is much more common in Bipolar II than in the general population.
2. PMS is much more common in women with seasonal affective disorder than in those whose mood does not shift in the winter. In one recent study, 46 percent of women with SAD had severe PMS, whereas in women without SAD, only 2 percent had severe PMS. The association has

been shown in the other direction as well: in women with PMS, 38 percent had seasonal affective disorder; by comparison, in those without PMS, only 8 percent had SAD.
3. Both PMS and seasonal affective disorder have atypical symptoms, which as you know from this chapter are associated with bipolarity.

Obviously these are all *indirect* connections. These conditions might not be related at all. But this is not just idle speculation. Remember, antidepressants are recognized to sometimes make bipolar disorder worse. This is true not just in Bipolar I, but all the way across the Mood Spectrum. Therefore we *should* wonder, using the model presented in this chapter, whether concerns about antidepressant effects could extend even to PMS and peri-menopausal depression. Not that we shouldn't use antidepressants in these settings; but we should wonder about how it would look, if indeed these medications could somehow worsen a condition that looks unipolar but has bipolar features, at least in some sus-ceptible individuals. How would we know? Might we eventually see women who were treated for PMS with antidepressants who later look bipolar? I have not seen this yet, but I'm looking.

Can You Still Be Bipolar Without Depression? Diagnosing "Normal"

Remember that for the entire Mood Spectrum we assumed that depression was present. This is a very safe assumption in most cases. As discussed in Chapter 2, patients with bipolar disorder spend about half their time symptom-free. The other half of the time, they have some symptoms. In Bipolar I, the person spends about two-thirds of this symptomatic time depressed. In Bipolar II (shown in Chapter 2, Figure 2.3), the asymmetry is even more dramatic: in one study of patients with Bipolar II, over *90 percent* of symptomatic time was spent depressed.

But what happens to a diagnosis if depression is *not* present or is so mild that it's almost unnoticeable? After all, some people periodically have full manic phases, but never have depression. (I've seen estimates between 2 and 10 percent of all Bipolar I patients.) What would a person who never has significant depression look like if he or she has *subtle* hypomanic phases? In other words, what might a person who is farther down the Mood Spectrum toward the unipolar end look like if he only has the manic, not the depressed, side of things? Let's say a patient named Paul has this pattern. He almost certainly will not regard himself as having bipolar disorder and probably would not even regard himself as having any kind of mental health problem. If the mild hypomania tends to be *dysphoric*, Paul might recognize that he periodically becomes irritable and hard to please. He might even notice that these phases coincided with a shift in sleep pattern— periodically sleeping less total hours or having difficulty with frequent awakenings, when usually he sleeps solidly through the night. On the other hand, if his mild hypomania tends to be *euphoric*, then Paul almost certainly will not regard himself as having a problem, right? Periodically he would experience increased energy, confidence, and pleasure in everyday events, for no clear reason. But he wouldn't have much incentive to go looking for a reason, right? Paul would simply regard himself as quite a happy person, especially at certain times.

Indeed, some research on *temperament*, a person's habitual mood style, suggests that people who experience euphoric hypomania tend to be more positive, confident, and gregarious in their "normal" state. By contrast, people whose hypomania is more dysphoric tend to be grumpier, more brooding, and ill-humored.

Are these mild states mental illnesses? Once again the labels run the risk of causing more trouble than they solve. Everyone knows that the phrase "mentally ill" casts a dark shadow. No one wants that thrown over them. The phrase itself is so tarnished by its history, we psychiatrists have been avoiding it for years. (For example, we have "mental health" or "behavioral health" programs.) When people ask me if I think they are mentally ill, I try to reframe the entire question in different language.

If no clear dividing line exists between "normal" and "clearly ill," how do psychiatrists decide who to treat? That turns out to be pretty easy. First of all, we clinicians can only treat those who come to see us—that's a big hurdle. You can almost assume that anyone who gets as far as my office may be worth treating—although, of course, treatment is entirely up to the person, at least in the case of mild to moderate symptoms. (Severe symptoms may pose risks to the person or others, and then the issue of who needs treatment becomes much more complex.) But the cutoff we clinicians really use is this: how much do the symptoms interfere with life? Some pretty dramatic symptoms may be present, but if you are coping with them so well that you don't really create much trouble, then there is probably little reason to take the risks or spend the time and money to be treated by a psychiatrist. Granted, "create much trouble" is pretty vague. It leaves a lot of room for interpretation, perhaps just shifting the gray zone of "who to treat?" to different language. But it beats "mentally ill," don't you think?

You've learned in these first three chapters about the Mood Spectrum: a new way of thinking about the relationship of unipolar and bipolar mood problems, which is rapidly becoming mainstream. By having learned more about this spectrum way of thinking, I hope you can directly help with the making of your own diagnosis, to which we finally can turn.

CHAPTER 4

Making *Your* Diagnosis

There are no lab tests for psychiatric diagnoses. Because we psychiatrists still have no biologic underpinnings for our diagnoses, doctors in other medical disciplines continue to view us with a mixture of scorn, pity, or relief (relieved that at least they don't have to do it). Like it or not, psychiatric diagnoses currently are based on four factors:

1. Symptoms
2. Symptom course over time (including age of onset)
3. Family history
4. Response to prior treatments

As you've read repeatedly in this book, the diagnosis of bipolar disorder tends to be based on the presence or absence of hypomania or mania, rather than on the latter three factors. But as was shown in Chapter 3, these other factors are very relevant.

In this chapter we'll look at two factors that affect the gathering and interpretation of the diagnostic data: first, your doctor's diagnostic biases and second, your own insight into your symptoms. Then we'll look at the risks of the underdiagnosis and overdiagnosis of bipolarity. In Chapter 6 we'll return to all this, putting together a plan for working with your doctor or therapist—first on your diagnostic evaluation and then during ongoing treatment.

Why Searching for Hypomania Can Be Difficult

As you now know, hypomania can be very subtle, and there is considerable controversy about where it stops and where unipolar depression begins. Since in a DSM system your diagnosis hinges entirely on whether hypomania is judged to be present or absent, how your doctor looks for it is extremely important. In the DSM system, the doctor, whether she thinks of it this way or not, must establish that hypomania is *not* present. Here's why:

1. Antidepressants can make bipolar disorder worse.
2. Therefore, antidepressants can only be used safely (i.e., without the risk of worsening bipolar disorder) if bipolar disorder is not present.
3. Bipolar disorder is present if hypomania is present.
4. Therefore, only if hypomania is *not present* can antidepressants be prescribed safely.

So diagnosis often comes down to the search for hypomania. Since this search is so important, you might think there would be an agreed-upon system for doing it. Nope—and that's one of the main reasons I'm writing this book: there is no system for finding hypomania. Part of the problem is that logically it is not possible to be certain that something is *not there*. Here's a long analogy to illustrate this problem.

One Cannot Prove Something Is *Not There*

Suppose someone loses his or her keys at your house. How do you go about looking for them? You start with the obvious places, hoping to easily spot the keys. A big, bright key ring would help, right? But if you don't find them after a quick look, you get a little more systematic, cruising through each room in the house. It would sure help if you knew exactly what you were looking for, but in this case you do not know the color, size, or even number of keys you are hunting. You begin to think the keys are not in the house. But how about that big swimming pool out there? Suppose you have reason to think the keys could have landed in the pool? Eventually, if you really have to find those keys, you will end up pacing around the pool and finally, if necessary, jumping in. If it really matters, you might get your snorkel and mask and spend quite a bit of time underwater looking.

Mind you, in this scenario you are not certain the keys have been left at your house. This makes the search more frustrating. You also don't know if you're looking for a big key ring with ten keys on it or a small one with three keys. But suppose these keys belong to your boss and you might lose your very important job if you can't find them. OK, now the pressure is on. You have to be *sure* the lost keys are not at your house. If you find them, you can stop looking. But if you don't find them, can you be sure they aren't there? Think of how thoroughly you would have to look! After searching for an hour or more, you might finally say, "Well, I'm not sure there are keys here; but I know I looked really hard. They could be here, but I know I can't find them."

The medical field has a phrase for this: "Absence of evidence is not evidence of absence." (You might have to read that sentence a few times.) In other words, looking for keys and not finding them does not make it certain they aren't there. It just means you didn't find them. Establishing the absence of something with certainty is nearly impossible; you can only increase the probability that it isn't there.

Not Enough Time and the Stakes Are High

Why are you running through the house looking for a key ring? Because the search for keys of unknown size and number, which might be underwater in the swimming pool, is rather like the search for hypomania. Think about it: the doctor cannot be exactly certain what she is looking for. There are many places to look—sleep pattern, energy level, activity level, risk-taking, plans, mood, thought speed. The thing she is looking for could be underwater—that is, underneath the more obvious depression that is the patient's original reason for seeing the doctor. The stakes are high, because safely taking an antidepressant requires establishing that bipolar disorder is *not there*. A mistake could lead someone to become manic, or enter a bipolar mixed state with its risk of suicidal thought or action.

According to current diagnostic practices, when a doctor finds depression, he or she should *also* go looking for "the lost keys." Before prescribing an antidepressant, the doctor must establish that there are no keys to be found. Never mind that the key ring can be large, small, or even submerged depending on where you are on the Mood Spectrum. Never mind that the doctor, especially a primary care doctor, has limited time for this search. Never mind that she knows she might be searching for something that isn't there. And never mind that as a primary care doctor, she may not have had much training about bipolar disorders. Despite all these handicaps, we expect her to pronounce: "You have no hypomania, so you are unipolar, and you may therefore safely take antidepressant medications." As I mentioned before, even the FDA put forth this expectation, saying (in their March 2004 announcement and now in every antidepressant package insert) that all patients should be *screened for bipolar disorder* before they are prescribed an antidepressant.

Most doctors look for hypomania sticking out of the patient's depression symptoms. They think that if mania or hypomania is there, they should be able to see it. They do not believe hypomania is something they should hunt for with a magnifying glass or a snorkel. They belive hypomania is supposed to be evident to the naked eye. Of course, a good psychiatrist tries to bring out a patient's history of mania or hypomania with questions such as, "Do you sometimes find yourself sleeping less than usual and not really missing it?" and "Have you had times where you do things that later seem like poor judgment, or risky activities, such as having sex with people you don't know or spending money you don't have?"

But do you see what can happen here? How many such questions should they ask? In my practice, I have the luxury of spending half an hour or more, if necessary, conducting this search for hypomania. I can use several different methods, from direct questions to open-ended questions that are designed to give me broad information about sleep quality or activity levels. Or I might have the patient complete a screening questionnaire as a starting place for further discussion. Most doctors, however, do not have this time luxury.

Doctors' Diagnostic Bias

Here's what I really worry about: doctors might have the chance to screen as I do or could arrange it (particularly my psychiatric colleagues), but *they don't* because they do not believe a diagnosis of bipolarity should be made this way. They expect hypomania to be obvious enough that searching with a comb (much less a snorkel!) is not necessary. Thus you can see what can happen: your diagnosis could end up having more to do with which doctor you see and his or her diagnostic belief system, than with you and your symptoms.

In recognition of this risk, I routinely tell my patients about my bipolar lenses. I offer what another psychiatrist with different lenses might say, as best as I can imagine it, including treatment recommendations that result from looking through different glasses. I also ask my patients to read "Mood Swings but not Manic" on my website, from which this book derives, describing the Mood Spectrum and linking many articles from mood specialists on this subject. (Don't worry, you know much more now than you'd have gotten from the website!) I want my patients to see that the notion of subtle hypomania is not mine. I want them to understand that together we are trying to make their diagnoses as accurate as possible, that I need their help, and that they can help just by *understanding what I'm looking for.*

On the other hand, is it possible to go too far the other way? Suppose you get a doctor who believes entirely in the model presented here. He pulls out a strong magnifying glass, as well as a comb. If he looks long and hard enough, might he almost always find *something* to suggest hypomania? In that case, nearly every patient examined will be bipolar, right? We'll look at the risks that might go along with such a possible overdiagnosis in the next to last section of this chapter. First, though, I must consider a limiting factor on your end. How well can *you* see your own hypomania?

Can You See Your Own Hypomania?

Sometimes, you could be so accustomed to having phases of being mildly energized and accelerated, or irritable and negative, or agitated and anxious, that you do not perceive these states as abnormal. For you, these are normal. How would you or a loved one know you need to go see a psychiatrist? If you did go, unless the psychiatrist asks very deliberate questions designed to bring out such experiences, neither you nor the psychiatrist will recognize that hypomania has indeed occurred at times. Thus the diagnosis of bipolar disorder will be missed.

I hope you're thinking, "Wait a minute, how can people not know they have symptoms? If *they* don't know they have symptoms, how is anyone else supposed to know?" Again, the problem is that you are so used to having these experiences and have had them for so long, that you don't really have a way to look at your lack of sleep, for example, as a symptom. It's like asking a fish if it ever tasted water.

On the continuum of symptom intensity that makes up the Mood Spectrum, some symptoms can be so minimal that not even you really notice them, and yet your doctor might want to know about them. For example, do you sometimes find yourself much more talkative than usual? On some such occasions, the reason could be obvious: you just had a fun time on a trip to your cousin's, and when you get together with your family afterward, you want to tell them all about it. But suppose that kind of talkativeness occurred with no particular reason? That's what we're looking for. In this chapter we look at each one of the features of hypomania in this way, including *who* might notice: you, your family, your doctor, or even your friends or coworkers.

Getting an Accurate History: How Family and Friends Can Help You

Upon whose recollection of your symptoms will your diagnosis depend—yours, your family's, or your friends'? The doctor's, after she interviewed you for less than an hour? Of course, the best answer is the usual one for such multiple-choice questions: *all of the above.* Using your history alone runs the risk of missing something that you, the fish, can't see. Your family may have their biases, and I would never want to make a diagnosis based on family input alone. But their input can be very valuable in making up for any of your possible blind spots. Your doctor will ask you questions, as well as listen to your initial explanation of the problem, but her time will always be limited.

Remember the drill cores from Chapter 2? Recall that in Table 2.1

- Column D symptoms are so severe they can be recognized even by strangers.
- Column C symptoms (at the lower intensity) may be recognized as you "not being yourself" by a friend or coworker.
- Column B symptoms are so subtle that they generally go unnoticed by anyone except someone who knows you very well, such as family members.

But, wouldn't *you* be able to recognize all three levels? Well, that depends, actually. Some people maintain the ability to recognize what is happening and when they are not their usual selves, from subtle hypomanic symptoms to the extremes of mania. This ability is usually termed *insight,* meaning that a person can see him- or herself clearly and recognize changes in behavior.

But often in mania, and somewhat less often in hypomania, the illness itself interferes with this insight. People become overconfident, start making big plans, start acting a bit erratic and irritable, and may not recognize—even when it is pointed out to them by family or friends—that they are not acting like themselves. When symptoms are most severe, such as in Column D, lack of insight can readily add to the problem and create some very dangerous situations. For example, one young woman once became my patient at the psychiatric hospital where I was working because she was writing checks for thousands of dollars to churches, theaters, hospitals, and other such institutions. She was convinced that she could give money away at this rate because she could easily turn around and make more money whenever necessary. Her family tried to convince her that something was wrong, but her confidence was unshakable. She was finally brought to the hospital after, in irritation with someone on the telephone, she threw her cell phone out of the car window into traffic while driving eighty miles an hour down the freeway.

By contrast, in hypomania the main problem with a lack of insight is that the person having these symptoms will not recognize them and thus not be able to report them. His symptoms might not be dangerous in themselves. For example, he might periodically go to karaoke bars and perform, when usually he is rather shy. He might think this is odd, yet never think of it as a *symptom*. Since the diagnosis of bipolar disorder in the *DSM* system hinges on detecting these kinds of symptoms, a person's inability to recognize them can interfere with receiving an accurate diagnosis.

Allowing Friends and Family to Help You Fill in the Gaps

Diagnostic accuracy is almost certain to be higher when several different points of view are obtained. This is clearly the case when insight is limited. Many psychiatrists have come to recognize that they and their patients benefit from opening channels for families to provide information. They emphasize that such input is welcome and valued. But this may not be routine for the doctor you see. You may need help getting additional views of your symptoms onto your doctor's radar screen. At minimum you can have family members complete one or both of the bipolar screening tools described later in this chapter. (But you'll have to explain that you want them to complete the form as though they were you, based on what they have observed.) At best, the doctor will ask your permission to have family members comment, and offer them several ways to do so, including coming to sessions with you during the diagnosis phase, for part of the time you spend with the doctor, or perhaps to be interviewed separately.

An Extra Pair of Eyes

Remember that ruling out hypomania is similar to making sure your boss *didn't* leave keys at your house. Having family members help is like having extra eyes for the search. Think about it: if your hypomanic symptoms are obvious, you may be able to see and report them, your doctor may be able to bring out a story about them, and you might even act them out right there in the doctor's office. Or the symptoms may pop out when the doctor asks the routine questions about mania. But when your symptoms are *subtle*, your doctor is likely to need some help determining the presence or absence of hypomania. At this point, some additional input about you from someone who knows you well could make the difference between an accurate diagnosis and a diagnosis that is too heavily dependent on a biased point of view (yours or the doctor's).

Moving across the Bipolar Spectrum from the relatively obvious Bipolar I to subtle versions of Bipolar II, it takes more and more time, effort, and diligence to establish that hypomania is present, or that it is not. *Therefore, the more uncertain you are about whether you really have a Bipolar Spectrum condition, the more you'll need input from others to make your diagnosis an accurate one.* Read that sentence again, please—it's really important. As is true for you personally, the biggest aid to accurate diagnosis that your family or significant others can provide is to *understand what you're looking for* in the search for hypomania.

What If They Call Me Bipolar When I Really Am Not?

Although current evidence suggests that missing bipolar disorder by calling it unipolar is the main diagnostic problem, could we end up making as significant a mistake in the opposite direction, calling you bipolar when you really are unipolar? If so, what would happen? To answer this question, let's take a moment to consider what "really" means, in this context. Then we'll look at the consequences of a mistaken diagnosis.

What Does "Really" Being Unipolar or "Really" Being Bipolar Mean?

Obviously these phrases imply that behind the names are some real things. An accurate diagnosis matches the right name to the real thing. An inaccurate diagnosis uses the wrong name. These phrases indicate that we all, doctors and patients, seem to believe that there truly are right and wrong diagnoses, because there truly are real conditions that these names are supposed to reflect. But this belief may be, at the very least, dramatically oversimplified.

Let's take a simple example to illustrate the problem. Suppose someone begins to have difficulty breathing and starts breathing very rapidly. She might have pneumonia, or she might have severe asthma. The medical field uses some relatively easy ways to know what she really has. If a sample of what she's coughing up is placed in a Petri dish and a colony of streptococcal bacteria grow there in forty-eight hours with no other bacteria (a *pure culture*), and there is a blush on her chest x-ray that shouldn't be there, then pneumonia is pretty likely. If she unfortunately dies from this pneumonia, we can reach near complete certainty of pneumonia if, after her death, an autopsy showed that her lungs are full of that same bacteria.

However, this woman's case shows how the level of certainty increases with each new finding: from suggestive symptoms, to bacteria in the Petri dish and a suggestive chest x-ray, to finally the clincher: a matching finding at autopsy. This is how doctors know about what *really* is causing a problem: there is a progression from symptoms and clinical signs (such as rapid breathing) to laboratory findings, all of which increase certainty, and the highest certainty comes with the autopsy result.

In contrast, diagnoses in psychiatry almost never have this kind of certainty. Most of the illnesses we clinicians treat do not consistently cause a recognizable physical change in the brain that can be detected with a brain scan or even at autopsy. There lies the diagnostic dilemma. For most psychiatric conditions in general and for Mood Spectrum conditions in particular, clinicians have no equivalent of a chest x-ray, and worst of all, we don't have a clincher finding like bacteria in the lungs to establish what really caused the problem.

There will be great excitement when someone comes up with a lab test for bipolarity. As of this writing, a research group just recently proclaimed to have developed a test that might be useful, if not perfect. Yet when such sunny possibilities are announced, they only begin to penetrate the clouds of uncertainty. Think about it. How will we know a test for bipolar disorder is really correct? Won't we need a group of patients who are somehow known with complete certainty to have bipolar disorder, in order to show that the test can *find them* and name their illness *accurately*, distinguishing them from a group who don't have bipolar disorder? But how will we have determined that the bipolar people, for such a "test of the test," are really bipolar?

Increasing the Probability of "Likely" Bipolar

You can see the problem: there is no perfect reference point. The presence of bipolar disorder cannot be established with certainty: there is no x-ray, brain scan, blood test, or even autopsy finding. I hope this will change, perhaps in the next few years and likely in the next decade, as the understanding of the cellular and genetic basis of bipolarity continues to improve. But for now, how will we know whether a test can really find bipolarity? Fortunately, the situation is not hopeless. We can find groups of patients whose symptoms lead to strong agreement about their diagnosis of bipolar disorder, and use them as the standard for evaluating how well a test performs at identifying bipolar versus not bipolar. Two questionnaires that have been validated in this way are discussed later in this chapter.

Yet even with such tests, we only can increase the *probability* that bipolar disorder is present. We cannot really know, even through the most expert interview (which is one of our best current ways of knowing, believe it or not), that a person has bipolar disorder. Thus we can't know whether a diagnosis really is correct or not. But we can make the probability quite high. For patients with classic symptoms typified in the *DSM*, we can easily get psychiatrists to agree that a particular patient does have bipolar disorder. But for patients with more complex and subtle symptom patterns, psychiatrists can easily disagree, and there is *no perfect standard* to use to know which psychiatrist has the right diagnosis.

Sorry, that does leave you wondering, doesn't it? How are *you* supposed to know, if we clinicians have so much trouble knowing what you really have? Look at it this way: the more you know about bipolar variations and how they lie on the Mood Spectrum, the more you can help your doctor or therapist arrive at the most accurate conclusion possible—even if it is not possible to be *perfectly* accurate.

Instead of trying to establish with certainty whether you do or don't have bipolar disorder, whether you have unipolar depression or Bipolar II, you can establish a sense of the likelihood of some degree of bipolarity in your case. If you're out at one end of the Mood Spectrum, either clearly bipolar or clearly unipolar, having diagnostic confidence and selecting a treatment are easier. But people in the middle of the Mood Spectrum—whose symptoms can be interpreted either way, unipolar or bipolar—have to weigh the risks and benefits of being treated as though they are *unipolar*, and then compare the risks and benefits of being treated as though they are *bipolar*.

The Consequences of a Mistaken Diagnosis

If your symptoms place you rather clearly at one end of the Mood Spectrum, you may not need to read this section. This information is intended primarily for those in the middle. There are four possibilities:

1. You really have unipolar disorder and are treated for unipolar disorder.
2. You really have unipolar disorder but are treated for bipolar disorder.
3. You really have bipolar disorder but are treated for unipolar disorder.
4. You really have bipolar disorder and are treated for bipolar disorder.

Obviously it's numbers 2 and 3 that you have to worry about, right? For you visual-learner types, Table 4.1 shows you the possible outcomes.

As you can see, when what you really have (as if there is some magic way to know) and your diagnosis match up in the table, this ought to lead to a satisfactory outcome. However, problems arise when there is a mismatch, as in the lower left and upper right

TABLE 4.1 What You Really Have Versus Your Diagnosis

		What You Really Have	
		Unipolar	Bipolar
Your	Unipolar	1. Satisfactory	**3. Problem**
Diagnosis	Bipolar	**2. Problem**	4. Satisfactory

TABLE 4.2 Consequences of the Two Major Misdiagnoses

		What You Really Have	
		Unipolar	Bipolar
Your Diagnosis	Unipolar	• Satisfactory	• Risk of mania, mixed states, rapid cycling
			• May decrease response to mood stabilizers in short and possibly long term
			• May increase suicide risk in some people
			• Delay effective treatment
	Bipolar	• Stigma of bipolar label	• Satisfactory
		• Greater medication risks	
		• Ineffective treatment	
		• Delay effective treatment	

boxes. Turning to those two problem areas, Table 4.2 summarizes the risks associated with the two types of misdiagnosis, as described in the next several sections.

Really Bipolar, but Called Unipolar. We're in the upper right-hand box now, right? Treatment options for unipolar disorder (in the *DSM*, that's Major Depression) include psychotherapy and exercise—and medications. When a medication is considered, it will almost certainly be an antidepressant. There is considerable controversy about just how often antidepressants cause trouble in bipolar disorder. Despite some skeptics, however, I think the research literature convincingly shows that *some people* can have very severe negative reactions to antidepressants when their depression is really bipolar in origin. These reactions include having

- A full manic episode
- Rapid cycling from one mood state to another
- Mixed-state symptoms—including the most dangerous of all mood states, the combination of agitation and depression

Some evidence suggests that antidepressants can alter the course of bipolar disorder, leading to more symptoms than you would otherwise have experienced. Though still quite controversial, some evidence also suggests that antidepressants can cause people to have suicidal thoughts and actions. This reaction is more common in people with bipolar disorder. Finally, a more theoretical concern is that antidepressants could somehow make the manic or hypomanic symptoms more severe, bring them on sooner, and perhaps make the entire condition more difficult to treat later, requiring more medication, than otherwise might have occurred. This theory is called *kindling* (discussed in more detail, along with the rest of these antidepressant-associated risks, in Chapter 9).

Finally, there is a very unfortunate paradox in this diagnostic process: if you are under twenty-five years old and have had only depression so far, with no bipolarity (using our magic way of knowing), your diagnosis should, indeed, be Major Depression. But this must remain a *provisional* diagnosis until you are at least in your late twenties, because it is possible that the manic-side symptoms just *haven't shown up yet*. Dr. Barbara Geller is one of the leading authorities on bipolar disorder in children. She and her group followed up on a group of children who were treated for Major Depression (at age ten, on average). By the time the children had reached twenty years old, *half* had developed bipolar symptoms sufficient for that diagnosis. Dr. Joe Goldberg, a brilliant bipolar researcher, and his colleagues found the same result in young adults (average age twenty-three) hospitalized for Major Depression. Over the next fifteen years, *half* of them developed bipolar symptoms.

You can see the unfortunate implication: you may look truly unipolar now, but if you're young and especially if you have several of the soft signs presented in Chapter 3, you'll have to *keep* considering this issue of bipolarity as you select your treatments. Doctors ask me: How soon can I relax about all this if my patient gets a good response to an antidepressant? My answer is that in my experience, negative reactions to antidepressants have occurred in anywhere between twenty minutes, such as my patient who said that twenty minutes after his first dose of paroxetine (Paxil), "I felt like I was shot out of a cannon," and seven years, such as my patient who developed a clear negative reaction to sertraline (Zoloft) after doing very well on it for seven years. (I published the latter as a case report because of its implications.)

Really Unipolar, but Called Bipolar. Finally, here is the promised section on what might befall you, if you really are unipolar and find yourself being diagnosed as bipolar by a doctor or therapist wearing bipolar lenses. There are multiple risks.

First of all, there is the stigma factor. It's bad enough to have to accept the label "depressed," right? But a label of "bipolar?" Whoa, that is a completely different level in the mental-illness department store. You came in looking for a new shirt, and all of a sudden someone is showing you a new suit and tie as well. Or so it may *seem*. Having read this far, you now know that this distinction between unipolar depression and bipolar disorder is just a matter of degree—a matter of your position on the Mood Spectrum. But *society* doesn't know that. It is embarrassing enough for someone to know you are being treated for depression, but for them to know you are being treated for bipolar disorder? Most people find this a very big jump, even after they have learned about the Mood Spectrum. I generally counsel my patients to be very cautious about whom they tell that they've been diagnosed as having bipolar disorder. There is just too much risk that their boss, friends, or schoolmates will react to this label as though it means Bipolar I (remember, that's the new name for the former *manic-depressive illness*, which includes full manic symptoms such as psychosis). There is nothing morally wrong about having Bipolar I, of course. Yet the term calls up an image in most people's minds that is far from the symptom patterns of the Mood Spectrum and thus is misleading, as well as potentially more stigmatizing.

Second is the issue of medication risks. Most people look at the list of potential side effects that can occur with mood stabilizers and think they look worse than the potential side effects of antidepressant medications. This is a bit of an apples-and-oranges comparison. How do you compare the risk of something that can cause a severe skin rash, which requires hospitalization 1 time in about 3,000 and occasionally, though very rarely, is fatal, versus the risk of a medication that can make you suicidal, perhaps rarely but perhaps as often as 1 time in 100 or 200? Antidepressants look pretty innocent in the advertising they receive, complete with happy white-teethed smiling models and cheery colors, yet they can cause weight gain, problems with sexual function (far more often than do most mood stabilizers), and the usual long laundry list of uncommon but serious problems. Nevertheless, when my patients look at the list of risks associated with mood stabilizers, they generally seem to regard the risk column as considerably worse than that for antidepressants (more about this in the Chapter 8).

Third, mood stabilizers may simply not work when the problem really is unipolar. Yet, some actually do: lithium is routinely recommended as an add-on option for unipolar depression that is not responding well or fully to an antidepressant. More limited data exist for several other medications used for bipolar disorder, suggesting they might be beneficial even if used mistakenly.

Finally, barking up the wrong tree potentially delays effective treatment. Since it can take several weeks before the benefits of antidepressants begin to appear, adding further delay by using mood stabilizers first (perhaps even several different ones, if the initial one doesn't work) can lead to a long period of time during which the depression symptoms persist. This delay is also an issue when the diagnostic error is reversed (that is, if someone who is bipolar is diagnosed as unipolar), so it is included in both sides of Table 4.2.

Where the Error Likely Lies

Right now, if any erring is going on, it appears to be in the direction of overdiagnosing *unipolar* disorder (depression). In my view, erring in the direction of bipolarity presents no greater risk. In fact, you can pretty easily make a case that if a diagnostic error is going to be made, fewer people will be harmed by leaning in the direction of overdiagnosing bipolar disorder (with the possible exception of the stigma factor for some people). Many other psychiatrists would strongly disagree with me here. It all depends on how risky you think antidepressants can be, and I worry about that more than most of my colleagues—which is why I wrote the rather elaborate essay "Antidepressants in Bipolar Disorder: The Controversies" on my website, summarizing what little data there are on this risk.

Disappointing, I know: if you might be on the left end or in the middle of the Mood Spectrum, there is no firm way to make your diagnosis. As you can see, my recommendation is to understand as much as possible about the nature of bipolarity and then work closely with your doctor or therapist. You start with a *working diagnosis*, a tentative framework and not a final conclusion, to see if this leads to a good outcome. If not, you rethink the diagnosis, repeatedly if necessary. As Harvard's Gary Sachs says, telling someone after one interview that he or she has bipolar disorder and needs treatment for it is like "asking someone to marry you and have children on the first date."

Suppose you don't have a psychiatrist to help you with your diagnosis. Couldn't you take some sort of test that might shed some light on the issue? It depends on where you lie on the spectrum, as you're about to learn.

Bipolar Tests

Many people finish learning about the problem of subtle hypomania and the soft bipolar variations of the Mood Spectrum, but still want to know: "Can't someone just give me a yes or no?" After all, when you see a psychiatrist or even your primary care doctor, before they can start treatment—especially with a medication approach—they have to decide one way or another, don't they?

Well actually, no—and yes. I don't mean to confuse you, but it really depends on which way you think about diagnosis. You now understand the Mood Spectrum model, which does not offer a yes or no. In this model a diagnosis is an attempt to place you somewhere on the spectrum. By comparison, in the *DSM* category-based system you *can* answer the question, "Do I have bipolar disorder?" with a yes or no.

In some people, all the diagnostic clues point in the same direction: symptoms, symptom course over time, family history, and response to previous treatment. These people are likely to be at one end or another of the Mood Spectrum. The *DSM* system works fine for them. A yes-or-no answer is appropriate and will lead directly to appropriate treatment. These people don't need any additional tests to help establish their diagnosis.

Ironically, the people who might need a test result to clarify their diagnosis are the very ones whose test results are most difficult to interpret, as you will soon learn. There *are* tests. Two of them are very easy to take, even on your own without a doctor or therapist involved at all. But you must remember: *the test result is not a diagnosis*. Even a positive test, a yes answer on the test, does not mean you have bipolar disorder. Many doctors have forgotten why this is so, though they once learned it. Therefore, to be safe, *you* need to learn this if you are going to use these tests either on your own or in a doctor's office.

You're anxious to look at the tests, aren't you? All right, they're coming. But first, you must know how to interpret the results. Usually this is left to doctors who are supposed to have been trained to do what you're about to learn. But it won't hurt for you to know, too.

What You Should Know Before Taking and Scoring the Tests

Before you learn how to score your test, you need to understand the warning that *a test result is not a diagnosis*. Wait a minute, isn't diagnosis the point of the thing? Well, yes and no. Yes, the point is to help establish a working diagnosis for you. But no, a positive test doesn't mean you have bipolar disorder. Why not? That gets a bit complicated. Here's a short answer.

Medical diagnostic tests, even the very best ones, don't give a diagnosis. They *shift the likelihood* of a diagnosis. Remember that most diagnoses in psychiatry are based on four things:

1. Your symptoms
2. Your symptom course over time
3. Your family history
4. Your response to treatments

When your doctor, with your help, has assembled those four parts of your diagnostic database, he or she will have at least a hunch as to what's going on. If the doctor is nearly certain you *don't* have bipolar disorder, or nearly certain that you *do*, there is no need for a test. But between those extremes, a test can sometimes shift the hunch in one direction or the other. That can be useful.

Though they were taught this logic in medical school, many doctors have forgotten that even a very biologically based test like an HIV test for the AIDS virus does not give a diagnosis. That's because the tests, even very precise tests like that for HIV, are not perfect. They can produce *false-positive* results. A positive is supposed to mean the disease is present, but sometimes this is a false signal. Sometimes the test is positive even when the disease is *not* present. The HIV blood test, for example, used to have a 1.5 percent error rate. (It's better now.) This means that if the test was given to 10,000 people whom somehow we knew did *not* have the HIV virus, 15 of them would have a false-positive test result.

The bipolar tests have error rates like this, too—worse, in fact. Some studies say quite a bit worse. That's why you have to be careful with the test results. They are supposed to be used to *shift a hunch*. They can be helpful in this way, especially if your test result is clearly positive or negative. But by themselves, they cannot make a diagnosis, because of their error rates. Just like any test, even the more biologically based low-error-rate tests, the bipolar tests give results that must be interpreted in the context of the other four factors for a diagnosis: symptoms, symptom course, family history, and response to previous treatments. This statistically correct way of using the test results is discussed in great detail (which doctors will recognize and perhaps shudder to see again, as these statistics are not easy and often are presented very quickly in medical school) on my website, in the plainest English I can muster.

That's why the test result is not a diagnosis: the result must be interpreted in the context of a hunch. Your doctor or therapist is supposed to gather the information to create that context and then the hunch. There is no statistical reason why *you* can't gather the information, arrive at your own hunch, and then use the test to adjust your hunch. If you've read and understood the first three chapters of this book, I think your hunch can, indeed, be more accurate than that of many primary care doctors (though their skills are beginning to improve rapidly).

The next step is using your test results to adjust your hunch. If you read and can understand my Web pages describing the details of that process, then I think you can do as well or better than most primary care doctors. Mind you, this is diagnostic heresy: the guild of medicine does not allow patients to make their own diagnoses. Let's put it this way: if you have not read and understood my Web pages about interpreting your test results, then you should not trust your interpretation of them and should talk with your doctor and therapist about what they mean.

Yet all this fuss over a test result is leading us away from the main point of this entire book: patients can be found all the way across the Mood Spectrum. Therefore, we'll look at the test that can help determine your position on that spectrum: the Bipolar Spectrum Diagnostic Scale (BSDS). By contrast, another test, called the Mood Disorder Questionnaire (MDQ), generally is used in a *DSM*-like way to provide a yes or no about whether you have bipolar disorder. Thus the MDQ is not as useful in a Mood Spectrum way of thinking. However, it has quickly become the more standard of the two tests, so your doctor is more likely to be familiar with it than with the BSDS. (If for some reason you need or want to use it, on my website is an MDQ and a scoring guide for it with information on how to interpret the results, just as you'll see in a moment here for the BSDS. Use the Notes page, psycheducation.org/notes.htm, for a link.)

The Bipolar Spectrum Diagnostic Scale (BSDS)

The Bipolar Spectrum Diagnostic Scale gives an answer in terms of a range of possibilities and thus works well with a Mood Spectrum diagnostic model. This test was developed primarily by a very smart and creative psychiatrist in Boston, Dr. Ron Pies. The accuracy of his test was subsequently evaluated by Dr. Nassir Ghaemi and colleagues. You'll recall Dr. Ghaemi from Chapter 3, which featured his research on the Mood Spectrum concept. These psychiatrists wanted to develop a paper-and-pencil test that could gather information about hypomanic symptoms in a systematic and quantifiable (put a number on it) way, and yet remain consistent with the idea of a Bipolar Spectrum. If you haven't taken the test yet and think that you might *ever* want to, you should do that now before you read about scoring it. Otherwise, if you take it later, you might be thinking about the scoring instead of just being yourself as you read the paragraph. Here is Dr. Pies' test in the sidebar.

The BSDS

First read the following paragraph all the way through ignoring the blanks, and then follow the instructions that appear afterward.

Some individuals noticed that their mood and/or energy levels shift drastically from time to time _____. These individuals notice that, at times, their mood and/or energy level is very low, and at other times, very high_____.

During their "low" phases, these individuals often feel a lack of energy, a need to stay in bed or get extra sleep, and little or no motivation to do things they need to do_____. They often put on weight during these periods_____. During their low phases, these individuals often feel "blue," sad all the time, or depressed_____. Sometimes, during the low phases, they feel helpless or even suicidal _____. Their ability to function at work or socially is impaired _____. Typically, the low phases last for a few weeks, but sometimes they last only a few days _____. Individuals with this type of pattern may experience a period of normal mood in between mood swings, during which their mood and energy level feels right and their ability to function is not disturbed _____. They may then notice a marked shift or switch in the way they feel _____. Their energy increases above what is normal for them, and they often get many things done they would not ordinarily be able to do _____. Sometimes during those high periods, these individuals feel as if they had too much energy or feel hyper _____. Some individuals, during these high periods, may feel irritable, on edge, or aggressive _____. Some individuals, during the high periods, take on too many activities at once _____. During the high periods, some individuals may spend money in ways that cause them trouble_____. They may be more talkative, outgoing, or sexual during these periods _____. Sometimes, their behavior during the high periods seems strange or annoying to others _____. Sometimes, these individuals get into difficulty with co-workers or police during these high periods _____. Sometimes, they increase their alcohol or nonprescription drug use during the high periods _____.

(continued)

The BSDS, *continued*

After you have read this passage, please decide which of the following is most accurate:

- This story fits me very well, or almost perfectly.
- This story fits me fairly well.
- This story fits me to some degree, but not in most respects.
- This story doesn't really describe me at all.

Now please go back through the paragraph, and put a check mark after each sentence that accurately describes you. When you are done, total the number of check marks.

Scoring the BSDS. If you want to use this test yourself, now is probably the best time to follow those instructions and take it. You can tally your check marks on a separate sheet of paper if you'll be giving this book to a friend later.

When you're ready, here's how the original author, Dr. Pies, recommends scoring your result. Add your total of check marks from the first nineteen sentences. To that total, add the number in parentheses that follows the line you selected earlier:

- This story fits me very well, or almost perfectly. (6)
- This story fits me fairly well. (4)
- This story fits me to some degree, but not in most respects. (2)
- This story doesn't really describe me at all. (0)

The maximum is 19 points from the paragraph, plus up to 6 points from "how well it fits." Here's how to interpret your score:

19 or higher = bipolar spectrum disorder highly likely
11–18 = moderate probability of bipolar spectrum disorder

6–10 = low probability of bipolar spectrum disorder

< 6 = bipolar spectrum disorder very unlikely

If you were hoping for a yes or no answer from this test, that's understandable. But remember, the whole point is to estimate your position on the Mood Spectrum, and that is not a yes-or-no matter. Remember that these tests are supposed to shift a hunch, not make a diagnosis. Talk about this test result with your doctor.

OK, before we leave Part I of this book, on diagnosing these different bipolar variations, let's examine some other conditions that can *look like* or *accompany* Mood Spectrum symptoms.

CHAPTER 5

What Else Could It Be? Ruling Out Conditions That Mimic Bipolar Disorder

You probably don't need to read this chapter if you have a good doctor whose diagnostic abilities you trust, you've received the same diagnosis from multiple providers, or your diagnosis already has led to effective treatments. But if you're just beginning your diagnostic learning, and especially if you think ensuring a correct diagnosis might somehow be up to you, then before settling with a working diagnosis of a Mood Spectrum condition, you'll want to consider four alternative explanations:

1. Medical conditions that can look like bipolar disorder
2. Medications that can produce similar symptoms
3. Psychiatric conditions that might better explain your symptoms
4. Conditions that commonly occur *with* bipolar disorder

Were this chapter to name and describe every condition related to these four possibilities, you'd have a small medical textbook.

Instead of lists and descriptions that you can find in more detail elsewhere, here are some *concepts* that may guide you when considering alternative explanations for your symptoms. Most doctors approach the issue this way: first use these concepts to think broadly; then consult the lists when necessary.

Medical Conditions That Look Like Bipolar Disorder

Other illnesses can cause symptoms that resemble bipolar disorder. But imagine what could happen here: I could give you a whole new set of worries, right? You pick up this book looking for help with your mood symptoms, and all of a sudden, you find yourself worrying about having a brain tumor or immune system problem. Thanks a lot, Dr. Phelps.

Well, we'd better start with a lesson from medical school: "Common things are common." This is a nonstatistical way of saying a statistical thing. It's simple, really. Imagine that two different illnesses can produce the same kind of symptoms. For example, say a person can get pain in his or her neck from either muscle tension or a spinal cord tumor. (Of course, neck pain has other causes, but for now let's consider just these two.) OK, you're the doctor, and Roger Samuels shows up in your office with neck pain. Before you get the story of this pain and examine his neck, there is already a certain likelihood that he has muscle tension. That likelihood is much higher than the likelihood of a spinal cord tumor, because muscle tension is a very common illness whereas a spinal cord tumor is not.

Getting a little closer to home, suppose you have phases of irritability, insomnia, and agitation, and at other times you have phases of extremely low energy, low motivation, and an inability to enjoy things you usually enjoy. While a brain tumor can *on very rare occasion* cause this set of symptoms, a mood condition is hundreds of times more likely to be their cause because such tumors are very rare and mood disorders are common. So if you have such symptoms, then without even considering things like family history, you can establish a *probability*—a likelihood for each different diagnostic explanation (depression, bipolarity, brain tumor, autoimmune disorder) based on how commonly they occur.

Therefore, we doctors were taught in medical school, "common things are common." Our teachers emphasized the importance of this idea: think about whether your proposed diagnostic explanation is actually a common condition or not. Medical students, being what they are, commonly translate this to, "When you hear hoofbeats, think horses, not zebras." Get it? Horses are common, zebras are not (at least at U.S. medical school locations). When a medical student sees a symptom, such as cough, she should think about common possible causes, or "horses," *first*. Later, she can consider much more unusual causes of cough, the "zebras" of medicine.

So as you consider lists of medical conditions that can cause depression, please take into account that they only very rarely produce bipolar-like symptoms, with three major exceptions:

1. Thyroid problems
2. Reproductive hormones in women
3. Medications for other conditions

Let's take a closer look at these three.

Thyroid

You'll want to know about your thyroid status for at least two reasons:

1. Thyroid problems can *cause* mood symptoms.
2. Even normal thyroid hormone levels can affect how you respond to Mood Spectrum treatments like antidepressants and mood stabilizers.

Low levels of thyroid hormone (*hypothyroidism*) can cause depression. High levels (*hyperthyroidism*) can cause anxiety and agitation. In my experience, *hypo*thyroidism can *also* be associated

83

with anxiety. Some kinds of anxiety can be part of a bipolar disorder, as discussed in the anxiety sections of this chapter. Thyroid problems are common—these are definitely horses, not zebras—so an evaluation of mood problems should include a check of your thyroid hormone status. If your doctor does not arrange this, you can gently wonder aloud about whether it might be wise (following the general approach discussed in Chapter 6 on collaborating with your doctor).

Whereas the importance of checking thyroid status is generally well-known, the concept that normal thyroid levels can affect treatment or mood problems is not widely recognized. Several studies in both major depression and bipolar disorder have shown that people with thyroid levels close to *hyper*thyroidism (too much thyroid hormone), but still in the normal range, responded better to treatment. By contrast, people with thyroid tests in the normal range but close to *hypo*thyroidism responded to treatment more slowly or did not respond as well. The authors' conclusion from one of these studies has such important implications that you better hear it from them: "Our results suggest that nearly three-quarters of patients with bipolar disorder have a thyroid profile that may be suboptimal for antidepressant response." In other words, 75 percent of people with bipolar disorder may be too close to *hypo*thyroidism to respond well to treatment for depression. Mind you, this is only one study regarding this relationship in bipolar disorder; a repeat study with similar results would help firm these conclusions. However, the importance of topped-up thyroid levels is supported by the fact that a similar study in patients with major depression found a similar result.

These authors stop short of recommending treatment with thyroid hormone for patients with bipolar disorder, because their research did not directly study such an approach. They clearly imply that the approach should be considered, though. Treatment with thyroid hormone, even starting from within the normal range, carries little or no risk unless you are given too much and become *hyper*thyroid. Therefore, adding thyroid hormone to any treatment you receive, long recognized as a strategy for *treatment-*

resistant depression, is an option to consider if things are not getting better and if your thyroid tests close to the hypothyroid end of the normal range. See my Web pages on thyroid and bipolar disorders (via the Notes page for Chapter 5: psycheducation.org/notes.htm) for a description of these tests and ranges, as well as more updated information on the relationship between thyroid changes and mood symptoms.

Reproductive Hormones

I have to include something about reproductive hormones and mood because

1. Everyone knows there is some sort of relationship.
2. Whatever's going on is common.

Unfortunately, medical science has avoided studying women of reproductive age until very recently. Despite watching the literature for several years on this topic, I have found little research on the treatment of mood problems that seem directly related to hormones, except concerning the treatment of PMS.

Yet the PMS research proves disappointing also. At least twelve randomized trials (the optimal research design, described in Chapter 7) have been done for serotonin-type antidepressants, which all seem to work quite well. But we have only one tiny study on exercise as a treatment for PMS, one large study for calcium, none for black cohosh, and only old preliminary studies for chasteberry—at least that I am aware of at this point. I may have missed a study or two, but you still see the point: there are well-designed research studies for the medications that will make money, but no such data, or very little, on the treatments that are cheap. This, of course, is not a coincidence.

Conditions Associated with Depression

The list of diseases associated with depression is so long that it is of little use: nearly every common disease you can think of is on it, including heart disease, stroke, diabetes, and cancer. So I'll focus on a few (other than thyroid) that are particularly relevant to Mood Spectrum conditions.

Sleep apnea is not on the depression lists very often, yet it is a growing problem because it occurs more commonly in people who have gained a lot of weight. In the United States, weight gain is completely out of control. Since 1991 obesity has increased 75 percent in the United States. One in every five Americans is obese—we're eating ourselves into a corner. Stress may play a huge role in this as well. Then there are medications with weight gain as a side effect: most antidepressants can cause weight gain, and the worst culprits are among the mood stabilizers. Unfortunately, the standard test for sleep apnea, an overnight sleep study in which breathing is monitored during sleep, is very expensive. Frankly, I'm not sure the United States can afford to test everyone who might need to be tested. But sleep apnea can make depression worse and make Mood Spectrum variations more treatment resistant.

I'm certain the United States can't afford to treat the diabetes wave that is coming, estimated at 30 percent of the Medicare population in the next decade by an endocrinologist who described a routine regimen of five drugs *minimum* to treat it—all expensive. I thought psychiatry's end of the drug-budget boat was sinking until I heard this. But I digress—or perhaps not. A tiny bit of evidence shows that obesity can worsen mood, not just through how people feel about themselves and through the limitations in their physical activity, but directly. (You can see more speculation, including a remarkable case report on my website page: "Metabolic Syndrome—*Causes* Mental Health Symptoms?" found on the Notes page at psycheducation.org/notes.htm.)

Notice that I've been talking about only depression so far. What about bipolarity: do any medical conditions look like bipolar disorder? Again, yes, many do. The standard lists include too many rare conditions to be of much use to you. Head injury and stroke are very commonly associated with bipolar symptoms showing up in someone who never had them before. However, generally we clinicians think of these conditions as bringing on true bipolar conditions, rather than as mimics.

How can you know whether you have a mimic and not bipolar disorder? In general this matter is best left to your primary care doctor, if you have a good one. Here are some clues the doctor looks for: symptoms that just don't fit, such as shifting levels of alertness; lab test abnormalities on routine screening tests; or unusual findings on a physical exam. Another simple clue is the absence of other features of bipolar disorder—no early onset of symptoms, no repeated mood episodes, no shift in mood after childbirth, and (perhaps most important) no family history of any mood, anxiety, or alcohol problems. When *some* of these features, as well as bipolar-like symptoms, are present, the likelihood that a bipolar diagnosis best explains all these findings increases.

Medications That Can Produce Bipolar-Like Symptoms

My prescriptions can certainly cause problems that other doctors end up having to deal with, such as weight gain, increased blood pressure, or increased cholesterol levels. (You'll also learn about some medications that *don't* do that kind of thing, when we get to Chapter 10.) But you have to watch out for a few of those other doctors' medications as well.

As a primary colleague of mine often says: "medications are guilty until proven innocent." (This important way of thinking about medications has actually been around a long time; see Notes on my website.) If mood symptoms worsen *after* a medication is introduced, then it may be the cause. The only way to prove innocence is to stop it, as long as the medication is not absolutely essential in some way, such as an antibiotic for a severe skin infection. However, DO NOT STOP ANY MEDICATION ON YOUR OWN. Your doctor could know something you don't about the risks you face when stopping a medication. The doctor can help you plan a tapering-off schedule. *Taper everything*, at least any psychiatric medicine, following the plan you worked out with your doctor. (Do I sound a little anxious about this?)

When my patients come in and are not doing well, I look at their medication list, wondering if something on that list might be preventing a good response. Every single medication must be considered in this way. Indeed, if you search the Internet for a list of medications that can cause depression, you'll get a huge list. It's so long that it's impractical: there are too many medications for anyone to remember and too many that cause depression only rarely. So even though the list of possible culprits is very long, a few of them turn up frequently (including causing everything from mania to plain depression).

Steroids

In my experience, steroids are one of the worst offenders. (The only other medication that causes serious trouble so frequently is alcohol, discussed in Chapter 11.) The common form is prednisone for poison oak, asthma, or a really creaky joint. One or two doses can cause mood symptoms to worsen or reappear if they were previously well-controlled. The steroids to be concerned about are the oral versions—pills that you swallow. This includes estrogen, progesterone, and testosterone. As noted earlier, these hormones are quite famous for causing mood symptoms: progesterone causes primarily depression; testosterone causes primarily mania (at least at first). Estrogen is a wild card—it can cause agitation and anxiety. Some women can't take birth control pills for just this reason. It can also cause depression, though that's less common.

How about inhaled steroids, such as for allergies and asthma? Although there is a case report of mania associated with an older inhaler, beclomethasone, such problems are quite rare. Steroid creams for the skin are also only very rarely a problem, with high doses on skin that's irritated or has high blood flow for some other reason. The rest of the medications on the typical lists are, in my experience at least, not very commonly a problem.

Other Medications to Watch Out For

The famous candidates are pain medications (particularly ones that are opiate-based such as Percocet), tranquilizers (Valium and its cousins, including Xanax), and blood pressure medications of all kinds. In my experience, however, these often are not the problem. They can sometimes be *part* of the problem. Yet, it is important to consider them, particularly when treatment is not working well. Using the guilty-until-proven-innocent approach, they are all traditional suspects.

Psychiatric Conditions That Might Explain Your Symptoms

This section looks at psychiatric diagnoses that might better explain your Mood Spectrum symptoms. That is, they might be alternative diagnoses—*instead of* a diagnosis of bipolar disorder. Two conditions in particular can create virtually all of the bipolar symptom set: substance use and borderline personality disorder.

Substance Use

Substance use is the politically correct term for drinking alcohol or taking street drugs. If you can manage to stay off the stuff for a few months, then figuring out whether substance use is your *only* problem should be pretty easy. If you're clean for months and you have no more symptoms, then it is pretty likely that the drugs or alcohol were the problem, not bipolarity. But if you are off substances for months and your symptoms are still around, you might have *two* problems—a mood problem and a substance use problem (although by that time the latter would be in short-term remission).

However, many people are using alcohol or street drugs to treat their Mood Spectrum symptoms. For example, people use alcohol or marijuana to dampen the agitation that can accompany hypomania. They conclude that their mood symptoms are worse than the consequences of using drugs or alcohol. These people can have a tough time going drug free long enough to figure out if they've got one problem or two. Their symptoms come back when they try to stop using. Sometimes we clinicians just have to presume there might be an underlying depression or bipolarity and treat it, hoping the substance use will ease up as a result. This approach used to be scorned—fifteen years ago when I was in training—but now is a more common approach, with some good data to support it.

Borderline Personality Disorder

Borderline personality disorder is described by an expert as "a common personality disorder that involves difficulties with intimate relationships, problems handling emotional states like anger and sadness, impulsivity, and suicidality." If you are not familiar with the borderline concept, you'll get a quick idea of the diagnostic problem simply by looking at the *DSM* criteria for Borderline Personality Disorder alongside a Mood Spectrum interpretation of bipolar symptoms, as shown in Table 5.1. The point, I hope, is obvious. The two conditions nearly completely overlap, with the exception of two symptoms not found in bipolar variations: chronic empti-

TABLE 5.1 Borderline and Bipolar Symptoms

	Borderline Personality Disorder (*DSM* list)	Bipolar (broad view)
Cognitive	Unstable self	Unstable self
	Transient paranoia	Psychosis, especially paranoid/grandiose
	Chronic emptiness	
	Abandonment fear	
Energy	Impulsivity (sex, substances, self-harm)	Impulsivity (spending, sex, substances, risk sports)
Mood	Affective instability	Affective instability
	Reactive mood	"Rejection hypersensitivity"
	Episodic dysphoria	Dysphoric hypomania or mania
	Irritability, intense anger	Irritability, intense anger
	Anxiety	Anxiety
Behavior	Suicide (~10%)	Suicide (~10%)
	Self-harm	Self-harm

ness and abandonment fear. Different psychiatrists seeing exactly the same symptoms could easily apply different diagnostic labels.

The very concept of personality disorders has a complex history in psychiatry. (A less judgmental and more descriptive terminology cannot come too soon, in my opinion.) This history cannot easily be summarized, but one thing is clear: distinguishing borderline personality disorder from bipolarity is quite controversial. If this topic is of interest to you, take the Notes route to see my essay "Borderline Versus Bipolar," which links about thirty important references and is periodically updated. The bottom line of that essay is that treatments for both labels can be useful for both conditions, and neither type of treatment is likely to make either condition worse if there is a misdiagnosis—so why not just get on with selecting treatments and skip the worry over the label? You may recognize this as a "lumper" approach. Treatments may become more specific in the future, making a "splitter" approach more necessary. For now, however, I think lumping makes more sense, especially because it may prevent potentially destructive disagreements about diagnosis, which serve little purpose but can increase patients' distress.

Conditions That Commonly Occur *with* Bipolar Disorder

Unlike substance use and borderline personality disorder, which represent *alternative* diagnoses, the following conditions do not include mood symptoms, at least in their technical definitions. Thus they do not represent alternative explanations. In this section, we look at conditions that often *occur with* bipolar disorder but are less likely to fully explain your symptoms, because they do not typically have a strong mood component. In other words, sometimes a patient is very unlucky and gets *two* mental health problems, each independent of the other and requiring separate treatment. (In doctor lingo these are given the unfriendly label *comorbid conditions*, meaning that you have two different co-occurring problems.)

However, often the symptoms seem to improve simply by treating the bipolar component, suggesting that these symptoms were part of the mood condition in the first place (or it made them sufficiently worse to reach symptom level).

Bipolarity has this occur-with or part-of relationship with nearly all the major classes of psychiatric diagnoses:

- Anxiety disorders
- Attention-deficit disorders (ADD)
- Personality disorders
- Substance use disorders
- Psychotic disorders

Psychotic disorders overlap primarily with Bipolar I. A spectrum view has been applied to psychosis as well, placing schizophrenia at one end of a continuum and Bipolar I at the other, with *schizoaffective disorder* in between. Substance use and borderline personality disorder (discussed in the previous section) are very commonly comorbid conditions, occurring with bipolar variations. That leaves anxiety and attention deficit disorders, both of which have extensive overlap and co-occurrence with bipolarity.

Anxiety Disorders

The following is not just a tour through the diagnostic classes of anxiety. This overlap with anxiety disorders really matters. Here's why: the medications most commonly used to treat anxiety disorders are antidepressants. Seems a bit odd, perhaps, but they work quite well for many people. The problem comes when anxiety overlaps or actually is part of a Mood Spectrum condition— that is, when some degree of bipolarity is present. We must consider the risk that an antidepressant for the anxiety condition could make the bipolarity worse.

Fortunately, all the anxiety disorders have specific psychotherapies, which in many cases work as well or better than medications. But these are not widely known nor widely available. As a result, many patients whose anxiety is prominent, but whose cyclic changes in mood and energy (their Mood Spectrum component) are not, will end up getting treated with an antidepressant. I'm writing this book in large part because of all the patients I've seen who were treated this way, whose symptoms only came under control when the antidepressant was tapered off after mood stabilizers were started. Don't get me wrong: antidepressants can be great medications. They help many people. *If you're taking one, you definitely should not stop yours based on having read this book!* However, talk to your doctor about what you've learned. If you have anxiety symptoms as well as Mood Spectrum symptoms, and especially if the anxiety symptoms are not coming under control while the mood symptoms are treated, then you may need to seek out one of the specialized psychotherapies.

But sometimes anxiety is just part of the bipolarity. It only looks like an anxiety condition when the Mood Spectrum condition is not well controlled. Granted, anxiety generally is not regarded as a bipolar symptom. Yet the originator of the bipolar concept, Dr. Emil Kraepelin, clearly recognized it as part of the condition back in 1921. He described "anxious mania" and also "excited depression," which included a "great restlessness." (If the idea that anxiety can be a bipolar symptom rouses your curiosity, take the Notes page link to this topic on my website, which includes a recent review.) Space does not permit a thorough explanation of each of the anxiety disorders, if you are not familiar with them. If you would like more basic information about any of them, go to the Notes page for a link to a condition-specific website. Here I'll highlight major issues regarding overlap with bipolarity.

Social Phobia or Social Anxiety Disorder. *Social phobia* (the *DSM* term), or more politely, *social anxiety disorder*, is an anxiety that is limited to social situations. When away from other people and not facing contact with others soon, anxiety goes away. This is in contrast to all the rest of the anxiety disorders, in which anxiety persists even when alone.

Some degree of social phobia can be part of bipolarity. One of my patients once said, "The opposite of *manic* is not just *depressed*, you know; it's also *lack of self-confidence*." Think about what the mirror image of manic grandiosity looks like. This mirror image is one of the worst aspects of this illness—a self-loathing, self-critical state in which your mind keeps generating very negative assessments of your abilities, your attractiveness, and your very worth. If this combines with the accelerated thoughts from hypomania or mania, you can feel pummeled by a rapid stream of negative thoughts. (You can see why this is commonly associated with suicidal thinking.) But now consider the mirror image of milder, mid-spectrum grandiosity, which manifests as great confidence and assurance that things will go well. You can see how this mirror image can be experienced as lack of self-confidence. People who are not confident are likely to be shy in social situations. Thus bipolarity itself can create a social anxiety.

Unfortunately, while this anxiety often becomes worse when bipolar disorder is worse, it often does not go away when bipolarity is treated. In many people it appears to be a separate, additional condition. Yet they need not turn immediately to treatment with antidepressants. A specific psychotherapy for social phobia, a cognitive-behavioral approach, is nicely described at socialanxiety.factsforhealth.org. An excellent manual, *Managing Social Anxiety: A Cognitive-Behavioral Therapy Approach* (client workbook) is also available. If you need this treatment but can't find a therapist who does it, you can get a manual like this and ask any good psychotherapist with cognitive-behavioral skills (discussed in Chapter 12) to go through it with you.

Obsessive-Compulsive Disorder (OCD). An excellent starting point for OCD education is the very readable *Brain Lock*, from the UCLA OCD program, or the OC Foundation website at ocfoundation.org. Sometimes when hypomania is controlled, obsessive thoughts that look like OCD completely stop. But sometimes, relatively classic OCD obsessions and their attendant rituals—such as checking locks or washing hands—remain. In general the OCD worsens when hypomania worsens. In any case, psychiatrists strongly agree that when both conditions appear to be present, one should *treat the bipolarity first.*

If mood stability has been achieved but OCD symptoms remain and create enough trouble to warrant additional treatment, there are basically two options:

1. An OCD-specific psychotherapy called *exposure and response* (or *ritual*) *prevention (ERP)*
2. Antidepressant medications

Since the latter run the risk of destabilizing the bipolar disorder, starting with ERP makes sense—except for one thing: it's difficult to find an ERP-trained psychotherapist. The treatment is becoming standardized, so you could find a good therapist with cognitive-behavior skills and use the same approach discussed earlier for social phobia therapy: decide with the therapist on one of the several ERP workbooks available, and go through those steps together.

Only as a last resort, in my view, should you consider adding an antidepressant medication to treat OCD if you clearly have significant bipolarity. However, the use of antidepressants in bipolar disorder remains controversial (as summarized in Chapter 9).

Panic Disorder. Panic attacks are sudden episodes of intense anxiety lasting twenty to thirty minutes before gradually fading away. Panic attacks are frequently confused with phases of bipolar-driven anxiety, which can last for *hours* (but often last less than a day). Fortunately, a cognitive-behavioral therapy (CBT) for panic disorder, requiring only twelve sessions, has been shown in one major research study and several smaller ones to work as well as medications in the short run and better in the long run. Which medications would that be? Yes, antidepressants again. Granted, even when people respond very well to CBT, there is a 50 percent relapse rate; however, those who were panic free on an antidepressant then tapered off six months after responding have a *75 percent* relapse rate.

In my view, almost any patient with panic disorder, not just those who also have some degree of bipolarity, should consider the psychotherapy approach before the antidepressant approach. Panic attacks are like a big lake backed up behind an earthen dam: when the water level is at the very top of the dam, it takes just one raindrop to start a flood. Once a small overflow begins, the dam quickly erodes and the whole lake flows out all at once. When it's over, people look back and wonder, "Wow, what was it about that raindrop that made me panic?" Obviously, the problem is not the raindrop, but the *water level*. Anything that raises the water level will make panic attacks more likely. The psychotherapy uses several different techniques to lower the water level.

Hypomania commonly raises the water level. Treating it often stops panic attacks. If not, then psychotherapy may be useful to lower the frequency and intensity of any panic attacks that continue or recur. If you can't find a therapist who knows this method, get the manual *Mastery of Your Anxiety and Panic* (MAP-3, client workbook; amazon.com has them) and work through it with any good therapist who has some cognitive-behavioral skills.

Post-Traumatic Stress Disorder (PTSD). The human nervous system learns well, sometimes all too well. A life-threatening experience, just once, can teach your brain to be cautious about anything even remotely resembling that experience, for years. Fortunately, well-refined psychotherapies for PTSD help many people. These are summarized on an excellent website, ptsd.facts forhealth.org.

Bipolarity interacts directly with PTSD: that is, each makes the other worse. So getting your bipolarity well-controlled is an important part of PTSD treatment. The reverse is probably also true, but harder. In medicine, we often think that if one condition has many treatments, that's because none work very well, such as some cancer treatments. This could be said of PTSD treatments. Many kinds of psychotherapy have been tried. Most clinicians would agree on one thing: when a person is in the grip of uncontrolled *bipolar* symptoms, that is not the time to explore the memories of the triggering event for the PTSD. Use self-control and self-soothing behavioral techniques at such times, and get the bipolar cycling under control before using exploratory psychotherapy. Similarly, almost every medication class in psychiatry has been used in PTSD (except stimulants). Most medications help a little, particularly—ah yes, here they are again—antidepressants. Fortunately, mood stabilizers are often helpful. Once again, my general approach is to maximize all other treatments first, and thereby try to avoid adding an antidepressant.

Generalized Anxiety Disorder (GAD). Characterized by intense worry about anything and everything, this kind of anxiety almost completely overlaps with bipolarity—except the mood component. In Table 5.2, a list of well-recognized bipolar symptoms appears on the right. In addition are two symptoms, marked in brackets, that I frequently hear about from patients who *clearly* have bipolar disorder (not mid-spectrum cases), but which are not as well accepted as bipolar symptoms.

Common medication approaches to GAD include—ah, here they are again—antidepressants. However, GAD also has a specific cognitive-behavioral therapy, taught in *Mastery of Your Anxiety and Worry* (Client Workbook), although it has not been as effective as the CBT for panic disorder. At minimum, people who

TABLE 5.2 Generalized Anxiety Disorder and Bipolar Symptoms

	Generalized Anxiety Disorder (*DSM*)	Bipolar (broad view)
Cognitive	Worry	[Free floating anxiety]
	Difficulty concentrating	Difficulty concentrating
Energy	Keyed up, on edge	Agitation
	Restlessness, tension	Restlessness, tension
	Easily fatigued	Extreme fatigue
	Difficult to fall or stay asleep	[Profound insomnia]
Mood	Irritability	Irritability

have not responded to antidepressants for GAD should wonder whether their condition has a bipolar component, particularly if they have significant depressive episodes.

Attention-Deficit Hyperactivity Disorder (ADHD)

For basic information about ADHD, try the fact sheets at CHADD (Children and Adults with Attention-Deficit/Hyperactivity Disorder: chadd.org). Two issues arising from the overlap between ADHD and bipolarity affect diagnosis and treatment.

Are Bipolarity and ADHD Really Separate Conditions? Here's a research result that will stun you: the percentage of kids in prepuberty who have bipolar disorder, by rigorous research criteria, *and* have ADHD is *90 percent*. While you try to make yourself believe that number, notice that it refers to children who are diagnosed with bipolar disorder *before puberty*. In adolescents with bipolar disorder, the figure in that same study was 30 percent. In adults, the figure was lower yet. What does this mean? First of all, trying to diagnose bipolar disorder in kids requires looking underneath the ADHD symptoms, which according to this research are very likely to be present.

What distinguishes *ADHD Plus* (bipolarity) from *plain ADHD*? After all, many of the symptoms are common in both disorders, such as high energy, distractibility, and rapid speech. But remember, bipolarity is a *cyclic* condition, so symptoms of any kind that *come and go* are more likely to come from a bipolar basis. Among the symptoms of bipolar disorder, hypomania and grandiosity are not part of ADHD.

What do these symptoms look like in kids? Sure enough, here is the same diagnostic dilemma you witnessed in Chapter 2. No clear dividing line exists between obvious mania and normal child behavior either. In fact, making that distinction is even harder! As Dr. Barbara Geller, the principal author of this research, points out, it is hard to imagine how children could have "functionally impairing, pathologic happiness" or how they can be "pathologically too happy and grandiose." She notes, for example, that kids don't have maxed-out credit cards or four marriages. Her group found that four factors best indicate hypomania and mania in children, because unlike high energy, distractibility, and rapid speech, they are not at all common in ADHD. These are

1. Abnormal elation
2. Grandiosity
3. Racing thoughts
4. Decreased need for sleep

Yet she emphasizes in her research report that distinguishing *abnormal elation* in a child is tricky, because kids (lucky for them) get elated a lot. Trying to determine with a yes or no answer if bipolar disorder is present in a child is clearly harder than it is in adults. Once again, using the spectrum model presented earlier in this book as a lens can make it easier to see one's way in the diagnostic process. Use the excellent resources at bpkids.org for more information, including the introductory essay on pediatric bipolar disorder.

Does the Presence of ADHD Change Bipolar Treatment? When both conditions are present, mood experts generally agree: "Treat the bipolar first." This means using mood stabilizers first, because they sometimes decrease or eliminate ADHD symptoms. If ADHD is a separate condition, mood stabilizers alone probably will not have much impact on these symptoms, and treatment with a stimulant—the standard medication approach to ADHD—might be necessary. However, the idea that one should treat the bipolar aspect first generates little controversy—perhaps in recognition of the possibility that stimulants, like antidepressants, can make bipolar disorder worse. The idea that using stimulants might be risky in bipolar disorder is a very serious, but still a theoretical concern. Such a risk has not clearly been shown. Indeed, stimulants might be able to undo some of the brain changes associated with ADD, at least according to the experience of Dr. Daniel Amen, in whose clinics this has been studied for years. I'm told they are now preparing to publish some of their results, which might address some of their skeptics' concerns. But other mood specialists worry about stimulants just as they worry about antidepressants.

However, the problem with trying to evaluate the risk of stimulants for patients with some degree of bipolarity is that some doctors wait to see hypomania with the naked eye, whereas others believe one must go searching, using a snorkel and a magnifying glass if necessary, to be certain it is not there. Thus when asking whether stimulants (or antidepressants) might bring on hypomania or mania, one must consider: how hard is one going to look? Might the intensity of the search determine whether one finds it or not? I hope this sounds familiar: a clinician's search process can determine the conclusion, perhaps even more than the patient's symptoms!

How have researchers looked for hypomania or mania during studies of stimulants? A recent prominent study used a scale designed primarily to detect mania, not hypomania. The authors concluded that stimulants are safe in bipolar disorder, at least when a mood stabilizer is in place, because no mania was detected in their study. They proceed as though hypomania should be visible with the naked eye, or in this case, with a relatively insensitive instrument. There is no well-defined clinical test for more subtle hypomania, as discussed in the previous chapter.

As you can see, understanding bipolarity in the context of other conditions that resemble it is very complex. Bipolarity can be mistaken for other conditions, occur with other conditions, and be worsened by the treatment of other conditions. It can look like another diagnosis, yet respond fully to mood stabilizers. Or the symptoms of another disorder may become more obvious and recognizable when the chaos of uncontrolled mood instability calms down. You must keep an open mind and consider the entire course of symptoms (not just today's symptoms) as you weigh different explanations. But surely by now you're anxious to start looking at how we treat Mood Spectrum conditions. I hope the next section of this book will help you understand your treatment options.

PART II

Finding and Using the Right Treatment

CHAPTER 6

Getting Help: How You Can Work with Your Doctor

Your doctor may have a lot of medical training and experience. But you are even more of a medical expert on one thing: *you*. You know more about you and your symptoms than your doctor is ever likely to know (except perhaps your behavior when you're hypomanic). Since there aren't tests for bipolarity, except those that can help push the probability a bit in one direction or the other, your information about *you* is the key to accurate diagnosis and effective treatment.

However, you're not going to walk in and tell your doctor that you have bipolar disorder. Nor are you going to walk in and say you've been reading about the Mood Spectrum and figured out that you're at the bipolar end. Good. Because the *relationship* you have with this doctor also matters. It matters a lot. You have to be prepared to work with whoever this doctor is and however he or she likes to practice. That may take a little figuring out. In this chapter, we will consider each aspect of your interaction with the doctor: *what* information you need to prepare, and *how* to present it. If you already have a doctor you like, you may not need to read this chapter, but if things are not going so well, it may be useful.

If you're looking for a doctor or thinking about finding a new one, then I hope this chapter will help you be well-organized when you have your first session. (You'll find a very detailed guide to choosing a new doctor or therapist on my website under the home page heading "Finding a Therapist/Psychiatrist.")

Let's get ready to prepare some information for your doctor. You may have heard the phrase, "Don't let the *best* be the enemy of the *good*." I really like that because it warns against something people do all the time. We hesitate to try something if it might not turn out very well, and as a result, we don't try at all. Take exercise, for example: if Michael can't work out five times a week, which he knows is what he should be doing, he doesn't work out at all. How ironic. Wouldn't three days a week be better than none? Even one day a week is still better than none, right?

In the sections that follow, you can find yourself overwhelmed, thinking, "This is just too much, I can't do this." You'll find ideal examples written for someone who has good organizing skills and wants to put together a full package of information. But don't let those ideal examples keep you from putting together *a little something*. A list of current medications or a list of family members who've had mental health problems is extremely helpful. Just that much is definitely better than arriving at the doctor's office with nothing prepared at all. Simply getting to a psychiatrist's or therapist's office, however, is an achievement for many people; so if that's what you can do at this point, do that. Don't let the best, or the ideal document described here, be the enemy of the good, which might just be making the appointment and showing up.

We'll look first at documents you can prepare for a diagnostic interview, then at some ideas on building a collaborative relationship with the doctor, and, finally, at ways to show the doctor how you're doing during treatment. Here we go.

What Your Doctor Needs to Know About You

Your doctor is likely to focus on six standard categories during a first visit:

1. History of the present illness
2. Past psychiatric treatments
3. Past medical history (including current medications)
4. Alcohol and substance use
5. Family history
6. Social history

For each of these categories we will look at a brief description of what a doctor looks for and then an example that represents the maximum information you might prepare (more than this is likely to go unread, by my estimate). Remember, even just a small version of this information, or parts of it, would still likely help your doctor.

History of the Present Illness

Your present symptoms will get the most time and attention from the doctor or therapist. But remember the eleven *soft bipolar* features from Chapter 3. You may have to present these directly rather than wait to be asked about them. Just be careful not to sound like you're trying to make your own diagnosis with them. Remember, doctors like to be in control. Let your doctor make the diagnosis. You provide the information. Take a look at Joan Morton's example.

Past Psychiatric History

Summarize any medications you've tried and what they did. If there are a lot of them, organize them as shown in Table 6.1, Joan Morton's version.

Joan Morton's History

Main problem: depression. First episode at age 18, stressed at college. Next one at 26, lasted three months and then stopped on its own. Since then, they come about every three to six months, last a month or two, then go away. Had a bad one after son Joey; the OB-GYN called it *postpartum depression*. Never have had hypomania of which I'm aware. My BSDS score is 8.

TABLE 6.1 Joan's Medication Summary

Date	Medication	Side Effects	Notes
2002	Zoloft 100 mg	A little dizzy at first	Felt great for about a year; then it just stopped working
2003	Celexa 20 mg	No sex drive	Again felt great, this time about 3 months, then it stopped working again
2003–2004	Effexor 150 mg	Blood pressure up	A little better but anxiety and sleep were worse
Current	Lithium 600 mg	Dry mouth	Primary care doctor added this to Effexor, then tapered the Effexor; it helped a lot, but not enough
Current	Seroquel 100 mg	Really sleepy at first	Helps a lot with sleep and anxiety; still trying to figure out if my cholesterol is going up or not

Similarly, summarize any psychotherapy you've had: how long; with whom, if you can remember; and whether it helped or not.

Past Medical History

Name any medical conditions that are still being treated. Make a list of all current medications. Women who menstruate should give the date of their last period (so the doctor can relax a bit about whether you might be pregnant now). Men as well as women should explain how they are handling birth control and safe sex, just to be fair and help everyone remember that these are not just women's responsibilities. If you can dig up a thyroid test result from the last one to two years, do so.

Alcohol and Other Substance Use

Research studies have shown that more than 50 percent of people with bipolar disorders use alcohol or other drugs. Your doctor is not likely to be shocked if you come clean here (other than perhaps being shocked at your having come clean instead of underestimating or not reporting). Many people use alcohol or marijuana to dampen some of the agitation they can have with their bipolar symptoms. In my experience, most people find that directly treat-

Joan Morton's Past Medical History

I had my gallbladder removed at age 41. I have pretty bad heartburn off and on and take Prilosec for that when it's bad. That helps some. My menstrual cycles are regular. I'm sexually active, or was before the Lexapro anyway. We use condoms to prevent pregnancy. My last blood test was more than a year ago. I was told everything was fine. My current medications are:

- Lexapro 10 mg in the morning
- Prilosec 20 mg before bed
- Ibuprofen for muscle aches—about twice a week
- Fish oil for mood and cholesterol: the Kirkland brand, 4 pills daily

ing their bipolarity allows them to back off of these drugs (more on that in Chapter 11). So don't fudge, don't underestimate. Just put it out there. Hiding it doesn't make any sense: after all, you're seeing this doctor for help, right? The doctor needs to know what you're doing in order to help you. If you must, just put a note here: "I'll talk to you about this part in person."

Family History

This is very important, especially for young people, who have not necessarily had time to manifest hypomania and whose bipolarity will therefore show up primarily in family history. But most doctors spend little time on this aspect of the initial interview. They won't slow down and go through your family tree, one relative at a time. Therefore, you (with your family's help, if that's available to you) can really improve the quality of your doctor's information base by preparing an organized family history.

I know this looks like a lot of work. You may know much less about your relatives than Joan did in the following example. Remember, *any* organized information is good. Also, if there is *even one* close relative with a diagnosis of bipolar disorder, you can skip this entire project and just tell the doctor about that person. But if no one has a known mental health diagnosis or treatment, then highlight anyone who was very unusual in some way, as in Joan's example, seen in the following sidebar.

Joan Morton's Family History

My Generation	**Brother Jack**	Gets pretty wired sometimes, goes off fishing in Alaska on impulse, spends quite a bit of money (enough that people have commented on it); then can "crash" and seem pretty morose, much less active, for a few weeks.
	Sister	Doing fine, finished college and started a Ph.D. but never finished it; seems pretty happy running her little fishing-guide business. No kids.
	Cousins, mom's side	There are three. They're all fine, as far as I know.
Parents' Generation	Mom	Seems content, never any big mood or anxiety problems I could see. Very steady.
	Dad	Like brother Jack: gets really excited about an idea, has to know all about it, checks out a bunch of books on it from the library, talks about little else for three weeks, then poof, not interested in it anymore. Phases of low energy, but he always manages to keep working (runs his own small airplane business).
	Dad's brother John	Very religious, ran the Christian Science reading room for years, very active in church. Never drinks. No kids.
	Dad's brother Mike	Wild guy, was known to everyone in town, great but very daring skier, got himself pretty busted up twice doing that; then sort of fell off the map, Dad says, became a recluse, they don't hear from him now.
	Mom's sister Kate	Mother of three, no big news there; she lives in Alabama. Don't know much more about her. Seems nice, the few times I've met her.
Their Parents	Dad's dad	He was a preacher. He was known all over the South, they say. Once he had congregations going in three different states, apparently. He died when my dad was pretty young; haven't heard much more about him.
	Dad's mom	She has Alzheimer's now, lives in a nursing home. As far as I know, she never had any other problems in terms of mental health.
	Mom's mom	Died before I was born. Based on what I've heard, nothing unusual in behavior or mood.

	Mom's dad	Steady guy, worked until he was 70. Regular at church, volunteer work. I've never heard about anything unusual here either.
Kids	**My Joey**	12 years old. Saw the school psychologist because he wasn't "performing up to potential," year after year. They said he might have ADHD, but we didn't want him to take a medication for it. We have to help him a lot to keep his schoolwork organized, but with the system we've developed, he does OK. Seems like a really bright kid. No mood problems so far, as far as we know.
	Brother Jack's son Warren	He has been diagnosed with ADHD, but he keeps getting himself in trouble. He's 16 now. Really moody kid, but he can be a charmer sometimes, too. May have gotten into some drugs at school, his mom is worried about that.
	Brother Jack's son Zach	Wow, this kid is going to be a genius. He's only 12, but he already can play the piano at a concert level, and he created this science club at school that won an award from the state. He can really talk your ear off sometimes. Seems like he's always in a good mood.

Social History

This part of a routine medical history looks at social factors that might affect your diagnosis or treatment. Of course, you could write your entire biography here, because much of it might indeed be relevant, in some way. Obviously, that won't exactly fit in this document you're creating, will it? In practice, most doctors focus on a few features of your social history in the first interview. Here are the ones that I've come to use as a starting place:

- What was discipline like in your household when you were growing up?
- Any physical or sexual abuse then or since? (You can let the doctor help you describe these or offer a one-line summary.)
- Who do you live with now?
- Are you getting hit now?
- How do you spend your days now (e.g., running a household, doing other work, or going to school)?
- How are you doing financially (how much stress there)?

Joan Morton's Social History

Discipline while growing up was pretty rough, but no sexual abuse; only hit when dad was drunk, about once a month for a few years in grade school. Not being hit now. Husband sometimes yells when he is drunk, and I flip out. I live with my husband and two kids. We both work. Neither of us is making what we're worth, of course (who is?).

Remember, a minimal document, perhaps just a list of current medications and some notes about your family history, is definitely better than nothing. Don't let the best be the enemy of the good. Your doctor will almost certainly appreciate anything you bring—as long as it's not too huge, too detailed. Joan's example is getting about as long as you might dare, especially her family history. The longer it is, the better organized it must be so your doctor can look it over quickly and use it.

Strategies for Working with Your Doctor

You already may have a great doctor with whom you feel communication is going very well. If so, that's great. You can skip to the last section of this chapter on working with that doctor over time. However, after answering letters from patients online at bipolarworld.net for the last several years, I have the distinct impression that at least some, perhaps many, patients are effectively stuck with their psychiatrist. They may get treatment in a public mental health clinic and can't choose their doctor, or they may live in a location with only a few psychiatrists to choose from. If you're in that kind of situation, then the rest of this section may be relevant. There are ways to make the best of that situation. I hope you'll find a few of the following ideas useful.

Many doctors have big egos. (Fortunately, not me, of course. Why, I'm perfectly comfortable to practice psychiatry in complete obscurity. This book thing just happened to come along. . . .) You may have already learned that you could be in for a challenge if you're going to try to discuss with your doctor something he or she hasn't already recognized, such as

- Why he might consider a bipolar diagnosis
- Why a bipolar diagnosis doesn't fit *you*
- Why it might be worth trying a mood stabilizer
- That you *really* don't want to take lithium
- You would like a family member or significant other to sit in on the session to help make sure you understand everything

Fortunately, not all doctors resist input from patients about diagnosis or treatment. If you have a really open-minded doctor, who is in control of his or her ego needs, you may be able to walk right in and say what's on your mind. But if that's not the case, here are some suggestions:

- **Start small.** If you have no experience with this doctor at all, or believe that your doctor won't like you asking about things such as those previously listed, make sure you start with something small. For example, try asking for more information about an aspect of your illness. "I'm sorry, Doctor Ortiz, but I think I missed the point of checking my blood counts when I'm taking this medication. Can you help me understand that?"
- **Doctors need to feel valued.** Start by making them feel valued. But as you do this, *you must be sincere.* You'll have to find something the doctor has done that you truly appreciate. Then say, "Doc, I really appreciate the way you've . . ." Let's hope this step is not impossible. If it is, you might need to look for another doctor. Alternatively, you might need to look at whether your symptoms are limiting your ability to appreciate things, including this doctor. If that's the case, you likely won't get a better one very easily.

- **Assure your doctor that what you're asking won't take much time.** Doctors often feel rushed and fairly overwhelmed, and they may act as if they haven't much time (if you knew their schedule for the day, you might very well understand this). So they don't want to hear something that sounds like it could take a lot of time. Rather, say, "I just want to ask very quickly about something, and if I need to make a specific appointment to address it, that would be fine."
- **Doctors need to feel in charge.** There are some good reasons for this that are not based entirely on the doctors' egos, such as their constant vulnerability to lawsuits. Be understanding of their needs, but don't shortchange yours in the process, either. Instead, help doctors feel in charge by asking their opinion about something while not sounding very knowledgeable about it yourself.
- **If you are rebuffed, keep proceeding as best you can.** If the doctor doesn't hear you out or tells you that you are the patient and he or she is the doctor, you might consider saying, "Oh, I understand what you mean. Treating me surely isn't easy, I know that." Let's hope this is just a first exchange along these lines and that you will come back and try again. Perhaps start with something smaller next time?

These suggestions are usually even harder for family members watching a loved one being treated if they've been teaching themselves about that illness and think the doctor is off course on the diagnosis or treatment. If you're in this position, you don't even have a relationship, however strained, with the doctor. In that case, all these steps are even more important, especially if getting a second opinion is not practical (for example, you can't afford it, you can't travel 200 miles to get there, or your doctor won't listen to a second opinion even if it comes from the Emory University Bipolar Clinic). Perhaps the most important thing to remember, in my view, is that this doctor is human, too, and probably has some good reasons for being the way he or she is.

Maybe you can make some headway by learning about those reasons as you go.

Working with Your Doctor Over Time

Your doctor will want the same details every time you show up, such as what medications you've been taking (and not taking!) and what symptoms you've been having, if any. You can prepare this information in one of two ways: write up a brief summary before each visit, or track these details as you go along between visits.

Tracking as you go has one huge advantage: your data will be much, much more accurate. When you instead try to remember how you've been doing over a period of time, the most striking phases or events will come to mind and dominate your recall. This will almost certainly bias your report, as you forget the unremarkable parts in favor of the more memorable dramatic details.

Tracking as you go also has one huge disadvantage: it takes time and energy. Not much, but if managing an illness—which you don't want to have anyway—becomes just another thing you have to do, and you'd rather do plenty of other things, you can easily stop tracking the details.

Let's take a closer look at these two ways of reporting details to your doctor.

Preparing a Brief Report for a Follow-Up Visit

First, here's a little background on what the doctor is going to do with your information. One of the most time-consuming steps in medical care is writing the medical record. Traditionally, this includes four parts:

1. **S**ubjective data—what the patient is thinking and feeling
2. **O**bjective data—how the patient looks, talks, and acts
3. **A**ssessment—what the doctor thinks might explain these subjective and objective data
4. **P**lan—what the doctor and the patient have planned to do about the current situation

This record is commonly called a SOAP note, reflecting the four parts. The doctor usually writes all four parts, of course. But think about this for a minute: in the Subjective section, the doctor writes down how you've been feeling. This section is subjective because it's based on your report, as opposed to the doctor's observations (which go in the Objective part). If *you* were to write the subjective part, your record would not be less accurate. Indeed, it might be more accurate, because you would not be relying on the doctor to understand your subjective data and write them down correctly. Thus, there is a growing movement to encourage patients to prepare this subjective section of their medical record themselves. In a few years this may be a common approach. Some of my patients do this now according to the instructions shown in the following sidebar. They e-mail these reports before their appointment.

Sample Preparation Work to Do in Advance for Follow-Up Visits

The following is a sample of what you need to do to prepare for your follow-up visits.

Current Medications
Make a list of what you're currently taking. Save this section so you can start with it each time, adding any recent changes. Here's one example, but try another format if you think it would be easier or better.

- Lithobid 300 mg: one per A.M., two per P.M.
- Wellbutrin 150 SR: one twice daily
- Enalapril 10 mg daily
- Multivitamin: 1 per A.M.
- Aspirin: 1 baby size per A.M.

Current Symptoms

1. I usually want to start by looking at the big picture: are things getting worse, better, or staying about the same since you were last seen? On a scale of 0 to 10, where 10 is the best you've ever felt and 0 is the worst, how are you today?

2. Specifically, what has happened to your target symptoms since you were last seen (your main problems the medication is supposed to help)?

Side Effects

1. Any new ones?
2. Any old ones changing—for worse or better?
3. Weight: up, down, about the same?

New Targets or Issues

Do we need to adjust the focus of treatment and identify new target symptoms?

Important Life Changes or Relevant Current Events

This could be almost anything that you think might have an impact on your mood, now or later. Here are some examples:

- New job with different hours
- Getting divorced
- Dad moves in
- Considering getting pregnant (*Always* announce that one!)
- Stopped smoking or stopped drinking
- Started walking for 15 minutes every morning

Tips for Tracking as You Go

Sometimes, finding the best treatment for your symptoms can take a while. Although some people respond well to the first thing they try, others can go through one medication after another trying to reach the goal: as close to 100 percent symptom control as possible, with as close to zero percent side effects as possible. If you turn out to be one of those many-trials patients, you'll want to have a good record of what you took and what it did. The doctor will keep some notes, but these will be limited. If you keep even a minimal record *as you go*, it may prove very valuable for you later. You can choose from several charting systems. The hard part is actually *using* them.

Can you take thirty seconds every day to chart your symptoms? How about, say, right when you brush your teeth? If you do, then just bring your tracking sheet to your doctor's appointment. Your doctor may have a form he or she likes to use for this, or you can choose from several on the Internet. (See the Notes page at psycheducation.org/notes.htm for links to about six different versions.) Remember, "Don't let the best be the enemy of the good." You can do this with a typical store-bought calendar, if you can't get organized to make or download a chart. Just use a 0 to 10 scale to record your mood every day: 10 is the best you ever feel, 0 is the worst. Most of the downloadable scales use a system roughly like this. If you have room, you can track other things you'd like to view over time: exercise (how long, what type), irritability (on a scale from 0 to 3), or sleep (hours). When you've crammed your calendar too full of numbers, switch to a downloaded or even homemade mood chart and make your life simpler. All of these provide a thirty-one-day chart, with spaces to track mood, energy, sleep, and medications. Some also allow you to track exercise (as mine does) and other variables. My website has an electronic version for those who use spreadsheets all the time, and there is a computer program (all these are linked from the Notes page) that will put your data right into a research project (this way, your results can help others—your identity is fully protected, of course) and send you a graph by email every month!

Here are some tricks to make tracking easier to keep up.

- **Make it a routine.** That means the chart itself has to stay in some location where you'll pass it every night. I tell patients to put it on a clipboard, with a pen or pencil attached by a string; hang it on the back of the bathroom door or above the sink; and fill it out every night when they brush their teeth.

- **Don't list your medications every day.** Just note changes (mood, sleep, exercise, for example; or mood, exercise, irritability). This leaves only about three simple check marks to make per day. If you're organized, this should take, what, about fifteen seconds?

You just need to try this approach for a while to see if you can make it stick. If you succeed, you will have a record that is much better than your doctor's. You could look back months from now and know precisely what medications you were taking, what doses, and what results you were getting. This just can't be beat. And yet, unless you really work at it, this is not likely to be a regular part of your care. I have to admit, I don't have many patients doing it and have not made a point of it with them, primarily because I don't want to burden them with it. Many people don't want that daily reminder that they have a mood disorder requiring treatment. "Just taking pills is bad enough—don't make me *think* about how I feel!" However, some of the very best university clinics have built this tracking into their record-keeping process, demonstrating that it is doable, and there's no doubt at all about how helpful it can be.

Now, at long last, let us turn our focus from diagnosis and doctors, to treatment.

CHAPTER 7

Where to Start: Guidelines for Choosing Treatment

You're anxious to see what treatment looks like. Yet before we look at the full menu of options, we should consider *how* you will select from among them, deciding which to try first, which second (if necessary), and so forth. In the process, we'll look at how some of these treatments work, according to the current understanding.

You could simply follow your doctor's recommendations. If you have confidence in your doctor and he or she knows you well, your doctor's recommendations may be sufficient and you could skip this chapter. But your doctor could have personal biases, thus his or her recommendations might reflect personal assumptions and not be based *entirely* on your needs. For example, I routinely explain to my patients that I have strong views about antidepressant medication use in bipolar disorder that could cloud my judgment about using them, so I encourage patients to develop their own understanding of these issues.

If you're going to conduct your own evaluation of treatment options, there are many sources of information, including certainly your doctor; possibly your therapist, if you have one; definitely the manufacturer of the medication; likely your spouse, parents, or significant others; perhaps friends or even coworkers; and finally, through all sorts of subtle channels, society in general, which sends many messages, often contradictory, about whether a medication is a good idea. How are you to know whom to trust? I recommend this: *trust no one*. Instead, insist on evidence.

Evaluating Claims by Looking for Evidence

As you consider a treatment approach, you will be looking for evidence of two types, which you can think of as the good news and the bad news. First, look for good news: is there reason to believe this approach really works? You want to see evidence of benefit. Second, look for bad news: how much risk will you be taking? You want to hear about short- and long-term *risks*, as well as side effects that may not be risky but could be rather unpleasant.

You are evaluating probabilities—the likelihood that a positive or negative aspect of the medication will actually show up when you take that pill or start that therapy. Look for some hard evidence about those probabilities, not just someone's say-so.

An Example of Looking for Evidence: Using the Internet

Nowadays people routinely turn to the Internet for health information. Let's fire up your browser and do a search to illustrate just what you'll be looking for, and why. For example, you pull up Google and type in "lithium bipolar". What comes up? About 360,000 pages! Fortunately, many of the first listings are fairly unbiased sources that will give you the basics about lithium: what it is, how it is used, and some of its side effects (with no probabilities attached nor information on the probability that the medication will help you).

But even on that first page of results, there is a company trying to sell you—without a prescription—a form of lithium they say is "100 percent safe" and "nontoxic." Their version requires very small doses, they claim, because their version goes straight to the brain, an assertion that has not been tested in humans. They *could be* right. But we don't know that. Research on this form appears to have stopped around 1979 after one team found that it seemed to interfere with kidney function in rats.

See how easy it is to make grand claims about a health-related product? Indeed, this example shows that people can say just about anything they want, even claims like "100 percent safe" when the existing literature on this compound clearly raises concerns. Moreover, the people running that site are probably very nice and really believe what they're saying. Indeed, they surely have customers whose symptoms have greatly improved while on their lithium. But this doesn't prove it was their lithium that caused the improvement, and it leaves the question of long-term safety completely open.

The sidebar example makes an important point: people get better. They can do so on their own, and it happens all the time. Also, if you manage to convince people they're going to get better, this in itself increases the likelihood that they will get better. Isn't that a funny thing about us humans? So how can you know whether the treatment you are being offered isn't just a placebo, as the Internet-available low-dose lithium may be? And how do you find out about a treatment's safety record? Let's look at each of these factors in turn, in the next two sections.

The Best Kind of Evidence: Randomized Controlled Trials

As you know, getting better while taking something that might help but also might be a fake is known as the *placebo response*. A good research study has a group of people who get a pill containing only a little bit of sugar, or a *placebo*, instead of the experimental drug. In such a study, care is taken to ensure that no one, not even the researchers who deal directly with the participants, knows which people are getting the real thing and which are getting the sugar pill. The pills look identical; only a code number distinguishes the pill bottles and the participants' assigned group, and so forth. Thus the researchers and the participants are "blind" to who is taking what (called *double-blinding*, as opposed to a single-blind design where the researchers know but the participants don't).

The group that receives the sugar pill is called the *control group*, because they serve as a control over the placebo effect. Participants are randomly assigned to receive either the medication being studied or the sugar pill. This research design, called a double-blind *randomized controlled trial* (*RCT*), produces the most desirable results, because it controls for the placebo effect: a medication must *outperform the placebo* to demonstrate its effectiveness.

Without an RCT, it is much more difficult to be certain that a pill really does more than the power of suggestion. Suggestion has great power: in most research studies of depression treatment, for example, the placebo group improves at a rate of 25 to 30 percent! One person in four gets better, sometimes almost one person in three. Somehow, just suggesting to people that the pill they will take might help them (they know there is at least a chance they're getting the real thing) mobilizes some capacity that we humans have within to get better on our own.

So the people selling the expensive, minimal-lithium pills described earlier are very likely to hear back from many customers about how much the pills helped. The pill really did help—they really are better. Thus the people selling the pill believe it really works. And when they believe this, their medication becomes even more effective, because their ability to convince people that the pill will help improves with every reported success. You see what happens? Everyone in the loop reinforces everyone else's belief. Thus a pill that might contain no active ingredients (or almost none, in the case of the expensive lithium) becomes a truly effective treatment.

Here is a very important conclusion: because of the remarkable human phenomenon where *believing* something will work actually makes it work, anyone who claims that their pill, lotion, or potion "works" cannot really know this is so, unless they compare their product to a placebo. That's why randomized trials are so important.

There is one more reason for doing a randomized trial. The U.S. Food and Drug Administration (FDA) won't let you advertise the medication you just spent millions of dollars developing, unless you show them data from a randomized trial demonstrating that the medication is better than a placebo. Because of the FDA requirements, there are two different kinds of RCTs: those done by scientists who just want to know if a treatment really works, and those done by pharmaceutical companies to get their products through the FDA hoops. There are some good scientists running RCTs for drug companies, of course. But in some cases the study designs appear to have been influenced by marketing plans. For example, an arrangement called "enriched design" is a serious deviation from the usual logic of RCTs, yet has been accepted by the FDA. The conclusion here: not all RCTs are created equal. They must be interpreted with care.

The Open Trial

Before we proceed, you should understand one more research design, the open trial. This very common design is much easier and much less expensive to arrange than an RCT. Think of open trials as preliminary studies: they are supposed to point the way to treatments that might be worth studying in the more elaborate RCT fashion. Open trials have no placebo group. They simply study whether a medication seems to have any value at all. If you browse the medical literature, many of the research studies you will find are open trials. These results must be interpreted with great caution, because they are heavily influenced by doctors'— and patients'—initial enthusiasm, which can skew the results. This phenomenon leads to a standard joke about new medications: "use it quick before it stops working."

So now you know that not all research is the same, not even RCTs. But anyone who tells you "this pill will help you, take it" *without* an RCT to back up that claim may be trying to sell you something that is no better than a placebo. Let's now look at the other side of the benefit-risk ratio.

Considering the Risks and Benefits of a Treatment

We just finished looking at the kind of evidence required to establish that a medication works. What kind of evidence is required to establish that a medication (or herb or vitamin) is *safe*? The answer is that it's even harder to establish safety. Think about it: a medication can be in use for ten years, but if a problem that it causes takes fifteen years to develop, how would we know? It might be another five years before people start coming in with that problem. For example, a strong medication for severe bipolar symptoms called olanzapine (Zyprexa) was in use for several years before we recognized that it causes not only weight gain in many people—that became obvious quite quickly—but also diabetes in quite a few. How do medications' risks become known?

First come *adverse event reports*, which are submitted to the FDA, but not easily found in the medical literature. These reports are hard to interpret because there is no effort behind these reports to be sure the medication is really the culprit. They are merely reports of an event that occurred in someone taking the medication.

Instead, doctors prefer *case reports*, in which we can find a description of the patient and what happened. Usually these only are published when the apparent connection between a medication and a bad outcome is very likely, due to the timing: the problem shows up in such a way as to strongly implicate the drug and goes away when the drug is stopped. In the strongest such reports, the drug might be restarted and the problem reappears, only to go away again when the drug is stopped. Obviously the "rechallenge" results are considerably more convincing, because the likelihood that something *else* caused the problem goes down when the drug appears to be the cause twice in a row.

Then come *case series*, in which several patients appear to have the same experience with a medication. Next come larger "epidemiologic" studies, in which a researcher might compare the frequency of the problem among those on a medication with the frequency among those who have never been exposed to that medication. The latter group functions as a kind of control group, similar to those in randomized trials. When these epidemiologic studies are done with very large numbers of cases, the results can be very powerful; as in an RCT, the unexposed group allows a direct comparison of the impact of exposure to the medication versus never having taken it.

Finally, in some cases *randomized trials* are performed to see whether a medication actually carries risk, as well as benefit. Since risks may be much less frequent than benefits, these trials often require huge numbers of participants in order to see any differences between a medication and a placebo. A recent well-publicized study like this was the Women's Health Initiative, which looked at the risks as well as the benefits of *Prempro* (horse estrogens and synthetic progesterone). This study found that contrary to the beliefs that had accumulated for more than a decade, Prempro did not lower the risk of heart attacks, rather it was associated with a slight rise in this risk, as well as the risk of breast cancer. The result, of course, was a dramatic change in the prescribing of Prempro. However, note that it took years to establish these possible risks of Prempro. To be more certain would require a repeat study with similar results.

Thus we have the twin central issues in assessing medication safety:

1. Establishing that a medication carries a risk is much *slower* than establishing that it has benefit.
2. The smaller the risk associated with a medication, the larger the number of people who have to take this medication before a difference is recognized.

You can see the problem with all this: advocates will claim *benefits* for a treatment long before wary users are in a position to know about its *risks*. May I ask you to read that sentence again? Because now I'm going to sound like a doctor who wants to undercut the competition from herbalists, nutritionists, and other such folks. Yet hear me out, and think about this, please. I don't think undercutting the competition is my motive.

Herbs and vitamins are not regulated as are medications made by pharmaceutical companies. Even for the latter, discoveries of risk after years of use are rather common. Recent examples as I wrote this chapter included suicidality with antidepressants and increased heart problems with Vioxx. This is *not* the fault of the FDA letting medications onto the market too quickly or manufacturers rushing to make a profit. It is part of the *very nature of evidence*, pro and con, you see? Evidence of benefit can arrive long before evidence of risk.

Yet at least there is *some* oversight regarding risk of medications, compared to vitamins and herbs. The FDA's Adverse Events Reporting System at least creates a central database that can accumulate evidence of risk more quickly than can individual practitioners. There is no such database for herbs, vitamins, or other alternative therapies.

You could argue that herbs and vitamins are less likely to carry risk because they are natural. There may be some truth to that. But 60 international units (I.U.) of vitamin E is not "natural" (the average person consumes about 10 to 15 I.U. of vitamin E a day through food), let alone the 1,000 I.U. advocated by some. So don't necessarily assume that *natural* should mean "safer."

One more example can be found in the flurry of concern that serotonergic antidepressants like fluoxetine (Prozac) can raise the rate of serious bleeding problems after surgery. These medications have been around for more than fifteen years now. There were some reports along these lines at least as far back as five years ago, but a recent study reported an epidemiologic comparison (as described earlier) of more than 1,000 patients' experiences, strongly increasing the evidence for this risk.

The bottom line again is that it takes a lot longer to establish risk than to establish benefit. Unless you can find *some* reason to think an herb, vitamin, or other alternative medicine is safe, you are taking an *unknown* risk—rather like you would be if you use

Fish Oil: An Example of Evaluating Risk

In case I sound militantly antivitamin and antiherb, here's another example. Fish oil, as a source of omega-3 fatty acids, has been studied for potential mood stabilizing effects. In many respects it might be ideal for soft bipolar conditions—if it really works. Several randomized trials currently show some benefit, but a few randomized trials also do not, including some of the largest ones, so it is too early at this point to say whether omega-3s are really better than placebos. By the time you read this, the evidence will probably have improved, either for or against this strategy. But how are we to know that taking large quantities of fish oil in the form of capsules is *safe*?

In this case, there is at least the precedent that we humans have been eating fish, sometimes in very large quantities and even as the main element in the diet, for our entire history. Consuming large amounts of fish is "natural" and perhaps so is consuming a lot of their oils in the form of capsules. Well, close anyway. So far, there is no evidence that using fish oil to treat bipolar disorder carries risk. Several fish oil brands have been tested for the presence of mercury and other heavy metals, but since such metals are charged particles, they stay in the portion of the fish that attracts charges—the muscle—and are not extracted with the oil, which is thought at this time to contain none.

However, the point here is that it would take years to establish the safety of even something so seemingly safe as fish oil. That is the nature of evidence for risk. Somehow it might emerge years from now that something in the extraction process alters the fish oils in such a way that they can rarely cause cancer of the intestine. Again, it would take a long, long time to establish that.

a medication that had just been released for use. My dentist, Dr. Balkins, says, "I don't like to be at the front of the pack, and I don't like to be at the back of the pack; I like to be somewhere in the middle." When you choose a medication, herb, vitamin, or any treatment, you should know where you are in the pack.

Looking at Side Effects

Finally, to complete our study of the risk–benefit ratio, let's consider how you might look at side effects of the medication: things that are not risky, but could be pretty unpleasant. Again you are trying to establish a *probability*: how likely is it that this unpleasant thing will happen?

Although doctors are basically required to tell you about the bad things that might happen when you take a medication, they don't commonly have a good way to tell you *how likely* those bad things are. Figures like 1 in 1,000 are not very meaningful to most people. Does it sound very different to say 2 in 1,000? Not really, right? Yet that's double the rate! So we clinicians end up saying things that sound more meaningful but actually mean a lot less, like *rare*, *uncommon*, and *infrequent*.

However, there is a simple way to get a look at the likelihood of a side effect. The FDA now requires that drug manufacturers present their data about the frequency of side effects—along with a lot of other stuff that won't usually mean much to you—on that sheet of paper the pharmacist usually gives you with a new medication, the *product information (PI)* sheet. PIs for most medications can be found on the Internet as well. Around the middle of the PI is usually a table that compares the frequency of side effects in those who took the medication versus the frequency seen in those who took the placebo.

This is just what we need, of course, because not only do placebos commonly help people get better, they also commonly cause side effects! It's almost laughable in some ways, but it just shows how we humans work. *Expectation* has tremendous power. If researchers tell study participants, "This medication may cause a serious skin rash," the rate of rash in the *placebo group* roughly doubles.

When you need some real numbers for the frequency of side effects of a medication, get the PI. Find the table where the side effects of the medication are shown compared to the placebo, and skim down for instances where the medication side effects are clearly more common than those among the people taking the placebo. These are the *common* side effects (greater than 1 percent). Everything else is *infrequent* (less than 1 in 100) or *rare* (less than 1 in 1,000), usually shown just below that table. (A *word of caution*: if a patient in a research trial has a side effect for *even one day*, that side effect will be listed—even if it was gone the next day. So remember, the lists you see do not distinguish between the side effects that decrease or disappear, as many do, and the ones that never decrease and may force someone to stop the medication.)

Notice that for infrequent or rare side effects, *there is no placebo comparison*. So, when you read below the table, you have entered the realm of the unknown again: without a placebo, you can't tell whether those bad reactions were really caused by the medication. Some of them surely are, as we know from experience with the medications. As discussed in the Chapter 5, when a possible side effect arises, medications should be considered guilty until proven innocent by stopping the medication (but DON'T DO THAT ON YOUR OWN, REMEMBER? Whoa, there I go again). However, not all the side effects listed in the lower parts of the PI are really from the medication, right? Some of them, perhaps many of them, belong somehow to the patient (a negative placebo effect, if you will).

To conclude this discussion of risk and benefit, let me remind you that bipolar disorder carries its own risks. It can destroy relationships, lose jobs, interrupt education, and in severe versions, it can even cause death. So when you weigh the risks and side effects of medications, which can look huge sometimes, you may have to remind yourself about the risks of insufficient treatment. It's fine, indeed, it's a great idea to start by maximizing the benefits of non-medication approaches, which we'll examine in coming chapters. But if that is not enough, and often it is not, then carefully compare the risks when your doctor starts talking about medication options.

The next section of this chapter provides one more guide, besides research, for choosing among treatment options—our growing understanding of what causes the problem in the first place! Wouldn't it be nice to choose a treatment based on knowing how it works? This is the pipe dream of psychiatry, a distant goal for decades. But we are getting much closer to this goal. Take a look now at just how close. This may be more detail than you want—or can swallow! Skip to the end of this chapter if you're starting to choke (just breathe, breathe . . .).

What Causes Mood Disorders Anyway?

We now believe that mood disorders are produced when stress and other factors shift the normal balance between cell growth and cell shrinkage. Say that again? You thought it had something to do with serotonin, right? Well, that's true, but now more is known about what the serotonin is actually doing. Your brain cells (*neurons*) very actively reshape themselves all the time in response to your experience and your environment. This reshaping process requires that some cells shrink, while others grow. Just recently another important part of this process was revealed: *new* brain cells can be formed and become part of this reshaping process. Brain researchers have shown in several different ways that brains can indeed make new cells. (For some stunning pictures, go to the link on my website called "Depression Is Not a Moral Weakness.") The exciting part of this story is that these new cells form in the very parts of the brain where you're likely to need them—especially if you have a mood problem.

That's very nice to know, because the scary part of this story is that mood problems can make neurons shrink and even die. If this goes on long enough, one can even see, using research brain scanners, that a depressed person's whole brain has literally shrunk, as much as 10 to 15 percent in some sensitive areas. This brain shrinkage is called *atrophy*, and the chemicals that cause it are called atrophic factors. Effective treatments, however, may stop and even reverse at least some of this shrinkage.

We now know that feeling very stressed emotionally, such as through repeated major losses or intensely frustrating and yet uncontrollable situations, leads to increased brain chemicals that have an atrophic effect. Fortunately, several brain chemicals have the *opposite* effect. Many treatments for depression seem to work through these favorable brain chemicals called *trophic factors*.

In normal cell-shape change processes, the atrophic factors are balanced by trophic factors so that the result in your brain is merely a shape change, not an overall loss of cells. Mood disorders, including both unipolar and bipolar variations, seem to shift this trophic–atrophic balance. If the balance tips so that the atrophic processes just slightly exceed the trophic processes, this will lead to brain shrinkage over time, right? Slowly, if the shift is small, or rapidly, if the shift is very large, more neurons will shrink than will grow.

To understand the actions of antidepressant and mood stabilizer medications, you will want to know about some of the trophic and atrophic factors involved in this cellular balance. We'll look briefly at a few of these factors and then at how treatments affect the balance. Oddly, many of the trophic and atrophic factors have been discovered while researchers were trying to figure out how current treatments work. Researchers have been trying to figure out the root cause of mood problems by looking first at one effective medication and then at another to discover what all effective treatments actually do to brain cells. One of the main research teams producing these important advances is the Laboratory of Molecular Pathophysiology at the National Institutes of Mental Health. Led by Dr. Husseini Manji, a generous man as well as a dedicated neuroscientist, this team has studied how antidepressants lead to changes inside neurons. Although it has been known for years that fluoxetine (Prozac) and other antidepressants very quickly change the amount of serotonin found between neurons, what happens *after that* only quite recently has been discovered. To find that answer, researchers had to look inside cells. What did they find antidepressants doing at that level? Answer: they were increasing trophic factors.

Trophic Factors

These names may not mean much to you right now. But most people with mood problems want to know as much as they can about what's going on in their heads. Many people are encouraged to know that researchers are making very detailed headway in understanding exactly what has gone wrong when a person is depressed. This understanding is being used to identify molecular targets for new medications that might work closer to the root of the problem. In the hopes that some gritty detail might be helpful, here are some of the main players in this *neuroplasticity* story. Remember, you can find more detail, including some pictures that may help you really see this story, at the link "The Brain Chemistry of Depression" on my website. That version will be more up to date as well, as I hope to keep changing it as the story evolves.

Brain-Derived Neurotrophic Factor (BDNF). The word *trophic* comes from the Greek word meaning "to feed." Think of trophic factors as cell fertilizers, like putting a little Miracle-Gro in the cells' water supply. Thus BDNF does just what its name implies: it acts like a cell fertilizer for neurons. Antidepressant medications increase BDNF levels in neurons. This has been shown for several common antidepressants and at this point appears to be the likely way that they all work. *Electroconvulsive therapy (ECT)*—or more harshly, *shock therapy*—increases BDNF. Even *exercise* increases BDNF, at least in rat studies. This hasn't been shown directly in humans yet; that is a little tricky. (In one recent study, however, exercise was associated with brain growth in humans just as would be predicted if it did indeed increase BDNF in humans as well as rats.) Yet BNDF is not the only trophic factor on the farm.

Bcl-2. Whoa, you never thought you'd be getting in this deep— learning code names for brain molecules—did you? This one's worth knowing about, though, because it seems so close to the center of the story of mood and cell atrophy or growth. Bcl-2 controls the doors to the cell's powerhouse, the mitochondrion. When those doors get pushed open too far (by an atrophic factor you'll meet in a moment), Bcl-2 appears to be able to close them. If the doors are left too wide open, chemicals (especially calcium) and fluid can rush in and cause the mitochondrion to burst—not good. You need those mitochondria to keep a cell going. Lose too many, and the cell will shrink; lose more, and the cell may die.

BAG-1. Just one more, OK? Then we turn to a few bad guys. BAG-1 is something to really cheer about. Only recently discovered, it is one of the first mood molecules found because researchers *knew what they were looking for.* Until now, almost everything you've ever heard about the brain chemistry of psychiatric problems was discovered through research that was looking for something else or looking for some other reason. BAG-1 was found because Dr. Manji and colleagues went looking for another neurotrophic factor. The way they looked gives hope that yet more important factors may soon be found, because their search was very direct and successful. (Their process is described in the essay on my website.)

Atrophic Factors

Atrophy, literally the "lack of growth," is caused by factors that interfere with the neuron's ability to sustain itself. Remember, this is a *normal* process. But it becomes extreme and leads to brain shrinkage when stress and other factors shift the balance between growth and atrophy in the direction of cell death. So that you may recognize them in further reading, and keep your finger on this story as it develops, here are some of the molecules involved. (After all, we're poised on the brink of understanding one of the most dramatic medical puzzles in the last century. Psychiatrists are like the medical doctors of the early 1900s who knew of the illness called diabetes, but did not know about insulin. We are witnessing a medical breakthrough as this mood chemistry story unfolds, albeit slowly).

Cortisol. This is one of the main stress hormones of the human nervous system. It is not a bad guy as such. In fact, it's a vital hormone you can't live without. It helps turn on important body systems, including causing the liver to produce glucose to fuel the brain, under stress conditions. But (here's another part of the puzzle that's being investigated very actively) when stress goes on and on, cortisol begins to have very negative effects. Exactly how cortisol ends up switching from a useful to a destructive hormone is the subject of intense research, as this molecule has been known for decades to be involved somehow in mood problems.

BAD. Sounds like Hollywood got into the neuroscience lab, doesn't it? This acronym stands for *Bcl-2–associated death protein*, which is bad enough, one might say. It turns out that there is a whole family of Bcl-2 proteins. Some help cells grow, others mediate cell death, which is an important part of brain reshaping. They all seem to be involved in controlling the doors (pores) of the mitochondrion. BAD can cause those doors to open too far, if not sufficiently opposed by Bcl-2.

GSK-3β. Getting a little overwhelmed? This last factor is included because it is one of the molecules through which mood stabilizer medications appear to work. GSK-3β is an enzyme that when active leads to increased levels of BAD. Both lithium and valproate (Depakote) can decrease the activity of this enzyme.

Now we can go back to focusing on treatments since you know a little bit about how they work. We'll resume the discussion of how you choose a particular approach by first looking at the role of all the different tools available, and then considering three main strategies.

General Guidelines for Managing Bipolar Variations

Your treatment choices are based on weighing evidence about benefits and risks. There will almost always be less evidence than you would like. Your doctor may have his or her own biases and way of evaluating the benefit-risk ratio. Make sure that the treatment choices are made with *you* in mind, by evaluating the evidence for risks and benefits yourself, even if you must rely on your doctor to present that evidence. After all, you are the one who will go off to see the therapist or put the pill in your mouth. If you remain uncertain that the benefits really outweigh the risks and potential hassles, you are likely to miss appointments or doses—or even stop entirely. Talk to your doctor before you do that! But for now, let's focus on the basic principles of treatment so you will know how to approach the various medication and nonmedication approaches that are available.

First, Focus on Cycling, Not Symptoms

By its very nature, bipolar disorder is a problem of *cyclic changes in mood and energy*. In other words, people with bipolar disorder almost always have *phases* of one kind of symptom, then phases with none or with some other symptom. When you look at this pattern over time, you can see repeated cycles of symptoms. (An exception is mixed states, which can simply persist as a swirling mixture of agitation and depression. Although cycling might be going on, it is only from one combination of symptoms to another and can, instead, feel rather constant.) These cycles often have no clear relationship to human calendar time, with the notable exception of symptom increases around particular phases of women's menstrual cycles, and seasonal shifts in mood and energy associated with the timing of morning sun and total light levels.

Few would disagree with the commonsense notion that it's better to prevent symptoms than to wait for them to show up and then treat them. Therefore, arising from the cyclic nature of bipolar disorder, we have the first principle of bipolar treatment: *focus on a long-term goal of stopping the cycling*. Try to avoid focusing on treating your symptom du jour (symptom of the day), which in most cases will be depression. Instead, the goal is *not having depressions in the first place*!

Maintain Long-Term Focus on Your Goal. Two tricks may help you maintain that long-term focus. First, look for treatments that *can* keep depression from returning but *don't* make the cycling worse.

Not many true mood stabilizers meet both of these conditions. However, when you also consider nonmedication approaches, quite a few treatments fulfill these twin requirements *and* have antidepressant effects as well.

Here's the second trick for keeping a long-term mind-set. Most patients' depressive phases don't last very long: perhaps weeks and occasionally months. If they can just get out of the current episode and put a treatment in place to prevent falling back in, they may be able to avoid using an antidepressant approach with its possible risks. But how are you supposed to manage during the depression that you're waiting out? Fortunately, there are options (discussed later), which not only can prevent later episodes but can also treat the one you're in. It's important to recognize (especially when you are weighing the risks of such treatments) that for some people, one option is to take no risks and wait the depression out—as long as some steps are being taken to decrease the chances of going through depression again. For people with very long depressed phases, this may not be such a good idea. But if your episodes generally last a few weeks, or if they last months, but you're already two months into this episode, you might be able to stick it out knowing that you're adding a preventive agent and may be less likely to go through this again.

Maintaining this shift in mind-set is not easy, because of the very nature of depression itself. It can be awful. It can even be dangerous, when people start thinking about suicide, which unfortunately is common. You can just imagine what happens: a depressed person wants help, knows about antidepressants, and hopes to get one. His doctor knows that antidepressants can cause hypomania, or more cycles of depression, and she wants to avoid using them. But he is sounding a little desperate. He notes that he's been having thoughts about suicide: no plan, no real intent at this point, but he is frightened to even find himself thinking this way. He's not trying to talk the doctor into an antidepressant, but he wants to make it clear that he's having a rough time and is getting worse. If you were the doctor, what would you do? Wouldn't you

find yourself thinking very strongly about prescribing an antidepressant for this distraught person?

In fact, you'd have to have very firm beliefs that antidepressants
can make things worse, or you would probably go ahead and prescribe one. Even with such beliefs, you might find yourself having
to almost ignore the patient's desperation in order to stick to your
principles. A well-known mood expert suggests, partly in jest, that
doctors "plug their ears with wax" (invoking the story of Ulysses),
meaning they should try to ignore the patient's pleas for help with
their *symptom du jour* and keep the focus on the long-term goal.
The problem with this approach, of course, is that patients want
to be heard. They are suffering, and they want help with that suffering. Can't you just see the doctor getting ready to cave in?

The doctor needs a quick reminder and an alternative plan. The
reminder goes like this: many mood experts agree to avoid using
antidepressants wherever possible so as to avoid inducing cycling.
Indeed, it seems that the more experience one has treating patients
with bipolar disorder, the more one avoids antidepressants. According to one study, bipolar specialty clinics have only about 20 percent
of their patients on antidepressants, whereas general psychiatrists use
antidepressants in 80 percent of their bipolar patients.

Fortunately, much more is available for the treatment of
depression (in a Mood Spectrum context) than antidepressants
alone. So the doctor need not plug his or her ears. She can treat
depression very actively, in fact, yet emphasize approaches that do
not risk making the long-term picture worse while treating the
short-term problem. These are summarized in the next section.

Second, Use Antidepressants That Aren't "Antidepressants"

Sounds odd, doesn't it? Fortunately, the list is not short. It includes
several nonmedication approaches, as well as some pill-based
approaches with low long-term risk—which is important, because
in most cases people need to use these strategies for a long time.
(How long? Usually I duck that question at this stage, suggesting

that first we want to focus on finding a treatment that *works*. Later we can talk about how long the treatment might need to be continued, what kind of risks and side effects go along with it, and so on. At that point—since I emphasize finding treatments with no side effects, if at all possible—thinking about staying with that treatment for a long time may not look so bad, especially if it is already helping.)

Most of the strategies shown here will be discussed further in later chapters, but I want you to see them all at once. Knowing about this list helps many patients and doctors see that depression does not have to be ignored or always treated with an antidepressant. Table 7.1 lists the tools to which I turn when faced with depression symptoms in a patient for whom antidepressants might pose some risk.

Because the list starts with nonmedication approaches, you might think this whole collection looks lightweight, compared to antidepressants. Note that there are some heavies farther down the list. Looking at the nonmedication approaches first is a good place to start, especially since part of the goal is to keep overall risks low. The nondrug approaches here have almost no risk at all. You'll find details and links for all these strategies in the remaining chapters.

As you can see from Table 7.1, there are lots of things to try. You can make many combinations of elements. Each might be insufficient by itself, but when combined they can have a strong impact on your depression. The table roughly is organized from least risky to most—so you could start at the top and gradually combine elements, finally including one or two of the medication approaches as well, if necessary. But remember, time is on your side if you are adding *any* mood stabilizer—even if it does not have specific antidepressant effects—because you can prevent cycling back into depression, and you will come out of this episode as you have come out of those preceding it.

Third, Gentle Pressure on the Seesaw

Everyone faces destabilizing factors in their lives, such as emotional stress, but most have at least some stabilizing factors as well,

TABLE 7.1 Antidepressants That Aren't Antidepressants

Nonmedication Approaches	How It Works for Treating Bipolar Disorder
Exercise	The evidence is excellent: the hard part is to *do* it (Chapter 13).
Light and sleep shifts	Light boxes help almost 50% of people with obvious seasonal changes in mood; this is under study for PMS as well. Sleep timing also matters (Chapter 11).
Fish oil (omega-3 fatty acids)	The evidence that these can affect mood is slowly racking up. Best dose is not yet established. Slow to start working. No heavy metal or any other risk known at this point.
Psychotherapy	Many people shy away from this, but research has shown that a good therapist is as good as an antidepressant for several kinds of depression (Chapter 12).

Medication Approaches	How It Works for Treating Bipolar Disorder
Lithium (several generics)	Despite the stigma of lithium, this is a very good tool. Low doses have many fewer side effects and can still help a lot. Often used to boost other medications. Has anti-suicide effect.
Lamotrigine (Lamictal)	Slow to get started, to avoid causing a dangerous rash. Otherwise extremely useful: it has strong antidepressant *and* anticycling effects. Costs much more than lithium, though.
Olanzapine (Zyprexa)	Outstanding, rapid symptom reduction, often within hours or a day. Too bad it also causes people to feel too slowed down, it can cause diabetes and astounding weight gain, and is extremely expensive.
Quetiapine (Seroquel)	Like olanzapine, but not quite as effective, yet less likely to cause diabetes and weight gain. Sedating initially; expensive.
Other options	Several antimanic medications also have at least *some* antidepressant effects, though generally thought to be less than those shown here (including valproate and risperidone).

such as adequate sleep, good social connections, and perhaps even regular exercise. Think of these factors as sitting on opposite sides of what we used to call a seesaw, back in the old days before Xboxes. On one side of the seesaw are the destabilizing influences: alcohol, other drugs, sleep deprivation, uncontrolled stress, and for some people, their antidepressant medications. On the other side are the stabilizing factors, including regular daily rhythms, stress-reducers like having a secure job and a regular income, and (yes, here it comes again) regular exercise. (Really, even you. This is going to happen—you'll see.)

In general, the treatment of bipolar disorders requires steadily tipping the see-saw toward the side of greater mood stability. In addition to lifestyle changes, many people have to use pills as well: perhaps fish oil, usually something pharmaceutical. Some require several mood stabilizers, combining them at low doses to avoid the side effects that might accompany using one or two at high doses. But slowly, all these ingredients begin to tip the balance toward greater stability. Thus treatment is a *process* involving much more than medications alone. You have to look at your lifestyle, your social connections, your job and income, even what you eat (because weight gain can result from the condition itself, as well as from some medication options), when you sleep, and certainly how much you exercise. This is true for all types of recurrent mood disorders across the Mood Spectrum—even including Bipolar I.

There is nothing earthshaking in this third principle. It's just good medical practice to look at *all* the possible factors that affect you, and to try to shift the balance between the negatives and the positives. But notice what this perspective suggests when the next depressive phase comes along. Rather than trying to fix it or trying to make it quickly go away, one can see the recurrence as an indication that more pressure is necessary to stop the cycling. This is the first principle again (focus on cycling, not symptoms), but this time with a big-picture time frame around it: we're looking not just at the current episodes, but at *all* episodes and their prevention. We're looking to stop the cycling by *gently* tilting the see-saw back toward stability.

Why this emphasis on *gently*? Because we're dealing with your *brain*, OK? But (to speak more gently) also because the system we're dealing with seems to *react to change with more change*. That's what cycling is all about. If something shoves the mood system hard in one direction, in many people the system responds by pushing back in the other direction. This may be the basis of the most common cycling pattern, in which hypomanic or manic episodes go straight into depressive phases. It's as though the mood system overreacted to the hypomania or mania and pushed so hard in the other direction as to cause a depression. This same logic could explain why in some people, antidepressants appear to *cause* hypomania or mania, perhaps by pushing too hard and leading to an overshoot in the other direction. Occasionally, when increased quickly for mania or hypomania, a rapidly applied mood stabilizer such as valproate seems to cause a similar overshoot, leading to depression. So in general, slow and small changes are better than quick, big ones (as long as things are *safe* in the interim).

Three Main Strategies for Treating Complex Mood Disorders

The principles offered so far in this chapter form the basis of my three main strategies (what I actually *do*) for treating patients with complex mood disorders. These strategies have worked so well for me over the years that they have become almost a standard approach—almost a set of rules. Of course, with each patient I try to keep an open mind and look for reasons why these strategies may not be a good idea. My patients know that getting them a good outcome is the goal, not just following these rules! However, these almost-rules have been so useful, I'd like you to see them lined up:

1. Rely on *mood stabilizers* that the patient is clearly willing to use on a sustained basis, as generally we will be working on this for quite a while. Use low-dose combinations to avoid side effects.
2. Maximize use of low-risk and nonmedication strategies to address depression *without antidepressant medications*.
3. Use antidepressants only when *no signs of hypomania or mixed states* are present and other strategies are not working.

Strategy 1: Rely on Mood Stabilizers

Psychiatrists almost universally accept this first strategy, as reflected in virtually all bipolar treatment guidelines. (There are several, and some of the most prominent are summarized on the "Mood Stabilizers" page on my website.) However, you can see I place great emphasis on *sustainability*. This means looking even more closely at side effects and risks than you would for a medication you might take only briefly. For most people, one of the biggest factors they consider at this stage is whether the proposed treatment causes weight gain. Although many mood stabilizers do, a few do not. (A couple of them seem to block appetite and lead to weight loss in many people, but these options have other side-effect problems and some significant risks. Also, so far none have been clearly shown to function well as a long-term mood stabilizer.)

As you saw in Table 7.1, when depression is the main target symptom, two obvious mood stabilizer candidates are *lithium* and *lamotrigine*. Lithium can cause weight gain, but not as often nor as dramatically as medications like olanzapine, and it costs very little. It has some long-term risks to the thyroid and the kidneys, as well as risks of blood levels getting too high.

Lamotrigine is almost ideal in this role. It is weight neutral in almost all cases and has strong antidepressant effects, yet it has not been associated with causing cycling. (I think it may have some such risk, but far less than antidepressants, and perhaps none at all.) It has a serious short-term risk (potential for causing a severe skin condition), but once it is established, long-term risks are minimal. It is much more expensive than lithium, though.

Olanzapine and quetiapine have strong antimanic effects but also have antidepressant effects. For long-term use, quetiapine causes less trouble with weight gain and less risk of causing diabetes. Both have strong antianxiety effects, help slow rapid thinking, and help people sleep. But both are also very expensive.

Other mood stabilizers with less-direct antidepressant effects still have the capacity to stop cycling and can be completely effective in the treatment of Mood Spectrum symptoms. They are less likely, however, to treat *current* depressive symptoms while establishing that long-term prevention. These medications will be discussed in the next chapter.

Strategy 2: Maximize Use of Low-Risk and Nonmedication Strategies

Like the first guideline, this is not controversial. This is just good common sense. So why does it merit discussion? Because these obvious strategies are harder than swallowing a pill! I wish I could *require* anyone who is going to receive an antidepressant to show me they've already tried a reasonable exercise program *first*. Unfortunately, our society doesn't consider that as an acceptable professional practice. But think about it: exercise has very low risks for most people, has practically zero risks for young healthy people, and has other known health benefits. Overall it clearly has more side benefits than it has risks—for almost everyone. So why even consider an approach with known risks when another approach has known additional *benefit* instead? Because our society makes exercise so difficult to get on a regular basis, that's why (more on that in Chapter 13).

For the other strategies shown in Table 7.1, the evidence favoring benefit over risk is not quite as overwhelming. For fish oil, this is because evidence for benefit is not very strong yet (evidence for risk is still zero at this writing). Light therapy is worth trying if winters are clearly worse for you than summers. But my main point here is to underline the importance of exercise and give you another gentle shove in the direction of reading the exercise chapter—and then doing it!

Strategy 3: Use Antidepressants When No Hypomania Is Present—and After Other Strategies

In practical terms this means two different things, depending on whether you are already on an antidepressant or if you are considering starting one. We'll look at each of these situations in turn. The logic is the same, though, as presented in the earlier guidelines.

Not Currently on an Antidepressant. Let's say you've tried all of the antidepressants that aren't antidepressants and depression is still your main problem. In fact, it's your only problem. You don't have any signs of hypomania: you're sleeping too much, not having difficulty sleeping; your energy is very low, not agitated; and your mood is just depressed, not significantly irritable. In addition, you are not cycling at all, just depressed.

Not many of my patients reach this point. It's hard to really exhaust all the options from Table 7.1. Most commonly, when depression is still a problem after all the options were tried, it is mixed together with signs of hypomania, such as agitation, severe sleep problems, or irritability. Even if these may only appear briefly in cycles, that still counts as present in my book.

If an antidepressant is added when signs of hypomania or cycling are present (speaking from clinical experience; there are no data to go on here), commonly the depression will get better all right; but the hypomanic symptoms often get worse, the cycling becomes more prominent, or both. If one assumes that the antidepressant can cause those changes, then one immediately faces the need to remove the antidepressant to address the hypomania and cycling.

Therefore, in my experience, if hypomania or cycling is present, I treat that first. Although all along the way my patient and I discuss the probable benefits and possible risks of antidepressants, I try to hold off on using them until we are faced with a relatively pure depression, with no hypomania at all. But, of course, you remember the trouble we had ruling out hypomania because of the difficulty with being certain something is *not there*? Just as different doctors arrive at different diagnostic conclusions because of the way they handle the gradually vanishing iceberg of hypomania, so too might they have different treatment strategies (even when they agree on this principle of avoiding antidepressants when hypomania is present!) because of their different thresholds for detecting hypomania.

When a pure bipolar depression is identified, an antidepressant with relatively more energizing effects, such as bupropion (Wellbutrin), is generally my preference. This scenario is very common in the winter, when a seasonal shift in mood leads to a winter depression. In *seasonal affective disorder*, very low energy is recognized as a characteristic feature of such depressions; thus, again, buproprion is likely to be my choice of antidepressant. (Of course, one then has to guess when, nearing the return of the light in the spring, one should taper off the antidepressant. For me this is always tricky, as the patient doesn't want to stop early!)

I have spoken very generally here. In my practice there are numerous exceptions to this rule. For many of those patients, we've discovered that they do better by staying on the antidepressant, and most had to discover that by going off the antidepressant and watching things get worse. I've not yet read anyone describe how we might identify these patients in advance so that they don't have to go through this process. One frequently cited study, led by Dr. Lori Altshuler, speaks to this issue, but people often forget to note the design of the study, which makes drawing any conclusions tricky. A more recent study with a much stronger design supports a general approach of routinely, though carefully, tapering people with bipolar disorder off of antidepressants.

Already on an Antidepressant. When referred to me, most patients are already on an antidepressant, having been treated thus far as unipolar. I leave them on it while starting a mood stabilizer. If things clearly get better, we then begin to taper the antidepressant. Again, the assumption is that more people likely would become worse, in the long run, from continuing that antidepressant, than would benefit from staying on it. One mood expert points out that at present we have *no* randomized trial evidence demonstrating that people with bipolar disorder do better in the long run when given an antidepressant, and yet we have considerable evidence that antidepressants can make people worse.

However, note the word *taper*. I once heard Gary Sachs, one of the most widely known and respected bipolar experts, say that if a patient is doing well, one should take four months to go off an antidepressant, 25 percent per month. If a patient is not doing well, I might go much faster, perhaps removing it in only a month or two. But my patients have seemed to do much better since I started following Dr. Sachs' advice. "Wait a minute," you say, "haven't you been telling us that antidepressants can make people worse? Now you're saying you should keep them around for *months*?" Good, following right along, aren't you. Here's one more bit of information you need to understand this paradox. There is also a phenomenon called *antidepressant-withdrawal* mania, in which suddenly stopping an antidepressant seems to induce manic or hypomanic symptoms. I've seen this rather frequently in patients who've gone off antidepressants on their own. Stopping fast is not good. How slow one has to go to avoid this phenomenon is not clear, but you can see why Dr. Sachs' advice may be wise.

To summarize, then: maximize your use of antidepressants that aren't antidepressants. Be cautious with true antidepressants. And rely primarily on mood stabilizers, remembering that the goal is not to treat today's symptom, but to stop the cycling. The next chapter will look at mood stabilizers in more detail.

CHAPTER 8

Mood Stabilizers: The Core Ingredient in Medication Treatment

Your cat Felicia needs to see the veterinarian. Time to put her in the little cat-transport box—which, of course, she hates. Imagine you had to do this with one hand. She sees your hand coming from the right, and she scoots left. You move your hand to her left, but she shies to the right. Finally, you get frustrated and try to just grab her, but whichever side you come from, she's off in the other direction. You might be able to nab some cats with a one-handed approach, but most require two hands.

Using antidepressants to treat bipolar depression is like trying to grab Felicia with one hand. It might work once or twice, but after a while you will want something that comes at her from both sides at once. To stretch this analogy a bit, imagine that Felicia prefers to run to her left. In that case, you could get away with an approach that is more sure-handed on the left, even if it's pretty weak on the right. But the more skittish the cat, the more you need an approach that covers both sides.

That is the general idea behind a *mood stabilizer*: a treatment for mood instability that pushes toward the middle from both sides. Note there is no intention of squishing the cat while doing this! You want Felicia herself to remain unchanged while you get a good hold from both sides. Turning back to real life and mood stabilizers, surprisingly only one treatment meets this definition, according to one analysis. That is lithium; though even lithium is not perfect, as it is not equally powerful on both sides. Beyond this, there is some disagreement about which medications merit the term *mood stabilizer*. Now that bipolar disorder is more widely recognized and discussed, medication manufacturers have recognized this large potential market. All of a sudden, everybody wants to be a mood stabilizer.

Examining the Mood Stabilizer Menu

How can you avoid getting caught up in definitions? Once again, a spectrum point of view may prove helpful. In some ways, researchers must look at medications in strict categories: this medication *is* a mood stabilizer, that medication *is not*. But you and your doctor can use a spectrum way of thinking: each of the various treatment options can be laid out on a continuum from purely antidepressant to purely antimanic. First, we'll look at the "menu" of mood stabilizers from this perspective, followed by some general information about each medication. Then we'll look at several different ways of choosing among all these options.

However, first I must warn you. Of this entire book, this chapter is the most likely to be out of date. By the time you read this, there may be new tools or at least an improved understanding of the best roles for those shown here. Rather than providing details about particular medications, this chapter will give you a *framework* for thinking about them. When you've finished reading the book, look for updated information about the medications that are most appropriate for you.

You can find a basic primer about each of these medications, including their risks and side effects, on many Internet pharmacy websites (just put the medication name in a search engine like Google). More limited, bipolar-specific information about each can be found taking links from the Mood Stabilizers page on my website (go there via the Notes page: psycheducation.org/notes .htm.). Even this will not provide all the information you need to evaluate your options. Theoretically, your doctor is supposed to do that. However, as long as you keep the previous chapter's guidelines in mind, you can *supplement* your doctor's teaching with your own reading.

Mood Stabilizer Spectrum

In Figure 8.1 you'll see all of the medications commonly used as mood stabilizers on a spectrum, ranging from antidepressant to antimanic. This "map" reflects my interpretation of the literature on these medications; other psychiatrists might place some of them slightly differently. Medications in parentheses have less evidence than the rest for being able to *prevent recurrence* of symptoms once a patient is well, a very important characteristic in a mood stabilizer. (They have not been shown to be ineffective in this respect; rather, they do not yet have significant randomized trial evidence, or years of clinical experience, supporting their effectiveness in this long-term role.) Verapamil has *only* antimanic evidence, not recurrence-prevention evidence, and so appears at the bottom. On the far right are medications with only antimanic effects (verapamil, carbamazepine [cbz] and oxcarbazepine [oxc]).

FIGURE 8.1 The Mood Stabilizer Spectrum

Antidepressant   Antimanic

lithium
valproate
cbz/oxc

omega-3's
lamotrigine
optimized thyroid

olanzapine
(quetiapine)
(risperidone)
(ziprasidone?)
aripiprazole
verapamil

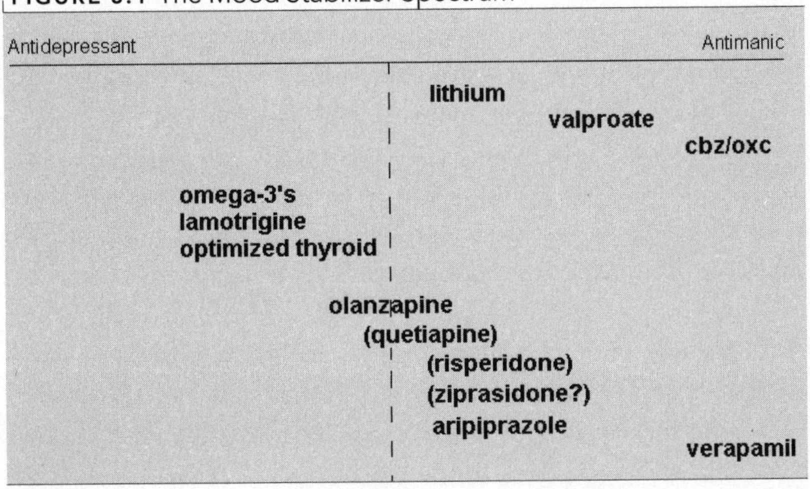

On the left are three approaches whose antidepressant effects are stronger than their antimanic effects: omega-3s, lamotrigine, and optimizing thyroid hormone. Olanzapine has nearly an equal balance of each and thus appears in the middle. Lithium has more antidepressant effects than valproate. The next section provides general information about each of these options.

The Original Mood Stabilizers: Lithium, Valproate, and Carbamazepine

This trio was all we had for the treatment of bipolar disorder until the late 1990s, so psychiatrists who've been practicing for ten years or more generally have had a lot of experience using them. Until recently, there has been little research to characterize their effectiveness compared to other agents, and this is still true for *carbamazepine* (cbz). Some mood experts think that these medications are underused because of all the research attention and industry promotion lavished upon the newer agents.

Lithium. Many people associate lithium with the treatment of severe mental illnesses. For people whose symptoms lie in the middle of the Mood Spectrum and whose primary symptom is depression, the idea of taking a medication they associate with severe mental illness is often hard to swallow (sorry). Yet lithium has one of the best track records as a mood stabilizer. It even has been shown to have an oddly specific antisuicide effect, much more so than valproate, for example. It has been shown to increase brain size, reversing the trend toward shrinkage (particularly in the frontal lobes and memory center) that mood problems seem to cause. It's cheap, and clinicians have many years of experience with it, so no new surprises are likely concerning long-term risks.

Yet lithium does have significant long-term risks:

- It can interfere with kidney function—though this usually takes more than a decade of use. (If you start now, however, I hope that by that time we'll have a much better treatment, developed on the basis of actually understanding the basis of bipolar physiology.)

- It can interfere with thyroid hormone production, requiring thyroid replacement (no risk there, if managed correctly, but it is another pill to buy and take).
- At full doses, it can reach too high a level in your blood and make you very sick.

On the other hand, at low doses this is an easy medication to use. It may boost the effects of other medications, so it can be used as an *adjunct* (not the main course, but a significant side dish in your treatment). It has significant antidepressant effects, though in one study this benefit was seen only at higher doses. In some recent large studies and an analysis of older data, it was better as an antimanic medication. Nevertheless, listening to international colleagues, it sounds to me as though they think we Americans are nuts, underusing lithium and overusing the newer, more expensive alternatives.

Valproate. Marketed as Depakote in the United States, this anti-seizure medication has long been recognized to have mood-stabilizing effects. Recently two small research studies have suggested that it has more "antidepressant clout" than previously thought—thus its position in the Mood Spectrum figure. (If not for this research, most doctors probably would have listed it in the same position as carbamazepine.) Valproate is still listed as a first choice in some expert guidelines but has recently been implicated in causing hormone imbalances in women. Because it also can cause abnormalities in developing fetuses if used in the first few weeks of pregnancy—more frequently than lithium, which can also do this—some psychiatrists have suggested that women of reproductive age not use it. However, every mood stabilizer either is known to cause fetal abnormalities or has not been shown to be safe, as that takes many years to demonstrate. So criticizing one particular medication for this is suspect. (Verapamil occasionally is mentioned as a possible medication for pregnant women with bipolar disorder. But it is not listed in this chapter, because the data on its effectiveness is weak.)

Carbamazepine (cbz) and Oxcarbazepine (oxc). Another anti-seizure medication, carbamazepine used to be a distant third choice after lithium and valproate because of its greater risks. These include

- Interference with blood cell production
- Liver irritation
- Potential for a severe skin reaction
- Complex interference with the metabolism of other medications

It's difficult to talk about positives after reciting a list like that: what could possibly justify taking those risks? Thus we doctors generally come around to it when lithium and valproate don't work. Although dramatic, the risks are quite uncommon. But many people think, "I don't care how uncommon it is; I don't want that to happen to me."

Stick an oxygen atom on carbamazepine and you have *oxcarbazepine*. This close cousin has fewer risks than carbamazepine. But after a period of initial excitement over having a low-risk version of carbamazepine, I discovered that I didn't have any patients doing well on oxcarbazepine alone, so I rarely start it anymore. (Research on this medication has been limited, for complex reasons.) Most of my colleagues agree this version merits its nickname "carbamazepine lite."

Stabilizers That Work Better Against Depression

Omega-3 fatty acids (from fish oil), lamotrigine (Lamictal), and thyroid hormone are a very odd assortment to lump in the same group. Yet all three have been shown to have both antidepressant effects and mood stabilizing effects—although the evidence supporting their effectiveness is variable.

Omega-3 Fatty Acids. Most likely you have heard of these as *fish oil*, as that is the source as well as the form you swallow. Most people immediately say, "Yuck," or some other colorful variation, perhaps thinking of mothers giving their children cod-liver oil or just imagining that fishy taste. But some fish oil pills are tasteless, and even some fancy emulsions taste pretty good, believe it or not, although they cost much more. One thing stands out about this approach compared to the rest: *it has no known health risks.* People have worried about heavy metals like mercury, but these appear to get trapped in the fish meat and don't come out with the oil. Fish oil can cause "fish burps" (one patient said to me, "When I burp, I feel like a seal"), though taking the pills with meals or keeping them in the freezer so that they release more slowly and thus farther down your intestine appears to minimize or eliminate this effect.

But does it really work? The evidence so far is rather weak, but seems to be accumulating. The current data are made somewhat more convincing by several studies showing that people in fish-consuming countries have lower rates of bipolar disorder than those who live in countries where fish are not a regular part of their diet.

Lamotrigine. If this medication were cheaper and faster to start, it would be just about perfect for general use in the middle of the Mood Spectrum.

- It has strong antidepressant effects, yet it can prevent cycling (for example, it has been shown to be an effective treatment for rapid cycling).
- It does not cause weight gain, a major problem with most of the other mood-stabilizer options. (Weight gain is such a problem, in fact, that it gets a whole chapter in this book—Chapter 10.)
- It has no other long-term risks that we know of at this point, after nearly ten years' experience with it as an antiseizure medication.

Unfortunately for some patients—once in every 1,000 to 3,000 exposed—it can cause a serious rash, which can be life-threatening. We've learned that by starting lamotrigine slowly, the risk of this rash is much lower than when this medication is started quickly, but that means it is not a great strategy when you're in a hurry.

Thyroid Hormone. What's this doing here, in the column along with antidepressant-like options, no less? Well, it turns out that an extremely complex relationship exists between thyroid hormone and bipolar disorder. Thyroid problems run in families with bipolar disorder. Bipolar symptoms sometimes show up for the first time, or at least become severe enough to require treatment, after some thyroid hormone change. But can thyroid hormone be a treatment? There are four reasons to consider it.

1. When thyroid hormone is low, people can become depressed. Doctors should check thyroid hormone levels in someone who is depressed because it is such an easy thing to treat.
2. There is a long tradition of using thyroid hormone as a booster for antidepressant treatments that are not working well enough. Although the data supporting this practice are limited (by the way, the data are much better for lithium in this role), it's a standard option for *treatment-resistant depression*.
3. At least two studies show that people with low-normal thyroid hormone levels (still in the normal range, but at the low end) respond less well to treatment for depression. This has been shown in both unipolar and bipolar depression.
4. Thyroid hormone has been used at very high doses as a treatment for rapid-cycling bipolar disorder. This has seemed to work for a few of my patients, but about twice as many simply become hyperthyroid as the dose goes up. My experience with this strategy is limited, in part because

thyroid hormone is not regarded as a routine mood stabilizer. Most of the research on this approach comes from one research group. Funding is very limited because thyroid hormone has been generic for years.

Olanzapine: A Stabilizer Class unto Itself

Directly in the middle of the mood stabilizer spectrum is *olanzapine* (Zyprexa). In addition to rapid effects on manic and hypomanic symptoms (often within an hour), this medication has been shown to have substantial antidepressant effects. Originally developed as a replacement for the old-generation schizophrenia treatments, it is technically called an *atypical antipsychotic*. You'll meet a few more of these in a moment. The name is unfortunate, because these medications all have very clear benefits in bipolar disorder even when no psychosis is present. In low doses they can be extremely useful in treating patients whose mood symptoms are close to the *unipolar* end of the Mood Spectrum. Indeed, olanzapine has repeatedly been shown to be effective in *treatment-resistant Major Depression*. (In other words, it can help in pure unipolar depression that is not responding well to antidepressants. I always wonder, however, how many of those patients might have had enough bipolarity to make them resistant to antidepressants, but not enough to be identified as bipolar.)

Olanzapine also has been shown to very effectively prevent *recurrence* of bipolar symptoms—a feature that many experts consider an important standard for mood stabilizers. It is even better at this than valproate. Unfortunately, it also stands out for causing dramatic weight gain (20 pounds or more in a few months, in many cases), and it can cause diabetes. This problem is shared by all the atypical antipsychotics but is worst for this one. Thus olanzapine is a very tricky medication: it is so effective that it makes doctors *want* to use it, but since it also carries very significant long-term risks, most of my colleagues have learned to avoid it. One of my colleagues said, "I hate it when they start people on Zyprexa in the emergency room. When these patients come see me the next week, they feel so much better they don't understand why I'd even consider switching them to something else!"

Quetiapine: Antidepressant as Well as Antimanic

Although this medication has not been studied for long-term relapse prevention (and thus appears in parentheses in Figure 8.1), it has been shown, like olanzapine, to be effective in bipolar depression. Quetiapine causes less weight gain than olanzapine and appears to push people less strongly toward diabetes. It also has very predictable side effects: almost everyone who takes it will be sleepy at first; then the daytime sleepiness will ease up, but the nighttime improvement in sleep will persist. A patient told me on the day I wrote this, during his first visit after starting quetiapine, that the medication seemed to be "multitasking," because so many different target symptoms had improved: sleep, anxiety, thinking too much, and negativity. I think this is a characteristic experience on quetiapine, and thus I prescribe it a lot, far more than olanzapine or risperidone (the two others in this class, aripiprazole and ziprasidone, are still new for me). But the risks of weight gain and diabetes are not small. Using this medication requires careful monitoring of glucose and cholesterol, especially when it is first started.

Stabilizers with Mostly Antimanic but Some Antidepressant Effects

In this category are all the rest of the atypical antipsychotics: *risperidone* (Risperdal), *ziprasidone* (Geodon), and *aripiprazole* ("Abilify"—Are you familiar with the word *smarmy*?). All of these are vying for the title of "mood stabilizer." Among these, currently only aripiprazole has been shown to have the ability to prevent recurrence of symptoms (as olanzapine has demonstrated), in a short study. Remember that these two properties are what we might hope to find in a true mood stabilizer. Ziprasidone appears in parentheses in Figure 8.1 because so far, this medication has only limited data to suggest that it does anything more than suppress manic-side symptoms. By contrast, risperidone can act too much like an antidepressant, inducing manic-side symptoms even while it partially controls them, so that I never quite know what to do next: raise the dose or stop the medication? It is extremely effective in older patients as a low-dose single medication, and it plays an important role in the treatment of Bipolar I as well. It's just not my favorite for symptoms farther down the Mood Spectrum.

None of these medications has had the rapid, dramatic mood-stabilizing effects one can generally expect from olanzapine. On the other hand, they don't cause weight gain and diabetes as consistently either, although they all can do so (ziprasidone and aripiprazole apparently the least, so far). At present these medications are still considered primarily for stabilizing mood from the manic side; they are quite strong at this. Many psychiatrists combine them with antidepressants, thereby creating a two-handed approach. If it weren't for the weight gain and diabetes risks, I'd probably consider this approach more often myself. After all, in the old days lithium was the only medication for bipolar disorder; if it didn't work people would often end up on a combination of an antidepressant and one of the original antipsychotics—which did work very well for many patients. We don't consider that approach very often nowadays, because the old antipsychotics tend to make people feel very odd, drugged, and unable to think, much more so than the newer (but vastly more expensive) atypicals. In addition, the newer agents are somewhat less likely to cause a severe movement side effect known as *tardive dyskinesia*.

How to Choose from All These Options

You've surely noticed that every one of these treatments has something wrong with it. Just when one starts looking good, along comes the bad news. Research on new treatments will eventually lead to completely different approaches, but it will take several years to establish their safety. So for now one must choose among options that all have some problem. How do you go about making a decision?

Some psychiatrists and other providers regard this choice as theirs and will not seek your input. Others may allow you only a small role in the decision making. You can still teach yourself about these options and slowly build that doctor-patient relationship toward a more collaborative approach (as discussed in Chapter 6). If you're fully involved, however, how are you supposed to choose among all these options? Here are several ways to approach that decision.

The Ideal: Treat Current Symptoms *and* Prevent Cycling

You certainly want an approach that can treat your current symptoms. But if one of your options *also* has the ability to prevent cycling into symptoms in the future, that would be best. I hope that sounds familiar? Remember the first guideline from the last chapter: focus on cycling. In other words, you want to prevent the return of symptoms once they have disappeared, as well as make them go away now. If you can find a medication that will do both, that's obviously better than having to switch to a different approach later for prevention of recurrences.

The ability to *prevent* cycling is much harder to demonstrate in a research study, compared to treating the present symptoms. Imagine how long a research study needs to last to be able to say that a medication prevents the return of symptoms. For a person who has only a few mood episodes a year, the study would have to run at least a year to show a difference between the medication and a placebo. Amazingly, some of our treatments have actually been studied this long, and their proponents can thus make such claims. So far these include lithium, valproate (Depakote), olanzapine (Zyprexa), lamotrigine (Lamictal), and recently, for a shorter period of study, aripiprazole. Everything else has so far been studied only as treatment for a *current* symptom. This does not mean the others do not have the ability to prevent cycling back into symptoms. It just means they have not been shown in well-controlled research studies to have this ability.

So we have a serious "asymmetry of evidence"—a lack of research on all potential candidates. Some experts have suggested starting with one of the five medications named in the last paragraph because they at least have some evidence for these ideal effects (although most have been shown to prevent recurrence in only one direction—either into depression or into hypomania or mania).

Another way to choose might be to look for the best match with your current symptoms, according to the spectrum diagram at the beginning of this chapter. If that match *also* points toward a medication that has been shown to prevent relapse into *your most common symptom*, you may have found your best option.

What Is Most Important to You

In business school they teach students about three criteria that often guide consumers' choices. These are shown in Figure 8.2, using hamburgers as an example. As you can see, you can sometimes get two out of three of these important qualities, but not all three.

FIGURE 8.2 Buying a Hamburger

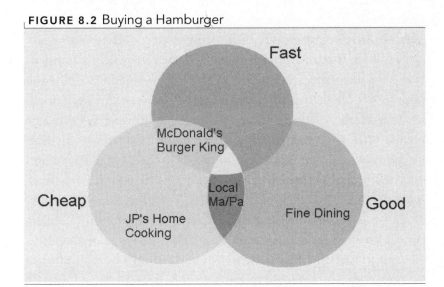

FIGURE 8.3 Choosing a Mood Stabilizer

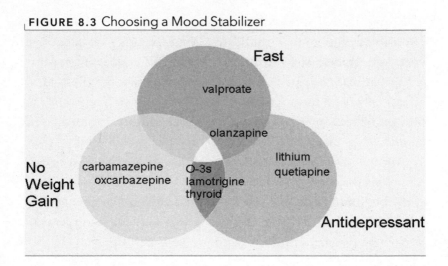

Mood stabilizers work in the same way, as shown in Figure 8.3. You sometimes get two out of three of these desirable qualities, but not all three in one treatment.

In my office, I keep an updated list of mood stabilizers handy, which lists the pros and cons of each option. As I present this list, I watch my patient's face. By the time we've gone through the list, I can usually tell which of these three criteria—Fast, Antidepressant, or No Weight Gain—will most strongly drive his or her decision. In America, avoiding weight gain is usually an important criterion: either people are already overweight and for health reasons cannot afford to gain more, or they fear gaining weight because of the culture's intense worship of thinness. For some people with very severe symptoms, the treatment must be fast. Finally, for most people in the middle of the Mood Spectrum, depression is by far the dominant symptom. For them, the treatment needs to include a significant antidepressant effect.

As you can see from these diagrams, a few medications can offer two out of three of these desirable qualities. A word of caution: I have positioned these treatments according to my understanding of current research and my experience. The diagram includes those medications that I think have been shown to approach the "ideal" characteristics of a mood stabilizer: able to prevent cycling as well as treat current symptoms. Some doctors would include the other atypical antipsychotics, placed as follows:

- Ziprasidone in the No Weight Gain circle with carbamazepine
- Aripiprazole either in the No Weight Gain circle or perhaps up with valproate in the Fast circle
- Risperidone with olanzapine in the Fast–Antidepressant category

Remember, these distinctions are based on my clinical experience, not entirely on research data. So if your doctor sees these categories differently, he or she is not wrong!

Approved by the Food and Drug Administration

You'll sometimes see people write as though FDA approval should guide your choice. After all, isn't that agency supposed to look at all the options and indicate the ones that have good evidence for effectiveness and low evidence for risk? Well, no, actually. That's not quite how it works. Here's a short version of a complex story about FDA approval.

A medication cannot be advertised for a specific purpose (such as treating bipolar disorder) until it is FDA-approved for that purpose. To get FDA approval, strict research guidelines must be met, including at least two randomized controlled trials, as described in the previous chapter. These trials cost millions of dollars. So if the manufacturer is not in a position to earn millions of dollars from promoting the use of their product, they have no incentive to bother getting FDA approval. It would just cost them money that they won't see coming back in return. This is especially the case when the patent on their medication is about to expire or has expired. After that happens, other companies can make a *generic* version of the medication. If the original manufacturer pays for studies to get FDA approval, when their competitors can make a much cheaper version (because they don't have to pay millions of dollars to sponsor such research), you can see this is not a good business strategy.

Therefore, the FDA-approved drugs are those where the manufacturer stands to benefit by supporting the expensive research. These tend to be the newer drugs, with at least several years remaining on their patents. So older drugs (oxcarbazepine, verapamil, and certainly thyroid hormone) are not likely ever to be FDA approved. No one wants to pay for the research the FDA requires.

As a result of this process and several other factors, no mood stabilizers have been approved specifically for Bipolar II. Some were approved for bipolar disorder generally, before the FDA started chopping up their approvals in the last decade. Most are approved only for the treatment of Bipolar I (this includes most of the atypical antipsychotics). Thus when given for the treatment of these different bipolar variations, most mood stabilizers are used *off label*. This jargon term means that the medication has not been officially "labeled" for this purpose by the FDA. It does not mean the medication doesn't work or carries more risk than other options. Ironically, medications that have been around a long time may actually be even *better* understood in terms of their risks than those that have recently earned FDA approval. The FDA label just tells you that the medication has been studied *directly* for the purpose described and meets the FDA's standards of evidence. As you can see, this is not particularly useful for guiding medication choices for spectrum versions of bipolarity.

Expert Guidelines (and Pharmaceutical Company Funding)

Finally, you could check to make sure the medication you are considering or being offered by your doctor is also recommended by expert psychiatrists. Three sets of expert opinion have been prepared in the United States (and more abroad):

1. The American Psychiatric Association
2. The Expert Consensus Guidelines series
3. The Texas Medication Algorithm Project (TMAP)

All three are summarized and linked in the introduction to the Mood Stabilizers page on my website. If you have a look at these documents—which I encourage you to do so you can get another point of view—you'll find that the presentation of medication options in this book is very consistent with those guidelines.

These expert opinion documents are created by gathering a group of well-known psychiatrists with an interest in mood disorders, then structuring their views into a consensus. You can imagine that the results could be somewhat political and that the companies that make mood stabilizer medications might want to influence the results directly or indirectly. Indeed, the TMAP has been criticized because many of the doctors involved have received honoraria (payments for presentations) and other support (grants and consultant positions) from manufacturers.

However, in the last five years almost all mood experts have gotten involved in this way with pharmaceutical companies—me, too. I use their money to pay for patients who can't afford care, as well as for time writing my website. Their money certainly could influence how I've written about their medications. But I try to watch for this and edit myself, imagining what I might have said without an awareness of the company's stake in what I say. This is tricky, because some of their medications I like, yet I don't think it's because of their money—I liked their medications before I had any connection with them. I grant you, at this stage I am certainly not in a good position to tell the difference. The point here is that gathering experts nowadays means gathering doctors who have worked with pharmaceutical companies and could be influenced by those relationships. Your own evaluation of benefits and risks, in which you compare claims and evidence for those claims, becomes all the more important to balance potential influence by manufacturers.

Finally, some might think that this entire book is a grand advertisement for these medications. This criticism is worth listening to. Some people who are being given mood stabilizers, and certainly some who are being given antidepressants, could be treated without such medications. In fact, some may not really have a Mood Spectrum problem, in the sense discussed in this book, at all. They might have family problems or life problems (a job they hate, or no job at all), that get interpreted as depression or perhaps even as bipolar disorder.

But I can tell you, after practicing psychiatry for fifteen years, when people get to me, they are usually really suffering. Most have tried getting help through their priest, friends, occasionally exercise, and sometimes herbs, naturopaths, acupuncturists, and such. Perhaps somehow we could restrict the use of the medications described here to those who are clearly in need, but who is in a position to make that judgment? I'm satisfied that those whom I treat really need these medications, even as I encourage them to pursue nonmedication approaches as well. They and I both recognize that our goal is to enable them to function, at minimum, and after that, perhaps to make them suffer less. I really don't think we're treating the worried well with these medications (though there are some exceptions here and there, as always).

One other concern about how we're using all these medications is that when subjected to a rigorous analysis, they don't look much better than lithium. Unfortunately, we don't do many research studies *comparing* treatments for Mood Spectrum versions of bipolarity. Notable exceptions include the BALANCE studies, now under way: one compares lithium and valproate for prevention of manic and depressive relapses; the other (BALANCE 2) compares lamotrigine and antidepressants for bipolar depression. Many experts outside the United States think we skip over lithium too quickly in favor of far more expensive but heavily advertised alternatives. As for me, I recognize the luxury of having all these alternatives at hand and the opportunity to make very broad choices in collaboration with my patients.

Balancing Hope and Realism When Using Mood Stabilizers

These medication approaches really work for a lot of people. In my practice,

- About 30 percent of my patients can get complete or very near complete symptom control with zero side effects (or very close to zero, easily livable).
- Another 25 to 30 percent get clear responses to treatment, but we are still making changes—either because of side effects we're trying to get rid of, or because they are not completely symptom free.
- Another 30 percent, roughly, respond only partially and often with side effects that are not acceptable in the long run (weight gain is one of the main problems).
- The remainder, perhaps 5 percent, do not seem to respond to anything I try (which usually leads, appropriately, to questioning the accuracy of the working diagnosis, and an offer to arrange a second opinion and transfer of care).

These response rates are similar to those from a large sample of patients with bipolar disorder, in the Stanley Foundation Bipolar Network. Overall, the likelihood of at least some improvement is extremely high. And overall, there is at least a 50 to 60 percent chance, in the long run, of finding a treatment that is clearly worth the risks, time, and money spent.

You can see I'm trying to raise your hopes that you, too, might get a very good outcome with treatment. However, you should be careful here. Dashed hopes, after a medication or therapy doesn't work, are a risk of treatment. If you've already tried many treatments, you know what I'm talking about. It hurts to discover, perhaps yet again, that what you thought might make a big difference in your life has not worked—especially if you were very hopeful when you began treatment. On the other hand, starting out skeptical can lower your placebo response rates, because hope is an amazing ingredient in treatment. I generally encourage caution, if not outright skepticism, in amounts roughly matching the number of previous treatments tried.

How Long Do You Need to Take This Stuff?

I usually duck this question initially, suggesting that we first find a medication or medications that clearly work. Obviously if we can't get that far, this question is moot. Yet people begin to realize that the medications may *control* symptoms but not *cure* the illness, and that in most cases treatment of some kind has to continue in order to prevent a relapse. With that realization comes one of the biggest hurdles: accepting that your mood disorder may be *chronic*, meaning that it probably won't go away. People begin to recognize that beyond getting rid of present-day symptoms, the next challenge is to stay well thereafter.

This realization can happen very early and very quickly—no matter how artfully I duck the question at first. This is why I so strongly emphasize that our goal in treatment is 100 percent symptom control, with 0 percent side effects. A patient with very severe symptoms may be willing to put up with significant sedation at first, or tremor, or even appetite increase. But once the symptoms are controlled, the burdens posed by treatment (including time and money spent on therapy and medications, as well as any side effects) must become the focus—and quickly. If these are not reduced to a tolerable level, the patient almost certainly will consider stopping the treatment: after all, the symptoms are now gone or much reduced, so what justification is there to put up with the treatment burdens anymore?

You can see why I steer patients toward treatment approaches that are sustainable for the long term, right from the beginning. Why start with something you'll want to switch away from, if it works? Why not start with those that, if effective, pose few problems when continued? For medications like lithium or valproate (Depakote), which have significant side effects at high doses but few at low doses, sometimes this means using several medications *together* at low, tolerable doses, rather than pushing a single medication up to its full strength. Historically this practice has been frowned upon, scornfully referred to as *polypharmacy* (literally, many medications). But polypharmacy is now generally accepted as a strategy in the treatment of bipolar variations, because clinicians understand the need to use treatment approaches that their patients will actually *continue using*!

Can Trying a Mood Stabilizer Make Things Permanently Worse?

Good question. You should wonder about this in order to evaluate the full picture of the risks you're taking when trying one of these medications. So far, mood stabilizers look better in this respect than antidepressants. As you'll see in the next chapter (Controversy 2b), a tiny bit of evidence suggests that antidepressants might be able to make things worse in the long run, perhaps permanently, in some people with bipolarity (and by the remotest stretch of the evidence, perhaps even in some patients who appear to be unipolar at the beginning of treatment). By contrast, I have never even heard *speculation* about such risks for mood stabilizers, with one exception: lithium, when stopped abruptly or tapered too fast (over a few weeks, instead of several months), appears to make some people *more* susceptible to a return of symptoms than if they had never taken it at all. If we stretch that evidence, as I'm obviously willing to do for antidepressant risk, we might conclude that all mood stabilizers should be slowly tapered. (This is based on *extrapolating* from the lithium experience; to my knowledge this phenomenon has not been shown directly for any other mood stabilizer).

Mind you, *any* treatment you try has some potential for risk. For medications that have been in frequent use for at least several years, these risks are fairly well-known. For newer medications and untested strategies such as herbs and other alternative treatments, it is difficult or impossible to fully describe the possible risks of treatment.

Risk of *side effects* is a different matter. Admittedly, most of the mood stabilizers have some nasty side effects to watch out for. In the view of most doctors, the side effect risks of antidepressants are not as concerning. For patients who are purely unipolar with no *soft* bipolarity, I would agree. For patients with some degree of bipolarity, however, one must also consider more controversial risks of antidepressants, which are discussed in the next chapter.

CHAPTER 9

What You Need to Know When Considering Antidepressants

Ever find yourself thinking that taking an antidepressant might be a good idea? Most people with milder bipolar symptoms have thought this. Remember the iceberg of hypomania we were looking for at the beginning of this book? It's only *2 percent* of the symptoms! (Well, 6 percent, as it is also part of the mixed-state phases, which you may recall seeing in Figure 2.3.) *Depression is the predominant symptom of the Mood Spectrum.*

Consider it this way: if pure hypomania accounts for only 2 percent of the time spent ill, and a person with this version of bipolar disorder is ill about 50 percent of the time, then that person is hypomanic only about 1 percent of the time. That means experiencing hypomania one day in a hundred—about one day every three months. But that same person is depressed about *six weeks* out of those twelve. You can see why people focus on the depression and often miss or fail to mention the tiny wedge of other symptoms.

Isn't this stunning? These data describe what it's really like to have Bipolar II: when symptomatic, you are *depressed*. Once in a rare while, hypomania appears, as likely to be mixed with depression as to occur by itself. If your bipolarity is subtle, perhaps very mild hypomania, you or your doctor could easily overlook it.

When Depression Is the Dominant Symptom

Now for the treatment implication of this depression dominance: *depression is very likely to be the patient's main target when coming to the doctor for help.* Many people have learned, from friends or from their own reading, that antidepressant medications can help with depression (lately they've had a lot of help from advertising by the manufacturers). Therefore, unless they learn about the complexities of the Mood Spectrum, as you have done by reading this far, they are very commonly looking for treatment with an antidepressant medication. Most often, they see their primary care doctor first. Unless she has learned about the complexities of the Mood Spectrum, an opportunity few primary care doctors have had, she is very likely to prescribe an antidepressant. You see the problem: antidepressants look like the obvious, right thing to do.

But antidepressants can make bipolar disorders worse. They can flip people into mania or hypomania, cause mixed states, increase the rate of shifting from one mood state to another, and may even worsen the long-term course of the illness—or so some mood experts believe. Let's take a look at the concerns about antidepressants in bipolar disorder.

The Antidepressant Controversies

Most of the debate you may see about antidepressant use in bipolar disorders is about *switch rates*: how often do antidepressants, given for depression, cause a person to have hypomanic or manic symptoms? In other words, how often does the medication cause a switch from depression to mania? This issue was part of the decision by the U.S. Food and Drug Administration to issue a warning about antidepressant use in children, because switching to mania may be the basis of some of the suicides and homicides in children taking antidepressants. But people with bipolar variations should be aware of additional controversies.

All of these are very active debates, so by the time you read this, there may be new data or new perspectives worth examining. I hope to keep my Web page on this topic up-to-date with such new views, although it is written for primary care doctors and is more technical than most of the rest of my website. This chapter presents a plain English version highlighting the issues.

Controversy 1: How Often Do Antidepressants Cause Hypomania?

At one time there was some doubt about whether antidepressants cause switching from depression into mania or hypomania. But after many analyses there currently is nearly complete agreement that this does indeed occur. Instead, now clinicians and researchers are asking, "*How often* does this happen?" For a person with a little or large degree of bipolarity, how much risk do antidepressants pose? That is, how likely is it that if you take an antidepressant when you are depressed, you will then get manic or hypomanic symptoms?

This is not an easy question to answer, for a wide variety of reasons, and as a result the estimates in well-conducted analyses still have a broad range. One recent and thorough review estimated that between 20 and 40 percent of bipolar patients experience manic or hypomanic symptoms in response to an antidepressant. Other rates also are quoted, including 3 percent in one widely cited study, which is problematic in design.

You might think that the risk of switching from depression to mania is greater the more bipolar you are—that is, the farther to the right you are on the Mood Spectrum. But establishing a reliable estimate of switch rates has been hard enough; comparing such rates *across* the spectrum has not been done yet. Some people are extremely switch-prone: give them even a tiny dose of an antidepressant and they become hypomanic, start cycling faster, or enter a mixed state. One of my patients could become hypomanic just by sitting in front of her light box a few minutes too long, and she could not take any antidepressant, no matter how low the dose, without accelerating toward mania. This was a major problem because she would routinely have severe winter depressions with suicidal thoughts and actions. (She has since moved to California, several lines of latitude south!) However, in my experience, patients who switch when taking antidepressants are not neatly clustered toward the Bipolar I end of the spectrum, as you might expect. I do not relax about the risk of antidepressant-induced hypomania even for patients whose symptoms place them toward the unipolar end of the spectrum.

On the other hand, a small amount of evidence shows that repeated exposure to antidepressants can *make* a person more switch-prone, which brings us to the next debate.

Controversy 2: Do Antidepressants Cause Mood Instability?

Most studies of antidepressant risk in bipolar disorder focus on the first controversy, the switch rate. But remember, depression is the dominant symptom in this illness. It comes back again and again. It is unusual for a patient with bipolar disorder to have only one exposure to antidepressant medications. Most patients receive these medications repeatedly or continuously. What impact does this have on their long-term outcomes? We'd want to compare them to a group without such exposure, preferably by randomly dividing a collection of people into a group that received an antidepressant and a group that did not. Unfortunately, we have no such randomized trial. In fact we have almost no experimental data to go on, though several authors have collected other data that allow an evidence-based approach to longer-term risks of antidepressants. These possible risks include

- Rapid cycling (as in the forthcoming example of John Hudson)
- The possibility that antidepressants might prevent response, or full response, to mood stabilizers
- A more theoretical concern about a long-term increase in mood episodes

Controversy 2a: Do Antidepressants Cause Rapid Cycling? *Rapid cycling* technically refers to patients who have more than four mood episodes per year. Surprising? In classic Bipolar I, patients can go for years without an episode of mania or depression. But in Bipolar II, particularly the more complex versions with additional symptoms of anxiety or problems such as alcohol abuse or a history of sexual trauma, cycle rates are very often far higher (so that my patients laugh at the idea of only four in a year).

And yet, as you know, antidepressants can make bipolar conditions worse. You've already heard that antidepressants can cause hypomanic and manic symptoms. A lot of clinical experience and a little research data suggest that antidepressants can also cause increased cycling, meaning an increased frequency of mood episodes compared to what might have occurred without the antidepressant. In other words, it looks like antidepressants can shift a patient to a more rapid cycling pattern, as appears to have occurred to John Hudson in Figure 9.1. The scale shown is one we clinicians often use for a quick estimate of how a person is doing. We ask, "On a scale from 1 to 10, where 1 is the worst you ever feel and 10 is the best, how are you doing today?" Most people who have no mood symptoms at the time answer, "OK, I

FIGURE 9.1 Antidepressant-Induced Rapid Cycling

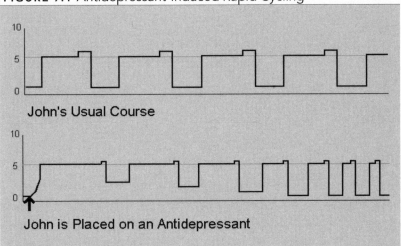

John's Usual Course

John is Placed on an Antidepressant

think, about 5 or 6." Thus the middle of this mood range is about 5, as shown by the straight line at that level.

As you can see, before John received an antidepressant, he was having repeated episodes of depression (with brief hypomanic phases preceding them—a very common pattern). After the antidepressant is started, he is not as depressed at first, but eventually he starts having the full depressive phases again—only *more frequently*. If you were the doctor and saw a patient's symptom pattern change like this after an antidepressant was started, you would probably suspect that the antidepressant was causing *increasing cycling*. In my experience, this phenomenon appears to be common. However, several factors could bias this observation:

- My own beliefs (causing me to see or remember increased cycling more frequently in patients whom I know are taking antidepressants)
- My particular patient mix, which might include patients much more likely to have this kind of experience, whereas in a more general mix of psychiatric patients, this phenomenon could be much less common
- Other factors in my patients themselves, which could account for the increased cycle frequency, besides the antidepressant (For example, they might be staying up too late because they started to feel better and went back to some of their old ways, or they might be drinking more alcohol, discussed in Chapter 11.)

Thus establishing a definite cause-and-effect relationship from such observations is difficult.

Granted, antidepressants often make the depressive phases less severe, at least at first. John appears to have had this experience, as you can see. He came out of his depression quickly after the antidepressant, and his next several episodes were not as severe as before. This beneficial effect is often lost, however, and sometimes quickly. In John's case the shift shown might have taken place over as little as three to six months, or even less if he was originally cycling quite rapidly. Occasionally this shift takes place much more slowly, perhaps even over years. By that time it's very hard to tell whether the antidepressant simply isn't working anymore, or whether it might be contributing to the problem. If the cycling stops when the antidepressant is tapered off, that obviously implicates the antidepressant. But usually by this time the patient is on a mood stabilizer, so perhaps *that* stopped the cycling? We also have to wonder if the illness we're trying to treat has become worse and would be cycling like this even without the antidepressant. As you can see, it is very difficult to be certain that the antidepressant is really the culprit, especially when things worsen slowly.

Several researchers have noted that rapid cycling was not as frequently observed, decades ago, as it is today. Perhaps we were missing it then, because bipolar disorder at that time was recognized only in the version now called Bipolar I (the classic, manic-depressive version). But some mood experts have wondered whether the use of antidepressant medications, stimulants for Attention-Deficit Disorder, or both may have contributed to the apparent higher rate. Do we have any direct evidence that antidepressants can increase cycle rates? There is one frequently cited study, conducted at the National Institute of Mental Health over several years. The research design is not the ideal randomized trial, but close. Although only a few patients were involved, cycle rates were observed for *many months*, which is exactly what we need for a longer-term look at antidepressant effects. Frequency of mood episodes was observed while patients were on, then off, then on antidepressants again. Their cycle rates went up, and down, and up again, just as one would expect if antidepressants do indeed cause rapid cycling, and in general, few psychiatrists doubt that antidepressants do just this.

A very standard recommendation for treatment of rapid cycling is to taper the antidepressant. In my clinical experience, this strategy has been very effective and has become a routine recommendation in my practice. I encounter quite a few patients who have been struggling to get their bipolar symptoms under control and who have been on an antidepressant the entire time they've been on mood stabilizers. At least this gives me an obvious new strategy to try! This presumed connection between antidepressants and rapid cycling leads us to the next controversy. My view here is strong and very unusual. Anyone with this much passion behind an idea should be doubted, so don't take it from me. Check out these assertions elsewhere, particularly for the next section.

Controversy 2b: Can Antidepressants Cause Depression? If you look at John's experience and can tentatively accept the idea that antidepressants can increase cycle frequency, you're ready for the next small step in this logical analysis of their effects in bipolar disorders. Think along with me carefully here, as this is extremely important for understanding the principles that follow. Here's the crucial step. If antidepressants do indeed increase cycling so that people have *more mood episodes* than before, then they also will have more *symptoms*. Ironically, these can include depressed symptoms. These patients may thus have more depressed phases, and thus more days depressed, than before they started the antidepressant. You can see this pattern in John's case, which I've drawn from the experience of many of my patients.

Since at this point, John's antidepressant is not helping and might be making things worse in this way, you might think that stopping it would be a good idea. But you wouldn't think about doing that with your own antidepressant, would you? Heavens no, you'd discuss it with your doctor first so that he has the opportunity to tell you why it is *not* a good idea in your case, and why there might be a major risk in doing so. Or the doctor might agree and then give you instructions on how to *taper it off slowly*, which is usually essential. In any case, you'd talk with the doctor about that first, right? Good, then I won't have to give you any further lecture about why it is so important that you not take the ideas in this book and run with them on your own.

Assuming for the moment that antidepressants can indeed cause increased cycling, one more small logical step leads to a very paradoxical conclusion: if antidepressants increase cycling and then *lose* their beneficial effects, they can effectively be causing depression. Pardon me? Antidepressants *causing* depression? My guess is that you've never heard of that idea. Neither have most doctors. This is my own way of looking at antidepressant effects, and not one you'll find in the standard writings about bipolar disorder and its treatment. So be cautious and remember I could be completely wrong about this. Notice that the whole idea of antidepressants *causing* depression depends entirely on whether antidepressants do indeed *cause* cycling from one mood state to another. Although generally most practicing psychiatrists accept the latter idea, only a little research evidence is available to support it. To my knowledge less evidence goes against it.

Wait just a minute here. Perhaps you find this idea that antidepressants can *cause* depression by causing increased cycling just too paradoxical to swallow. Here's an analogy that might make the problem clear. Suppose you love going to the amusement park to ride the roller coaster, but the newest one makes your stomach quite queasy. The big drops, from near the top to near the bottom, seem to really get you. Although you used to be able to ride these things with no nausea, now every time you get on their new Free-Fall Anti-Gravity Machine, you practically throw up. Your friend has a magic pill, however, that will decrease your nausea, she says. It blocks that feeling of going down and down so far. But she forget to tell you two things. First, this pill also accelerates the roller coaster. Second, the pill only works the first few times you try it; after that, the antinausea effect fades away, although the acceleration effect continues. Not knowing these two things, the pill sounds like a great idea, so you try it.

Off you go on the Free-Fall again—this time with the pill—and your experience is much better: no nausea at all. You are so pleased you hardly noticed that the roller coaster went a little faster this time. But a few weekends later, going back for the fifth time or so, the nausea returns. Now imagine going back for the eighth time since first taking your friend's pill. (You have a season pass for this thing, and while you need to do plenty of other things, your body wants to keep going back on the old Free-Fall.)

This time, the nausea is back to the same level it was before you took the pill, and the Free-Fall seems to go nearly twice as fast as it did back then. This is no fun anymore, and you wish you could get off and stay off.

To push this analogy just a bit further and prompt you to keep reading (which by now must seem pretty intimidating), here's one more aspect of the problem. A bit of evidence suggests that having accelerated your experience of the Free-Fall Anti-Gravity Machine, you might never be able to slow it down again, and you might be stuck riding on it. You might continue taking these nauseating rides, even though it has been weeks since you took your friend's pill. At this point, some people can't get the Free-Fall to stop until they start taking an additional (mood stabilizer) medication.

In real life, this analogy suggests that antidepressants could speed up mood cycling in such a way that the cycling remains accelerated long after the medication was stopped, perhaps even forever. But take this all with a very big grain of salt. This concern is still primarily a worried guess on the part of only a few psychiatrists.

And please don't go running off saying you just heard that antidepressants can *cause depression*. Out of context, that idea will generate a lot of confusion. In the context of this book, it means that antidepressants *might* bring about depressive episodes by causing episodes of all kinds to be more frequent.

Controversy 2c: Can Antidepressants Prevent Response to Treatment with Mood Stabilizers? Although it is not commonly discussed in the psychiatric journals, this controversy is one of the biggest issues facing patients and doctors. As for most of the issues in this chapter, however, there is very little evidence to go on. In my experience, antidepressants have so frequently seemed to interfere with response to mood stabilizers that I routinely tell patients, "If mood stabilizer X didn't work for you, but you were on an antidepressant at the time, you'll have to try X again *without* the antidepressant around to know for sure that it can't help you."

Are there any documented cases of patients who did indeed respond to a mood stabilizer that wasn't working when the antidepressant was present but started working when the antidepressant was tapered off? Yes, Dr. Rif El-Mallakh at the University of Louisville has published six such cases. Granted, six cases is not much to go on. To my knowledge, there are no research trials in which previously ineffective mood stabilizers were retried without an antidepressant around. But from my clinical experience, I'm pretty darn convinced my maxim above is useful.

Controversy 2d: Do Antidepressants Cause "Kindling?" As you know, a single spark can start a fire if you have laid the kindling well. Some patients with bipolar disorder seem to follow this *kindling* pattern. The intervals between episodes shorten, and the episodes become more severe. As you can see in Figure 9.2, this is what happened over years for Jason Brown (not his real name, but this example comes from a real patient's experience).

After his first episode of depression at age eighteen, Jason did not have another episode until he was almost twenty-five. His manic episode at age twenty-seven identified his mood disorder as bipolar. But the intervals between his mood episodes shortened as he became older, and the episodes became more severe.

Not all patients with bipolar disorder worsen over time like this. I'm sorry I can't offer you even a rough estimate of how often this occurs, because studying people for many years is not easy in research programs (they move away, they drop out, etc.). I can't guess from my own practice either, because the very goal

FIGURE 9.2 Some Bipolar Disorders Worsen Over Time

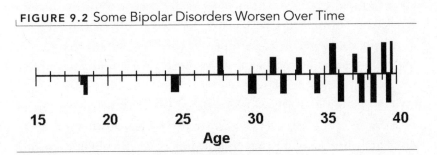

15   20   25   30   35   40

Age

of treatment is to stop the recurrence of episodes, right? As soon as this pattern seems to be emerging, we clinicians get more aggressive in trying to suppress any further episodes. Many bipolar experts think that patients whose symptoms are completely controlled—that is, who are not cycling at all—may not be as vulnerable to this possible kindling effect. In other words, if you stop the cycling, perhaps you can stop any possible worsening of the illness, or at least decrease the trend in that direction, if you happen to be someone whose bipolar disorder might follow this pattern.

Remember, this kindling pattern is observed in *some* people, not all. The idea that the mood episodes themselves are responsible for the accelerating course in these patients is a *model*, not an established fact. The model may explain some people's experience and guide our treatment—for example, suggesting that our goal might best be *zero* cycling in order to prevent possible worsening.

But this model has implications for antidepressant treatments. Again, I should warn you that the implications you're about to examine are not a common concern among psychiatrists, or even among mood experts. Since I seem to be one of the very few who worries about this, I could be taking the implications too far or missing something that others can see. You definitely should not take my concerns as the basis for refusing an antidepressant your doctor is recommending. I'm just inviting everyone to think.

Here are the implications of the kindling model, in my view. If for some people with bipolarity, each episode of mood symptoms can make subsequent episodes occur more frequently or be more severe, and if antidepressants can trigger mood episodes (by causing rapid cycling, which is generally accepted, or by causing hypomania or mania, which is not debated at all), then might not antidepressants be able to kick people forward into more frequent and severe episodes? Might they not push a patient forward on his or her personal timeline?

For example, imagine that Jason Brown's first episode of depression at age eighteen was treated with psychotherapy, exercise, or lithium. Note that he did not have his second episode until he was twenty-five. Now suppose he had been treated at eighteen with an antidepressant instead and went on to have a manic episode. Is it possible that the antidepressant might have kindled him so that his next episode occurred not at age twenty-five, but at twenty-two?

Or consider the experience of John Hudson. Remember that his episodes of depression at first were less deep, then became more frequent as well as more severe, until finally his episodes were as severe as when he started but occurring more often. What will happen to him when the antidepressant is stopped? Can we be sure he will return to the frequency of depressive episodes that preceded the antidepressant? What if taking the antidepressant has kicked him into a new phase of his illness, with more frequent episodes as his new norm? I've never had a chance to see the answer to this question, as I'm always busy trying to stop the cycling entirely by using mood stabilizers.

Imagine how hard it would be to know, for Jason Brown, that the antidepressant was responsible for the acceleration of his illness. How could anyone be sure it wasn't just the very illness worsening at the rate it would have regardless of whether he had taken an antidepressant or not? Although for one person it is impossible to know this, an interesting study done at Stanford University might support the concern I'm presenting here. In that study, people with Bipolar II, who were depressed, were treated with valproate (Depakote). The researchers found that people who had been treated previously with an antidepressant did not respond as well to the valproate as those who were "antidepressant naïve." As the authors acknowledge, it is unknown whether those who had received an antidepressant before entering this study had more severe symptoms than the other group and that is why they ended up getting an antidepressant in the first place. But these results are consistent with the idea of a permanent change in the nervous system that might result from antidepressant exposure. A small study like this doesn't prove anything, but it has kept me wondering. Dr. El-Mallakh, cited earlier, has wondered likewise. He and his colleagues concluded a review of this issue thus:

"Although far from conclusive, these data are consistent with the hypothesis that antidepressant treatment is associated with a manic episode earlier than might occur spontaneously."

Finally, let's return to the case of Jane Roberts, whom you met back in Chapter 3. As you'll recall, she had many bipolar *soft signs*, including a close relative with bipolar disorder, but she never displayed any hypomania at all (even when I looked very closely for it with my snorkel and magnifying glass). She let me give her lithium first, because of my concerns, but when that caused side effects, we switched to an antidepressant, and she got a very nice response. But consider her now in light of the theoretical concerns expressed here. Is there any chance that she'll respond nicely for a while, but later lose the benefits (as John Hudson did), and at that point find herself worse than she was when she started? I worried about that, but I gave her the antidepressant anyway, because, at this point, these concerns are so theoretical. (See the Notes page on my website for after-press follow-up on her case. Interesting.)

Beth: Did the Antidepressant Cause Her Mood Change?

I have had one patient whose experience certainly supports this kind of worry, so much so that with her permission I published a case report about her, which you can read about in more detail on my website. Here is a summary of her case.

Beth Carter is now sixty-two years old. She had been moderately depressed as long as she could remember, but she would worsen with severe depression every few years. She had no family history of bipolar disorder and no personal history of hypomania that I could detect (using a snorkel and magnifying glass). She did not get better with fluoxetine (Prozac) or paroxetine (Paxil) but had a dramatic improvement on sertraline (Zoloft). Her depression was gone, and she was not hypomanic. She continued to do well for *seven years*.

Then she began to have severe agitation, insomnia, and difficulty concentrating. Her primary care doctor thought she was having panic attacks and increased her sertraline from 100 mg to 150 mg. The agitation became extreme, and she started having suicidal thoughts again. She was referred to me at that point. We tapered her sertraline and added a variety of mood stabilizers, but none worked until the sertraline was completely gone.

Her case would not be so noteworthy except for what happened next. On low-dose quetiapine (Seroquel) she was no longer agitated, but she was mildly depressed again, just as she had been before the antidepressants. She started working with a good geriatric psychotherapist (thank you, B.G.) to address this and took low-dose omega-3 fatty acids. However, about a year later she went into another more severe depression, and on her own she restarted sertraline, though at only 25 mg per day. She called me after only two such doses to report, happily, that she was much better. In an office visit the next day though, after a third 25 mg dose, she was extremely agitated again. Her symptoms that day were almost as bad as they were when I first met her. We stopped the sertraline, but it took a month for the agitation to gradually fade away. Surprisingly, although her depression returned, it now responded very well to a tiny dose of lithium, even though a higher dose had shown no benefit earlier on when she was just coming off the sertraline the first time. (Note that this is consistent with my maxim described in Controversy 2b.)

Somehow the antidepressant switched from beneficial to clearly harmful. We must ask whether the antidepressant itself caused this change. Again, we cannot really know. She herself could have been changing. But the way she reacted to sertraline the second time, at such a small dose, seems (to me, at least) to implicate the antidepressant itself in *causing* this kind of agitation. If that is really what happened to Ms. Carter, note that the process can take *seven years*! If antidepressants can really cause this kind of sensitization, they may do so extremely slowly in some people.

Perhaps now you see why I hesitate to use antidepressants in people with symptoms that look a "little bipolar." Even though this is the current standard approach, we have all these variations of Controversy 2 to consider for such people. For example, think about Jane Roberts. She did not appear to have any hypomania to identify her as bipolar, but had many soft signs of bipolarity (a close relative with bipolar disorder), including early onset, recurrence, brief episodes, and postpartum depression. Recall that on this basis I hesitated to give her an antidepressant. She rather graciously allowed me to prevail and start with lithium. Because she had sedation and slow thinking at low doses of lithium, we then moved on to an antidepressant and she got a very good response. But can you see now why I worry that her story might not end there? The worst thing about this concern is that determining if this is a real problem, this risk of kindling, will take a very long time and a lot of questioning observation. Meanwhile, many people are taking antidepressants.

However, remember this is not a widespread worry among psychiatrists. I could have talked myself into believing we have a problem here. I will definitely regret raising this worry, years from now, if somehow we can establish that it pertains to only a few patients, if any. I recognize that having raised this alarm, if I am wrong I will have caused harm by making people fearful of antidepressants, perhaps not taking them when they might have benefited. (Again, please do not stop yours on the basis of reading this; talk with your doctor if you have such inclinations.) But I fear there is greater risk in overlooking the possible longer-term consequences of antidepressants. You'll see this bears directly on the next controversy as well.

Controversy 3: When to *Stop* Antidepressants

While discussing Controversy 1, I noted that some people are extremely switch-prone. But other patients with bipolar disorder do not seem at all prone to developing hypomania, rapid cycling, or mixed states when they take an antidepressant along with their mood stabilizer. In my practice I work with a few who clearly have bipolar features yet have done well for years on just an anti-depressant. (They usually were on this regimen when they first came to see me, and I've watched, usually with my knuckles in my mouth, as they go right along still doing well.) The fact that some people with clear bipolarity seem to do so well on antidepressants for years plays a large role in the disagreement within psychiatry about when to stop an antidepressant in a patient with bipolar disorder.

At one time, continuing the antidepressant indefinitely was the norm. Then came a phase of great concern about these medications, and many mood experts advocated routinely tapering patients off antidepressants (some prominent authorities still do—including, generally, the ones I trust the most). However, most recently, there has been growing recognition that some patients do better when they stay on a combination of a mood stabilizer and an anti-depressant. Now the debate is about how many patients are best treated thus: only a few? Or might it be many?

There are two strong driving forces in this debate. The first is a single article, which is almost always cited when this topic comes up. Yet even the authors caution that the design of this study makes it fundamentally very weak in terms of the conclusions that can be drawn from it. However, there are very few other data to go on regarding this particular issue: if a person is on a mood sta-bilizer *and* an antidepressant, and doing well with no cycling and no hypomania, how long should the antidepressant be contin-ued—indefinitely? As a result, this single article has had an unusu-ally strong impact on clinical practice.

The lead author is Dr. Lori Altshuler, now at the University of California in Los Angeles. She led a team of prominent bipolar experts looking at the experience of hundreds of patients who are participating in the Stanley Bipolar Treatment Network. In an analysis of these volunteers' treatments and outcomes, they found that in a select group of patients, those who stayed on their anti-depressants, did not relapse into depression as often as those whose antidepressant was discontinued. Sounds pretty clear, right? Bet-ter to stay on than go off?

185

That's the conclusion that is often implied or stated when this study is cited. But the most important phrase in that description is *not* "didn't relapse as often." Instead it is "in a select group." They had to examine the records of 549 patients to find 189 people (34 percent) who stayed on an antidepressant more than two months. The other 66 percent, for one reason or another, did not stay on an antidepressant even two months. Unlike the usual conclusion drawn from this study, the conclusion that only a minority of patients with bipolar disorder can take an antidepressant and stay well on it for over two months seems more apt. In any case, this study ought to be interpreted with caution. However, it does suggest that *some* patients do indeed fare better if they stay on their antidepressants, at least in the time frame of a year or so.

A clinical trial in which patients were *randomly* assigned to continue on to stop their antidepressant, while continuing their mood stabilizer, would provide better evidence to help us with this controversy. As noted earlier, a small such trial, led by Dr. Ghaemi, whom you met earlier in this book, has been completed but not yet published as of this writing. In this study, those who stayed on their antidepressant did *not* do better than those who were tapered off.

The other strong factor driving the debate about how long to continue an antidepressant is—or ought to be, in my opinion—your conclusion regarding Controversy 2. If antidepressants do accelerate cycling, and especially if antidepressants do create increasing long-term risk of mood instability, that would be very strong reason not to continue them indefinitely. (Indeed, in Dr. Ghaemi's recent study patients with rapid cycling did *better* when they were in the group whose antidepressant was stopped.) In fact, we would need some pretty strong evidence that antidepressants create good long-term outcomes in order to take this kind of risk. But in fact, we have no such evidence at all. That might sound a bit shocking, given that people advocate this approach and practice it all the time. (Remember the data about community psychiatrists' bipolar patients, 80 percent of whom are on an antidepressant?)

If you think about it for a minute, this is not so surprising. Think about the study design that would be necessary to demonstrate that patients on long-term antidepressants do better than those whose antidepressants are tapered off (or those who never started on them). This would be a long study (meaning expensive) and would require treating people with a placebo for a long time (meaning some ethical concerns, since these people would be depressed). No antidepressant manufacturer can make money from the study outcome (meaning there's no big-money funding source except our tax-payer-funded federal granting system, in which getting funding for a big study is very difficult). So we're not likely to see such research. That's why Dr. Altshuler and colleagues' study gets so much attention, you see? It's practically all we've got to go on. Only case reports such as you saw in the previous section can warn us of long-term risks with long-term antidepressants. How many canaries does it take before we should start telling people to change their practices?

That is not a simple question. Think of all the suffering that could result from concluding wrongly here about antidepressant risk. I use them frequently. I'd have had some patients commit suicide were it not for the antidepressants they took. Thus any conclusions, one way or the other, can have tremendous implications and place lives at risk if doctors are wrong. (Because of the nature of what we're treating, some lives are going to be at risk no matter what we decide. Yet doctors must try to make sure their decision does not *increase* that number.) Now you may understand why it is appropriate that this debate continue and that we keep looking for more evidence about both the risks and benefits of using antidepressants to treat people with bipolarity. The same issues arise in the last controversy to be examined here.

Controversy 4: Do Antidepressants *Cause* Suicidal Thoughts and Behaviors?

The FDA must make regulatory decisions for a country of approximately 296 million people. If they somehow make a decision that increases risk, the number of people affected is huge. Imagine what trying to make that call must feel like. You'd want to be pretty sure, wouldn't you? Yet you would be surrounded by stakeholders advocating their view, not the least of whom would be pharmaceutical companies, which by current arrangements actually fund a portion of the FDA's activities. Getting tricky now, isn't it? Then your neighbor across the pond, the British FDA-equivalent, goes and bans antidepressants for children. This is the situation the FDA faced in 2004 on this very issue. Many voices had raised concern that antidepressants might, in at least a few people, especially children and adolescents, *cause* suicidal and homicidal thinking and behavior.

Dr. Laughren and Dr. Mosholder and other FDA officials probably deserve a medal simply for not quitting in the face of this kind of pressure, let alone trying to work their way carefully through data and testimonies. Of course, once they made their decision, a vast surge of criticism came from both sides—which sometimes indicates the right decision in politics! Too bad this isn't politics, as then there would be only opinions to deal with. Instead, the expectation is that this issue will be based on evidence, and yet the evidence is difficult to interpret.

Unfortunately the debate about all this has been very polarized, with one side arguing that individual patients seem to have been *made* suicidal by antidepressants, and the other side arguing that antidepressants are important tools without which the suicide rate might go *up* again (in the last decade, it appears to have decreased slightly). To me it seems most likely that both groups are right: overall these medications help many people, and their use may be the basis of the apparent slight decrease in suicide rates overall. But among children and adolescents, perhaps two to four out of every one hundred who receive these medications can worsen, with suicidal (and sometimes homicidal) thoughts and occasionally actions. The number of adults so affected is probably somewhat lower yet. Ironically, finding those few who worsen is difficult when researchers look only at the outcome in the entire group of patients treated: the improvement in many of the patients could obscure the worsening in a few. In any case, I hope we will respect the difficulty of the decisions that FDA officials face, and remind ourselves how important it is to be cautious with our conclusions, given the magnitude of their potential impact.

While we're on the subject of evaluating and managing risks that come with treatment, we have to look at the risk of weight gain from mood medications. On to Chapter 10 then.

CHAPTER 10

Managing Weight Gain from Medications or Other Causes

Many medications used for the treatment of depression and bipolar disorder can cause weight gain. It's a big problem—especially since both conditions are themselves associated with weight gain. Add these two risks—the medications and the underlying condition—to the weight gain that is so common in the United States already, and you have three trends all leading in the same direction.

Worse yet, weight gain can easily worsen depression: people look at their bodies and behaviors and become even more discouraged and dissatisfied with themselves. They feel more uncomfortable when physically active, so they spend more time sitting and less time doing things that might positively impact their mood. Because they spend more time sitting or lying down, they may even begin to gain weight faster.

How ironic then that we might risk making this weight gain, depression, weight gain loop even tighter by adding to the problem with medications. Yet most of the medications we use for treating bipolarity can cause weight gain—not for everyone, but for many people.

There is some good news, however. A few medication options are clearly not associated with weight gain. Two medications occasionally used to treat mood (topiramate and zonisamide) even can cause weight *loss* in many people who take them, but their side effects are frequent and potentially severe, and their effectiveness is either unknown or doubtful, so they are not a rosy pair of options.

In this chapter we'll look first at the nature of the weight gain problem and then at three standard recommendations on how to deal with it and why these recommendations are so hard to actually do. Finally, you'll find out about some of the antidote medications that have been used to combat weight gain. The conclusion: the three standard recommendations, despite how difficult they are to follow, are clearly preferable to the antidote strategies.

Not Just the Medications' Fault

We now have very good evidence showing that bipolar conditions *themselves* can cause weight gain. Manufacturers of weight-increasing medications offer this evidence as an indirect defense: "See, it's not entirely our fault." Neither should we conclude that it's the patient's fault, mind you. It appears that some of the weight gain seen in these conditions comes from the very condition doctors are trying to treat, rather than from the medications. Medications can definitely make this problem worse, no question about it. But in interpreting their effects, you should understand how human physiology can change and make weight gain easier, even without medications.

Not Just "Calories in, Calories out" Anymore

Too much fuel coming in, too little of it burned up: weight gain does come down to this. But the last decade of research has shown that the story is much more complicated than the simple "calories in, calories out" model that has dominated dietary thinking for years.

When humans eat less, they can become more efficient, getting more mileage out of the fuel they do consume—as though you could improve your car's gas mileage when gas stations are few and far between! This is somewhat true for almost everyone, but in some people it is a quite dramatic shift (for example, in some Native American tribes and some Hispanic populations). How is our efficiency factor determined?

Just as you might guess, we see the usual suspects again: stress, lack of exercise, and refined sugar consumption. All are now thought to affect metabolic *efficiency* and thus affect whether people are gaining or losing weight on a given amount of fuel. There are probably other factors as well. Mood itself may be one of them, although trying to separate the weight effects of depression from the weight effects of the stress hormones that appear to (in part) cause depression is tricky. Most of the research on this subject has focused on a condition called *metabolic syndrome*, which we need to examine more closely, as the weight gain caused by many mood medications seems to be similar to this syndrome, perhaps identical.

Metabolic Syndrome

You may have heard of metabolic syndrome by now. It is the subject of much research, because it is associated with heart disease, the number one cause of death in the United States. Definitions for the syndrome can vary somewhat. Recently an entire conference of the National Heart, Lung and Blood Institute and the American Heart Association was devoted to clarifying how the condition should be defined. In general, metabolic syndrome includes elements from the following list:

- Increased abdominal fat
- Increased "bad" cholesterol (and decreased "good" cholesterol)
- Increased blood pressure
- Increased resistance to one's own insulin

Increased abdominal fat is a classic marker of this condition. Many people look at others with a large gut and think they lack self-control. I look at them and wonder what kind of stresses they must face and have endured during their lives (or if they might be taking one of the medications I sometimes have to prescribe to help my patients believe life is worth living).

The cholesterol changes seen in metabolic syndrome include increased *low-density lipoprotein* or *LDL*, which you know as one of the bad cholesterols because it is associated with increased rates of heart attacks and strokes. A related fat molecule called *triglyceride* is also increased in metabolic syndrome, which is not good, as triglycerides also appear to be another risk factor for heart disease. Finally, the *high-density lipoproteins* or *HDLs*, which have a protective effect against heart disease, decrease in this syndrome. As you can see, these changes are all going in the wrong direction for heart safety.

Blood pressure goes up in metabolic syndrome. The reasons for this are not clear. Stress hormones such as *epinephrine* (adrenalin) may be involved. Physical inactivity is probably also directly related, as increased exercise generally lowers blood pressure.

Finally, a complex series of metabolic changes interferes with the body's ability to respond to its own insulin. As you know, insulin is the hormone responsible for helping glucose get from the bloodstream into the cells that need it, such as your muscles and your liver. Metabolic syndrome seems to begin when your cells do not respond properly to insulin—a condition called *insulin resistance*. Because your cells are not taking in glucose well, its levels increase in the bloodstream. These high glucose levels call for more and more insulin. Your cells, seeing all this insulin, become more resistant to it (as to a neighbor who talks too much: eventually, you just stop listening). Ultimately the pancreas cannot make enough insulin to meet that need, and all the symptoms of diabetes appear. Even before that point, however, insulin resistance appears to be very directly involved in all the manifestations of metabolic syndrome. In many people, insulin resistance may be the most direct cause (in others, inflammation changes that suggest some immune system involvement may also play a role).

I hope you're asking yourself: What causes insulin resistance in the first place? Ah, there they are again, the usual suspects: stress, lack of exercise, and refined sugar consumption. Exactly how they interfere with insulin response is not clear, but at a simple level:

- Too much refined sugar overloads the system.
- Too little exercise leaves the system out of practice for moving large fuel loads.
- The stress hormone *cortisol* increases glucose release from the liver, further overloading the system.

Metabolic Syndrome and Mood. Why are we focusing on metabolic syndrome here? We do so because the condition has been shown to be common in depression and bipolar disorder, the defining poles of the Mood Spectrum. Does the mood problem cause metabolic syndrome or does metabolic syndrome cause the mood problem? Or does some third factor cause both at the same time? For now the answer appears to be all of the above, as follows.

The stress hormone cortisol, which we saw a moment ago causes increased glucose release from the liver, is also clearly involved in causing depression (although the brain systems that *regulate* cortisol are also involved in mood changes). Therefore, cortisol is a clear candidate for a third factor that might cause both metabolic syndrome and mood problems.

But depression can clearly cause metabolic syndrome through the self-reinforcing loop described earlier: mood goes down, energy goes down, activity goes down (and calories sometimes go up, particularly in atypical depression and seasonal affective disorder). This can lead to insulin resistance and from there to metabolic syndrome.

Finally, a slight bit of evidence suggests that somehow, metabolic syndrome itself might cause depression. For example, Dr. Natalie Rasgon, now at Stanford, and her colleagues at UCLA, published a very suggestive case report on this issue. They describe the experience of a woman who did not get better with an anti-depressant, but then got well and stayed well when her metabolic syndrome (a variant called PCOS) was treated. What was the treatment? The same medication that is commonly used for type II diabetes: *metformin* (Glucophage). A handful of other patients have also reported mood improvement on metformin, but this approach has not been studied. More on my website; see the Notes page.

From Epilepsy Came Clues for Bipolar Disorder

As you may know, epilepsy and some forms of bipolar disorder have some striking similarities. For example, several of the medications used in bipolar disorder, including in variations such as Bipolar II, originally were developed as medications for epilepsy. In fact, until recently, most of the medications known to act as mood stabilizers, except lithium, were antiseizure medications: valproate, lamotrigine, and carbamazepine.

Concern about medication-induced weight gain grew among us psychiatrists when we began using a lot of valproate (Depakote) for bipolar disorder. So when the neurologists began reporting an association between valproate and a metabolic syndrome variant called *polycystic ovarian syndrome* (*PCOS*), we began watching the neurology journals for information on this problem. PCOS causes not only abdominal obesity, but also *androgenization*: increased male hormone effects, most easily recognized by the growth of hair in places more typical of men than women (chin, breasts, and around the navel). It also causes fertility problems. What does this have to do with *weight*? Any metabolic syndrome variant, including PCOS, can cause weight gain.

Valproate was associated with PCOS in 1993 in a prominent article by a Finnish research team. Whether valproate actually causes PCOS has still to be established, however, despite continued research on this issue. In the process we've learned that epilepsy itself is associated with PCOS. More recently, bipolar disorder has also been associated with increased rates of PCOS, even without valproate treatment. (Data on the valproate-PCOS relationship, from my viewpoint, are presented in links from the Notes page on my website.)

When *other* psychiatric medications, such as olanzapine (Zyprexa), appeared to be causing large and rapid weight gain— particularly abdominal fat accumulation—our experience with valproate and PCOS had prepared us to look for *metabolic* changes. As noted in Chapter 8 on mood stabilizers, an association between olanzapine (and other new-generation medications like quetiapine [Seroquel] and risperidone [Risperdal]) and metabolic syndrome, as well as the related condition of diabetes, has already been established.

Antidepressants are also associated with weight gain, though not with metabolic syndrome. The older tricyclic antidepressants such as imipramine and especially amitriptyline are well known to do this. So do the rarely used monoamine oxidase inhibitor (MAOI) antidepressants. The commonly used serotonin reuptake inhibitors (SRIs), from fluoxetine (Prozac) to escitalopram (Lexapro), have also all been recognized to cause weight gain in some people. Paroxetine (Paxil) in particular is well known for this problem, more so than most of the rest in the SRI family. The more recent mirtazapine (Remeron) is a very potent appetite stimulant; substantial weight gain is very common on this medication. Only bupropion (Wellbutrin) does not appear to cause weight gain; it appears to be weight neutral, though it has been associated with a very minor weight loss in several studies.

Remember that when weight gain occurs, medications are not always the guilty party. The very conditions we are treating on the Mood Spectrum from depression to bipolar disorder can also cause weight gain. However, mood medications themselves definitely are often involved, and some very frequently. Medications for the bipolar end of the Mood Spectrum are most commonly associated with this problem, but even antidepressants can be a problem.

How to Handle Weight Gain

Although we look at several strategies here, a few of them far exceed the value of the rest and thus merit special attention. These include

- Exercising
- Using medications that are not associated with weight gain
- Avoiding simple sugars

Unfortunately, these most important strategies are also so unrealistic that the list should really read more like this:

- Exercise—you can't beat it, but you can't do it either, right?
- Use medications that are not associated with weight gain—great idea, got any?
- Avoid simple sugars—so don't eat what everything around you tells you to?

Let's look at each of these great ideas, and their problems, before we come to the less preferred solutions.

Exercise

This solution—and the reasons why it is not happening despite being so obvious—are so important that I'm going to drag you through an entire chapter about it. Chapter 13 focuses on why people *don't* exercise, and what you can learn from that.

Remember, exercise is one of the most logical, safest, and most effective approaches to controlling weight gain. It could be even better than that: it may even directly target the *causes* of weight gain from stress, mood problems, and the medications that often are used in treating these problems. Remember that metabolic syndrome appears to be caused by all three: stress, a prime cause of depression in the first place; mood problems, which after a time can become a separate cause of weight gain; and finally, mood stabilizing medications. At this point, it appears that much of the weight gain caused by mood disorders stems from the biochemical changes of metabolic syndrome, particularly insulin resistance. But *exercise reduces insulin resistance*! Should I say that again? Do you see how direct a solution is available through exercise? If insulin resistance is at the core of the weight gain caused by stress, mood problems, and medications, then exercise is a logical means of preventing the weight gain in the first place.

Remember this when we come back to it in Chapter 13: exercise is a highly specific antidote to one of the most significant side effects you could experience with Mood Spectrum symptoms and medications. Of course, it has other health benefits—including having its own antidepressant effects! You can understand why I'd love to have a system where anyone who wants me to treat their mood problem must first either become a regular exerciser or have a clear reason why no form of exercise is possible (a rare thing).

Use Medications That Don't Cause Weight Gain

Mood experts routinely recommend this strategy. When dealing with a medication that is *already* causing weight gain, they are unanimous: before trying any other strategy, switch medications. (For an example, you'll find this recommendation on the Expert Consensus Guideline series at psychguides.com.) But as you already may have noted, the problem is so common among mood stabilizers that finding an alternative is often difficult. Some noteworthy options so far (a situation that I hope will improve soon) are shown in Table 10.1.

TABLE 10.1 Medications That Don't Routinely Cause Weight Gain

Target	Generic Name	Trade Name
Depression	Buproprion	Wellbutrin
Bipolar depression	Lamotrigine	Lamictal
Mood instability	Carbamazepine	Tegretol, Carbatrol
	Oxcarbazepine	Trileptal

Avoid Simple Sugars

This solution shouldn't be quite as tough as adopting an exercise routine. True, it is also a matter of changing well-worn habits. But this time, it's about taking things out of your routines, not putting things in. For most people that is much easier. (Because of how exercise affects your insulin sensitivity, however, you might need to take out less if you are exercising regularly.) Let's look at places where refined sugars are routine for you. We start with a quick review of what *refined sugars* are and why they are such a concern. Then we look at where they may be hiding—or in plain sight—in your diet.

Why Simple Sugars Can Be Disastrous for Your Health. The term *simple sugar* refers to any form of sugar that very quickly can end up as glucose in your bloodstream. Glucose is the simplest form of carbohydrate, like a penny in the U.S. money supply. Dollars, fifty-cent pieces, dimes, and nickels can all be broken down into pennies, but that's as small as you can go. Likewise, your body breaks down complex sugars (*carbohydrates*) into simple ones by breaking the bonds between the glucose molecules that are usually linked in long chains in these foods. It's like turning your dollars into pennies after every meal (by contrast, the plants we eat are the ones who have done the work of linking those pennies together into dollars).

Your body uses glucose as the basic unit of fuel. It uses glucose pennies to pay for all the work that cells do. Some cells also accept euros—chains of fat molecules. But the brain, even though it is the greatest fuel consumer in your body, insists on glucose pennies for all the work it does. Because of the brain's dependence on glucose, the body regulates glucose levels very closely using the hormone *insulin*, which you recall is at the very center of the metabolic problems associated with mood disorders and weight gain. To make this glucose available to your brain and other organs, all the complex sugars you eat, such as wheat in your sandwich bread, are broken down into glucose before being absorbed into the bloodstream (with a few exceptions, such as fructose from fruits).

The problem with simple sugars is that they are very easily broken down into glucose units and thus lead to very rapid rises in blood glucose levels. High glucose levels lead to the release of large amounts of insulin, whose job is to store all that fuel. But recall that large amounts of insulin appear to be one of the major causes, if not *the* cause, of metabolic syndrome. I hope you follow the chain of events here: simple sugars lead to high insulin, which can lead to metabolic syndrome, which leads to abdominal fat and other health problems (including even higher insulin levels) through insulin resistance, which leads to higher insulin levels. As you can see, once this process starts, it can *amplify itself*.

Notice that this unhealthy cycle began with high insulin levels in response to simple sugars (it might also begin with stress hormones). The other important part of this story of insulin and metabolic syndrome is exercise—or the lack of it. Without exercise, your body can become increasingly resistant to your own insulin. When this happens, your pancreas releases yet more insulin, trying to get your body to respond to the insulin signal. Now you have the same problem that you saw earlier turn into a health nightmare: high insulin levels.

If you combine lack of exercise with a diet high in simple sugars, you have a recipe for disaster: two different factors converging to cause high insulin levels. No wonder metabolic syndrome appears to affect over a quarter of the U.S. population! Our population is very sedentary and eats large amounts of simple sugars. I hope you are now alarmed about simple sugars as a health risk and want to know in more detail: exactly what is a simple sugar?

What Exactly Are Simple Sugars? Table sugar, for example, is *sucrose*. Sucrose consists of one glucose and one fructose molecule hooked end to end. There are other simple sugars (dextrose, lactose, maltose), but glucose and fructose are by far the most common in the problem foods we face.

Fructose metabolism is more complex and not clearly as directly related to insulin as is glucose. We should not forget about it, though, because some researchers think that fructose may contribute to metabolic syndrome through other pathways, involving triglycerides. For a simple model, however, we could focus on the glucose. Most carbohydrates are long chains of glucose. Carbohydrates have had a confusing reputation in the last decade, recently undergoing a demotion from a preferred food, as in low-fat diet, to a villain, as in low-carbohydrate diet.

The proper role of carbohydrates in our diets is not clear at this point. For now let's keep it simple with a focus on how you should cope with the risk of metabolic syndrome—whether it comes from your mood condition, from the stress that may have caused the mood problem, or from medications you are taking to deal with it. The easiest way to simplify the carbohydrate story is this: focus not on glucose itself but on the *speed of its absorption*.

Foods that cause rapid release of glucose into the bloodstream are the problem. (All right, the purists out there are jumping up and down: the total amount of glucose you consume is also a problem—so when you find a glucose source, turn down the total amounts, too.) When you keep the focus on speed of absorption, the search for foods that might contribute to metabolic syndrome is rather simple. For starters, you can even limit the search to foods that contain sucrose (table sugar). Some authors want you to include fructose in your search as well. You can catch both if you think in terms of added sugar in any form. For example, check the label on any fruit juice drink. Corn syrup, composed of simple sugars, is often a top ingredient.

The next step in widening your search would be to include refined white flour, which also releases glucose rapidly. That's probably far enough, because if you just look for and eliminate any food made with table sugar or some other added sweetener, you'll be doing very well at lowering your risk of metabolic syndrome. Here are some particular villains.

Where in Your Diet Do They Hide? Public enemy number one: sugar-containing soft drinks. These are very high in calories, but worse, nearly every one of those calories is straight sugar. They should be a rare treat or eliminated entirely. Something about them makes them very enticing though: is it because they're so cheap, so available, or so acceptable in society? (Think about it: you can walk into most places with a Big Gulp, but not with a cigarette!) You may need a very specific plan for how you will avoid soft drinks and juices, at least for a while, as you break this habit.

Next source: dessert. An interesting word, from the French *desservir*, meaning to clear the table (and having nothing to do, in its origin, with the word *desert*, by the way). Here's the first trick, which we can take directly from the word origin: don't "clear the table." In fact, don't finish your main course. Leave at least one bite on the plate (since a clean plate more easily may trigger your years of expectation that dessert will follow). Next trick: practice skipping dessert until you can imagine routinely finishing a meal without it.

If you want to push your limits (in this case, pushing yourself to stay within yet more limits!), look for white flour. Shift toward wheat flour and whole grains such as brown rice. Sorry, I sound like some sort of granola-head, but I hope this makes sense to you. We humans like the refined versions better, because the sweet release *comes faster*. The manufacturers of these goodies know this. You don't see McDonald's hamburgers on wheat buns now, do you? But the consequences of eating refined sugars are directly related to the weight gain story here.

Low-Carbohydrate Diets. You may be thinking ahead. You've understood that avoiding glucose pulses is good because they lead to insulin pulses, and that avoiding insulin pulses is good because they can lead to metabolic syndrome. Finally, you've understood that avoiding metabolic syndrome, or even anything in that general direction, is good because, well, for one thing, that fat abdomen is not fashionable—not to mention the health problems. (There's also that bit of evidence that metabolic syndrome can cause mood problems, discussed earlier.)

If avoiding glucose pulses is good, what about avoiding glucose sources entirely? That is what low-carbohydrate diets basically are all about. Now for a speculation to tempt you to action. If metabolic syndrome and mood do *have* some sort of connection, might a low-carbohydrate diet *improve* mood? This is a logical conclusion given what I've said thus far, and it is a very important question. To my knowledge, however, all we have on that question is a single unpublished case report, which is equivalent to no evidence at all. Nevertheless, you may find it interesting that a woman wrote me describing her husband's mood shifts as he went on and off the Atkins diet. He was taking lithium and an antidepressant. When he went off the Atkins diet, he did so in a big way: eating an entire package of cookies at once, for example. When he did this, his irritability returned. When he got back on the diet, his irritability would go away. This case, by itself, means almost nothing, but it is an interesting story. After all, you might know of someone who can eat an entire package of cookies and *not* get irritable. That is, irritability does not *directly* result from eating a huge amount of refined sugar, as far as is known. But perhaps some people with Mood Spectrum symptoms might be more likely to experience such changes. That is just a guess at this point.

Overall, the entire story of metabolic syndrome drives home one point: we can't just sit back and blame the medications, even though they are part of the problem (often a big part). We also have to look at stress, exercise, and diet. But if you are stuck with a medication that can cause weight gain, a few antidotes have been tried. I warn you in advance: none is useful enough to have become a regular strategy in my practice, and so far I still don't have a single patient pursuing any of these strategies long term. I include them in the following section because you will hear about them when you look for information on coping with weight gain.

Blocking Weight Gain with Antidote Medications

Several medications have been tried as *antidotes* to block the weight gain associated with mood medications. The obvious disadvantage to this general strategy is that we're adding yet another medication, with its potential for side effects, long-term risks, and interactions with other medications. So it is not high on the list of options. But sometimes when a medication causes weight gain but works very well, and you really don't want to switch medications at that point, then you and your doctor might consider some of the following medications.

Metformin (Glucophage)

Metformin is used to treat diabetes and improves insulin sensitivity. Remember from this chapter that current research suggests that metabolic syndrome is strongly associated and may indeed by caused by insulin resistance. One form of metabolic syndrome, PCOS (also discussed earlier), is treated with metformin. It seems logical to connect the dots: mood medications can cause weight gain, weight gain (particularly in the context of a lot of simple sugars) can cause metabolic syndrome, metabolic syndrome can be treated with metformin, and therefore metformin might help reverse the weight gain caused by mood medications.

Indeed, this has been tried. In 2002 a research team reported treating nineteen young patients with metformin while they remained on the various medications that seemed associated with their extreme weight gain. Fifteen lost weight and the rest slowed down in their weight increases. Another team tested metformin for the treatment of PCOS, finding that it added to weight losses more than a placebo did. At this point, it is too early to say how useful this strategy might be. Metformin has its own risks, including a chemistry change called *lactic acidosis* that even can be fatal, although this may occur only in people who have well-known risk factors for this problem (e.g., kidney or liver problems).

At one point I tried using metformin for patients with apparent metabolic syndrome who also had mood symptoms. Contrary to what you might think from the preceding studies and the possibility (only very slimly supported at this point) that metabolic syndrome has mood effects, only one or two of twenty patients or so had any evidence at all of a mood shift with Glucophage, nor did they lose much weight (with two notable exceptions). That is just my limited experience with it. The study of nineteen patients by Dr. John Morrison and colleagues is slightly more useful because of the more systematic gathering of data. What really is needed is a randomized trial that tests a new treatment against a placebo. So far, that is not available for any of the antidote treatments described here except amantadine.

Topiramate

Topiramate (Topamax) was originally developed as an antiseizure medication. Now it also is used for migraines and has been used quite a bit by psychiatrists because it can cause appetite reductions and weight loss. That sounds good, doesn't it? Clear evidence of weight loss? Aren't we in an odd time in history, when a pill that can cause you to lose weight sounds so good even when many people in the world still can't get enough to eat? You know the phrase, "trying to get something for nothing"? Someone described drinking sugar-free, decaffeinated soft drinks as trying to get nothing for something. But I digress.

At one point topiramate was thought perhaps to have mood stabilizer effects and rapidly came into use by psychiatrists because it looked a lot better to patients and doctors than did many better known mood medications. However, several research studies of topiramate as an add-on mood stabilizer found that it worked no better than a placebo. Yet it seems to have mood effects in some people—sometimes too much: it can cause depression, as noted in the official product information (the long ticker tape the pharmacist sometimes gives you with a new prescription). But some people seem to get an *anti*depressant effect from it.

For other patients, it causes quite severe agitation, and yet others get some anti-anxiety effects from it. So I tell patients that this medication is like a wild card, where you might get something good, or you might get something bad. The most consistent side effect is appetite suppression and weight loss. But it also has some rather scary side effects, such as causing kidney stones in one or two people per hundred who take it. It has more uncommon but greater risks, including a vision problem called *glaucoma* and a chemical imbalance called *metabolic acidosis* that rarely can be fatal. But cognitive impairment, such as difficulty finding words and remembering things as simple as your neighbor's name, is the biggest limiting factor in using topiramate. This has caused most of my patients to stop taking it.

Another antiseizure medication called *zonisamide* (Zonegran) has appetite-suppression effects like topiramate does. This one currently seems to have more promise of benefits, but that is what was thought when topiramate first came along, so time and more experience with zonisamide will help. It has some pretty scary side effects, too.

H2-Blockers, Amantadine, and Others

Yet more medications have been proposed to block the weight gain associated with mood medications. Most of these have even less evidence supporting their use than do metformin and topiramate, or have been tried more extensively and found to be of too little use. For example, medications that interfere with stomach acid production, *histamine-2 blockers* or *H2 blockers*, such as *nizatidine*, appear to reduce the weight gain associated with olanzapine, the mood stabilizer with famous weight-gain-causing tendencies—but their effects are not enough to solve the problem.

Amantadine is used to treat early viral infections. For some reason, perhaps having to do with its effects on dopamine, it also appears to be able to halt or perhaps even reverse the weight gain caused by olanzapine (and thus perhaps others). Unfortunately, it also can cause quite severe tremor, which has limited its effectiveness for my patients so much that I no longer try this strategy. (As this book went to press, another small study showed amantadine stopped weight gain on olanzapine, though it did not significantly lower it.)

Weight-Loss Medications (Sibutramine, Orlistat)

As you can imagine, a furious research effort is underway to produce a safe, effective pill that causes weight loss. Think of the money it would make (even more than Viagra!). Again we see the irony of Americans trying so desperately to lose weight while elsewhere around the globe people struggle to gain it. But to make the list here complete, you should know that, yes, psychiatrists also have used medications such as *sibutramine, orlistat,* and others to combat mood-medication-induced weight gain. Remember it can take years to know how safe a medication is—much longer than it takes to find out if a medication really works. Recall what happened with the fen-phen weight-loss medications that after several years of use were discovered to be causing heart valve problems. I've only tried *sibutramine* once so far, when rather forced into it by the patient's circumstances.

I hope that after all this information the first three strategies (exercise, using medications that are not associated with weight gain, and avoiding simple sugars) now look like the most obvious and most important strategies for handling the weight gain associated with mood medications. Another is to maximize the use of non-medication approaches, discussed in the next three chapters on lifestyle changes (including exercise) and psychotherapy options.

CHAPTER 11

Simple Lifestyle Changes That Can Improve Symptoms

Three lifestyle management techniques can help control your symptoms: manage sleep closely, manage stresses as you are able, and be very careful with alcohol if you use any at all, while avoiding most other drugs. Exercise, a fourth technique, is so important that it gets its own chapter. (I know you're looking forward to it—if only because it's the last one!)

Some people might be able to manage their symptoms with these techniques alone, although that's uncommon. Even if the techniques don't end up helping you much, none will hurt you, at least not much. The problem is that you, like everyone else, also want to have as normal a life as possible. The challenge is to balance that wish with the need to do what you can to keep this mood thing under control as much as possible without relying on medications to do so. Remember, none of the following strategies are all-or-none. Each can be used to a limited extent if you don't go for the full version. Think about starting small and see how that goes first.

Watching Sleep, Light, and Darkness Closely

Everyone knows that sleep, light, and darkness are related. They appear to be even more related in most people with bipolar variations. Some people can use this relationship to their advantage, getting a mood-stabilizer effect by carefully managing their sleep and their light exposure. However, when you see what this involves, it may strike you as very unusual, perhaps even bizarre. Most important, it may strike you as far too restrictive on normal life. So I'm going to drag you through some brain physiology, which will help you understand why managing sleep and light is so important. It may also help you understand why current lifestyles may not be so normal, and why you may need to use a different pattern of sleep, activity, and light than is typical in modern Western societies.

Sleep Is Not Just a Good Thing, It Is an Essential Thing

Why do we sleep? Until about a decade ago, one sleep researcher answered, "Because if you don't, you get sleepy," expressing his humor as well as his frustration at how little was understood about the need for sleep. Recently sleep researchers have made it clear: sleep has something to do with learning. If research subjects are trained to perform a new task (a new computer game, for example) and are tested again after a night's sleep, they perform better than a similar group of volunteers who waited the same number of hours until retesting, but without sleep.

Clinical experience has also shown that sleep has something to do with health, especially mental health. People with bipolar disorders who miss too much sleep can have a manic or hypomanic episode. In other words, sleep deprivation is *pro-manic*. It promotes shifting toward mania. The opposite is true as well: getting too much sleep is associated with depression. Researchers have shown that if you wake a depressed patient at 4 A.M. and keep him up, his mood will improve that very day. (Unfortunately, when he sleeps again, his mood will worsen, so this is not a practical long-term solution.) So the right amount of sleep, which for most people seems to be about eight hours, seems to have a mood-stabilizing effect. This is a very powerful effect for some people. The good news is that you can strongly affect your mood stability simply by keeping regular sleeping hours. The bad news is that you sometimes will see your mood destabilized by variations in sleep that are forced upon you, by work, relationships, or even simply traveling across time zones. (We humans have no evolutionary experience with that kind of dramatic change in our relationship with the sun!)

What's the connection between sleep and mood stability? As yet, this is not known. It will be one of the exciting stories to watch in the next decade or so, during which the answer will, I hope, emerge. For now, enough is known to say that sleep management is a very important part of mood symptom management. To understand the connection, you need to understand a bit more about how your internal clock operates, because it very strongly determines your sleep patterns. (You surely know this from experience—that feeling you have, for example, when you get up at 4 A.M. for travel and stumble around, finally becoming truly alert around the time you usually wake up.)

Your Biological Clock

Your body has many biologic rhythms, of which sleep is just one. When you feel hungry, when you feel like going for a run (that happens to you every day about the same time, doesn't it?), when your body temperature peaks and bottoms out—all of these are determined by a clock in your brain. From research in animals, we even know precisely where the clock is located in your brain. Not surprisingly, from an evolutionary point of view, it is almost directly in the center of your brain in a structure called the hypothalamus.

The *hypothalamus* is the master gland for your entire body, determining the flow of many different hormones. Many of these hormone levels fluctuate daily, all under the control of your biological clock. One of the most dramatic demonstrations of the power of this clock is a bipolar variation known as *48-hour rapid cycling*. People with this variation have a manic day followed by a depressed day, over and over again. Every twenty-four hours they switch. (I've had two such patients, one of whom could predict weeks in advance whether she would be up or down and would schedule meetings at work accordingly!) The hormone patterns of such people have been shown to cycle up and down along with their mood. Graphs of these shifting hormone levels look like the pleats of an accordion (one day up, next day down, next day up, and so forth), and they flattened when a mood stabilizer was added. (See the Notes page on my website for a look at these graphs.)

This research shows that the biological clock has a very strong impact on bipolar patterns. This is not surprising in light of clinical experience. When people are manic, something is wrong with their clock. Their bodies don't seem to cycle naturally into *sleep mode* at night. They can be in daytime *action mode* all night (much to the disappointment of the hospital night shift, who otherwise can get a lot of work done and occasionally even sleep). Less obvious but equally as mistimed is the experience of bipolar depression, in which people can feel like they are in *sleep mode* nearly all day, sleeping as much as sixteen hours or more in every twenty-four. This can go on for days, sometimes weeks, and occasionally for months. Imagine what you'd think if this was happening and you did not know you had a bipolar disorder. If your family, friends, or coworkers did not know about or understand bipolar disorder, imagine what they would think. You may know from painful personal experience just how they would interpret one of these phases (saying you're lazy, have no gumption, are disrespectful, and so forth).

Thus the biological clock somehow is very deeply involved in bipolar symptom creation. Fortunately some clues about what's wrong with the clock are beginning to emerge, and this time one of the sources is a treatment, rather than a research team examining cells and molecules. To understand this treatment and what it may indicate about bipolar disorders, you need to understand a few more features of the clock.

Sorry Buddy, Your Clock Is Slow

For most people, the internal clock takes about twenty-five hours, rather than twenty-four, to complete a cycle! This finding was shown in an interesting experiment. A bunch of college students were told they could have all the food they needed, entertainment, telephone, and accommodations—if they were willing to spend several weeks without any natural light or any clock. Some of these experiments were carried out in underground caves. The volunteers were left on their own for about two weeks to eat, watch TV or play games, turn lights on and off, and sleep—all whenever they wished. The experimenters found that each day most volunteers stayed awake and active about one hour later than the previous day. As a result, after twelve days, and thus twelve hours of clock drift, they were awake and active during the real night and asleep during the real day! They had drifted to a pattern of activity completely opposite real time, at a rate of about one hour per day. From such experiments, we can conclude that our natural clock rate is about twenty-five hours, rather than twenty-four, for each cycle of sleeping and waking.

What keeps these volunteers, and the rest of us, on a twenty-four-hour clock when we are living in the real world and not in a cave? What locks our internal clocks to the reality of our earth's twenty-four-hour cycles of light and dark? The answer: those very cycles of light and dark. Morning light, in particular, is very important in this role. *The time at which our eyes first see light* in the morning most strongly resets our biological clocks to real time. If this is surprising to you, try closing your eyes and looking toward the light by which you're now reading. Notice that your eyelids only partially block the light; much of it gets through to your retina. Your retina has a direct connection to the biological clock center in your hypothalamus. So your brain knows when the light shows up in the morning, even if you are still asleep!

Making Sleep *Regular*

If the enforced-darkness approach in the following sidebar sounds too restrictive (which it does to virtually *all* my patients),

Darkness as Treatment: Dark Therapy

The disappearance of natural light at dusk also affects the clock, though not as strongly as morning light. Evening light exposure may be a very important variable in patients with bipolar mood variations. In modern societies, with our houses and window coverings, we live in simulated caves. Our eyes may not be able to see the real dawn while we are asleep, but even more artificial is the amount of electric light we use at night. Few people get to experience the gradual disappearance of the sun, shifting first to dusk and finally to darkness, every day. Most people live in prolonged day, and then finally turn it abruptly off at bedtime. They hope to fall asleep in the complete darkness that began only minutes before. Sounds a bit odd, doesn't it? Yet isn't that the norm in modern societies? Surely it's the norm at your house?

You're thinking, "I know where he's going with this, and I don't like the sound of it." Before you start reaching any conclusions, though, take a look at the experience of one patient whose rapid-cycling bipolar disorder was treated with *no medications*, and imagine what a smaller dose of the treatment he received might look like for you.

A patient treated at the National Institute of Mental Health (NIMH) had quite severe rapid-cycling bipolar disorder. When you're done with this chapter, have a look at the graphs of his mood over several years, and his dramatic response to treatment; use the NIMH link from the Notes page for this chapter on my website. What you'll see is simple: his cycling stopped completely, with no medications at all, under the NIMH treatment. What did they do? They required him to appear every evening at 6 P.M., at which time he entered a room with no lights, phone, television, or

you can still use its general principle: regular sleep in the dark is a crucial part of bipolar symptom management. Almost all people can tell that their mood stability suffers when they stay up too late (especially for several nights in a row). They are likely to find hypomanic symptoms creeping in, such as irritability and any other activity or light source. He stayed in that room until 8 A.M. the following morning. They did at least give him a bed, but he was not required to sleep. His cycling stopped so quickly that soon thereafter they lightened up the treatment, so to speak, allowing him to stay out another four hours a day—until 10 P.M. He remained stable for more than a year (at which point the graphs stop) on this regimen of ten hours of darkness nightly.

This "dark therapy" worked similarly for another patient in Switzerland with rapid cycling who was also taking a mood stabilizer. The researchers there noted that his rapid cycling responded immediately when he was given even just ten hours nightly of required darkness. (They called it a ten-hour dark/rest period.)

So for you, would perhaps a bit of dark therapy help limit the amount of medication you might need? We don't really know a minimum dose for this strategy yet, but it certainly is cheap, right? You might have to buy some extra-thick curtains. You could start by hanging dark towels to see if you can make this strategy work. Oh, the kids? What are you going to do with them while you're in the dark for twelve hours? Good point; that might require some significant negotiation with people who might benefit if your mood is more stable. Most people encountering this treatment idea are more concerned about boredom, or being stuck with nothing to distract them from the activity of their own mind. That, too, is an understandable concern. You might have to look at the NIMH patient's graphs to see how utterly dramatic and rapid his improvement really was, to prepare yourself to try even the Swiss ten-hour approach.

accelerated, fragmented thinking. Not long thereafter, depressed symptoms often follow.

To avoid all this, a regular bedtime is very important. Ugh, how boring. This idea does not have natural appeal, especially to the younger set. You might be able to convince yourself by temporarily adopting a regimen of regular sleep. (Use a mood chart discussed in Chapter 6 to record how things go.) You will have to be pure about it for a short while to get a good experimental result. How long you need to run this experiment depends on your typical cycle length. (Rapid cyclers might be able to detect an improvement in just a few weeks, as was the case for the NIMH patient.) The key is to stick with it long enough to get a good comparison with your usual loose sleep schedule. You can judge later whether it was worth it or not.

Similarly, it is also important to have a regular rise time. I can hear you saying, "I have to get out of bed on a weekend at the same time I get up on weekdays—6:30 A.M.? You *are* a nut, Phelps." Again, you can test this yourself. Compare your mood chart for several weeks during which you are regular with your rise times, versus several weeks when you get up late on weekends. If you can't tell the difference, you're not going to stick to this idea anyway, right?

To make these ideas more practical, try this: start by trying to limit your late-night bright light exposure. Even this is going to be hard for a lot of people: it means no television or computer use after, say, about 9 P.M. One mood and light researcher even suggests getting dimmer switches for all the lights you use late at night and gradually lowering them. At least you can get one for the bathroom, so you don't turn on the shaving lights at 10:30 P.M. to brush your teeth! That's the wrong message to be sending your hypothalamus, you see?

You don't have to place yourself in a dark room at 6 P.M. to benefit from these ideas. You could shoot for a gradual dimming starting at 9 P.M., getting in bed in darkness by 10 P.M., and having regular rise times. For people whose mood routinely goes down in the winter, a device called a *dawn simulator* can help make those morning start-ups easier. It gradually turns on your bedside reading lamp over thirty to forty-five minutes, mimicking the arrival of the sun. For some people, it helps prevent the depression itself (by tricking your hypothalamus into thinking it's still July!). This device is much easier to use than a light box, as by the time you wake, the treatment is complete. It is also far cheaper. An updated list of models and prices, and other details, can be found on my website Dawn Simulator page, linked from the Notes page.

Before we leave this topic, you should know that a research team has studied other social rhythms, not just sleep times. They looked at when you actually fall asleep (not just bedtime), when you eat your first meal, when you get exercise—twenty different daily rhythms. When they taught patients to try to maintain regularity in *all* these rhythms, those patients had better mood stability than patients receiving treatment as usual. But of all these variables, sleep was clearly the most important, regular exposure to darkness probably second, and regular morning light and rise times probably third. I strongly recommend that you work at making your own rhythms regular, in roughly that order.

Stress Management: Crucial to Stabilizing Moods

Stress worsens mood conditions, no doubt about it. Surprisingly, some people are far more susceptible to stresses such as losing a job, running out of money, or losing a loved one, than other people. A single gene may explain a lot of that variability (as described in an essay entitled "Depression Is Not a Moral Weakness," linked from my website's home page). The quality of one's childhood interacts with that gene to determine, for some people, their susceptibility to life stresses.

But few people can control life stresses such as job and money supply; fewer still can control the stresses of physical illness and loss of loved ones. You can't change your genes or your childhood. So what can you do about this stress-mood relationship? Well, quite a bit, in some cases. At the very minimum, you can use the strategies for finding a good cognitive-behavioral therapist (see the link "Find a Therapist/Psychiatrist" at the top of my home page) and ask for some help with stress management. Many people can benefit from standard Cognitive-Behavioral Therapy (CBT) techniques. (I discuss CBT in more detail in Chapter 12.)

These include learning the relationship between hot thoughts and your body's stress hormones. Cognitive therapists often quote a Greek philosopher named Epictetus, who said, "Men are disturbed not by things, but by the view which they take of them." You may not be able to control some of the stresses you face, but you can learn to control your reactions to them. Most people can at least learn to do so better than they did before CBT.

CBT also commonly includes techniques for managing the stress that does make it past your cognitive first line of defense. Tense muscles, overfocused angry thoughts, even increased heart rate and sweating: all of these can be eased with standard behavioral techniques such as relaxation exercises. Wait, wait—before you dismiss those exercises as too soft and fuzzy, you should know that several of them are standard parts of the lives of nearly half the people on this earth. Most religions emphasize prayer or meditation, and many meditative traditions are based on focused attention, especially on one's breathing. I routinely teach a breathing technique used in these meditative traditions, without the religious overtones. This method of *mindful relaxation* is simple, takes only minutes to learn, and is generally very well received, even by my patients who probably would not tell anyone about what they just learned (let alone where they learned it!). Some people may prefer to use meditative techniques such as yoga or tai chi rather than the more Western CBT approach for dealing with stress. Present research supports all these approaches. The more stress you have in your life, the more you need these tools.

Limiting or Eliminating Mind-Altering Substances

About one-half of all patients with bipolar disorder use some kind of mind-altering substance, far more if we include caffeine in one form or another. Managing symptoms may not require *completely* avoiding the use of these substances, but you have to be careful with them. We'll look first at alcohol, then caffeine, marijuana, and other common street drugs.

Alcohol

Perhaps you're not fond of it. Or maybe you avoid it because so many other people in your family have had trouble with it. But for everyone else, the following may come as a mild surprise: *you* are the one who's going to be in charge of how much you drink. Really? The doctor is *not* telling you that you can't drink any more alcohol?

Well, not exactly anyway. Here's what I tell my patients. While we're working on getting your symptoms under control, it's wise to take alcohol out of the picture entirely. Two weeks? Can you go that long? Four weeks? Some people drink so little and care about it so little, that this is not an imposition at all, and they readily agree. But others look at me as though I'm asking an awful lot when I ask them these questions. For them, I leave it at this: just a short while—basically as long as I think they might be able to go entirely without alcohol, even if it's only two weeks. Most people can see some mood improvement in that time. My goal at this point is to get them better enough that when they start drinking again, they can see that it's making them worse. When they come to see me, their symptoms often are so severe they can't even see the alcohol effect in the mess of cycling and symptom extremes. But if they manage to go without alcohol for a even a little while, and we manage to get their symptoms even a little better in that time, then they may recognize the sleep disruption and mood-destabilizing effects so common with even a little alcohol.

Some people require even more reassurance that I am not telling them they must stop drinking forever, right now. If they seem to need such reassurance, I add that in a few weeks, they'll probably be able to try adding back a little bit of alcohol, looking for destabilizing effects. In other words, I ask them to watch out for alcohol causing the opposite effect of what we're (hopefully) already achieving by then. Then I drop the bomb, gently or firmly, depending on what this particular patient requires: most people discover at that point that they can get away with about one drink per week, sometimes two, and usually no more than one drink at a sitting. More alcohol than this generally causes some instability that they themselves can recognize, particularly if we've achieved good symptom control by that time.

Again, the main point is to recognize that *you are going to be the judge about how much you can drink.* The trick is to be a good scientist and watch your results closely. Granted, this approach does not work for everyone. But most studies show that about half of all patients with bipolar disorder use alcohol or drugs, so it's almost the norm to have to approach this topic somehow. Some people, if they hear they must give up something they've already seen that they cannot manage without, may give up on treatment. So I tend to emphasize that *the patient* is going to make these decisions, and I support his or her efforts to take charge of the process—including efforts to control drinking. (This approach is called *Motivational Interviewing*; for more information, see motivationalinterview.com.)

How often do people use alcohol to treat bipolar symptoms? There is some debate about that. You'd think that people would drink when heading toward mania, trying to slow themselves down, and use stimulants when depressed, trying to get themselves going again. But often people use stimulants in the manic phase, trying for more of the same, and alcohol just about anytime. Many people use alcohol for two specific symptoms: sleep problems and social anxiety. Alcohol often helps people slow down their thinking, which makes getting to sleep much easier. Unfortunately it usually wears off about three to four hours later, at which point people rebound awake and have great difficulty getting back to sleep. Alcohol often helps with social anxiety, especially in low doses (higher doses tend to cause their own social problems!). But in both cases, the alcohol can easily make the bipolar disorder worse.

I recommend to you just what I tell my own patients:

- Take the alcohol out of your lifestyle entirely for starters, at least for a few weeks, but preferably until things are going quite well for you (however long that takes).

- Then you can try adding it back cautiously—but I suggest that you start with no more than one or two drinks per week and watch closely for any destabilizing effects.

Caffeine (That Means You Pepsi and Starbucks Types)

People with Mood Spectrum symptoms might use this drug for many reasons, most of which are the same reasons people with no such symptoms use it. But the symptom-specific purposes include trying to get energized during a depression and trying to cope with sedating side effects from medications. Caffeine is not an ideal solution for either problem, but it generally does not cause additional problems as alcohol does, unless used in large quantities. There is no clear reason to avoid it entirely, but high doses should be avoided. I am more concerned about the sugar that often accompanies caffeine in soft drinks.

Marijuana

For some people, marijuana seems to act as a "poor man's mood stabilizer." If they don't have another mood stabilizer on board, they seem to be better on marijuana than off it—or so they tell me. For some, I think this is true, as they go back on marijuana when they can't get my drugs, but seem to give up the marijuana without much effort or struggle when my drugs are available again. (Unfortunately, many people in the United States can float in and out of medical care, based on their employment, insurance, and disability status. We have a pretty good health care system if you're well-insured or rich, however.) Thus when both are available, they usually prefer my drugs to marijuana.

The psychiatric literature on marijuana has case reports of mood-stabilizing effects as well as concern about its effects on motivation. I do not suggest using marijuana. I also have little doubt that many regular users will be immune to psychotherapy until they get off the marijuana, and perhaps even relatively immune to life's attempts to teach them lessons of all kinds. But at present, alcohol seems more capable of making mood symptoms worse than marijuana, for most people. Worse yet are street stimulants such as cocaine and methamphetamine.

Street Stimulants

Increasingly, my colleagues voice concerns about the apparent long-term effects of methamphetamine (which in Oregon is far more prevalent than cocaine). Our mutual impression is that stimulants can lead to a persistent agitated state, similar to dysphoric hypomania, which can *last for years after the drug is stopped*, perhaps forever. (We haven't had long enough to watch to be sure yet.) This is just a clinical impression, not a research finding. But it sure makes the widespread use of methamphetamine a scary problem. I doubt that anyone who uses such drugs regularly could read this far in this book, but family and friends dealing with a loved one using methamphetamine may already know how difficult it can be to get that person into substance use treatment. Al-Anon can sometimes be useful, sometimes not, depending on the group in your area. Desperate parents, siblings, or spouses should seek the help of a substance use specialist.

One can wonder whether stimulant treatments for attention-deficit disorders might present some risk. This is still debated. We have the same problems gathering evidence for the possible long-term effects of such medications as we have for monitoring the long-term effects of antidepressants, as discussed in Chapter 9 (Controversy 2c).

Some authors would include other factors or strategies in this chapter. I certainly have not stressed substance use problems as heavily as others might. Beyond aggressive motivational interviewing and referral to substance use specialists where necessary, I generally have not been very successful when patients are not honest with me about their substance use and willing (or able) to eliminate it while trying mood-stabilizer treatments. Thus in my view the lifestyle management techniques in this chapter stand out more dramatically as those that the average person with symptoms can use most easily. Along with exercise, careful management of sleep and stress is essential in an overall treatment program. The goal is to maintain a sensible degree of control over these lifestyle choices without having one's life shortchanged by the illness. That's a tricky balancing act. Sometimes psychotherapy is worth considering just for help with this balancing process. But it also has specific benefits in bipolar disorders, as we'll explore next.

CHAPTER 12

How to Use Psychotherapy Across the Mood Spectrum

Many mood experts think that psychotherapy is underused: people do not turn to it as often as would be wise. This may be due to the stigma of therapy, the greater time and personal commitment that therapy requires compared to a medication, or simply because good therapists who know these techniques are unavailable. But does psychotherapy really work? Remember that any treatment you are offered—medication, therapy, or otherwise—should have been shown to be better than treatment with a placebo, because placebos work up to 30 percent of the time! If you're going to see a therapist, it would be nice to know that the treatment is better than some placebo equivalent. We now have such evidence for several psychotherapy techniques.

In most such research studies, all patients were given standard treatment (primarily medication-oriented); and the experimental group was offered the psychotherapy being studied *in addition* to the standard treatment. Two of these techniques, however, have been tested head-to-head against medications, with patients randomly assigned to receive either a medication *or* a psychotherapy (and in some cases both). In this chapter we look at five psychotherapies, all of which have been shown to be effective in this kind of research. We'll then consider where they fit on the Mood Spectrum, and how you might choose among them—if you are fortunate to have several available in your area. Finally we consider when you should start such a therapy (should you start right now or wait until you can sleep better and think more clearly?), and how you will know when you are done.

Five Effective Psychotherapies

Two psychotherapies for Major Depression (with no bipolar component) have been tested against antidepressant medications and shown to be as effective, in several large research studies. These are *cognitive-behavioral therapy (CBT)*—which you read briefly about in the last chapter—and *interpersonal therapy (IPT)*. If you are all the way to the left on the Mood Spectrum and thus have unipolar depression, these are the two therapies generally recommended. For people whose symptoms lie farther to the right on the Mood Spectrum, variations on CBT and IPT have been developed that address hypomanic and manic symptoms as well as depression. We look first at two specific tools, called *prodrome detection* and *social rhythm therapy*, then at three more comprehensive approaches: *psychoeducation*, a bipolar-specific *CBT*, and *family-focused therapy*.

Prodrome Detection

As the name implies, this therapy teaches patients to look for symptoms that might warn that another mood episode is coming. This technique is suited primarily to people whose episodes are discrete, separate experiences with "well intervals" in between. Many people with mood symptoms lack clear well intervals and would find this approach difficult to apply. However, in Bipolar I especially, a coming episode often has warnings, such as a decrease in sleep, an increase in speed of thought, or increase in impulsive action. These might be far too subtle for a psychiatrist or therapist to spot, but recognizable by the patient him- or herself, if the patient has rehearsed in advance what to look for. In this method, devised and tested by a brave research psychologist with little previous clinical experience, patients created a relapse plan for either manic or depressive symptoms, including their personal symptoms to watch for and three health professionals to whom they would turn for help at the first sign of recurrence. Their plan was printed on a laminated card that they carried at all times. As with all the therapies described here, this approach decreased the rate at which patients had episodes of mania or depression, presumably because they could nip some in the bud.

Social Rhythm Therapy (SRT)

As discussed in the previous chapter, sleep is an important regulator of mood, and our internal biological clocks are important regulators of sleep. It appears that our clocks imprint with our usual daily rhythms. You know how this works. When your alarm always goes off at the same time every morning (and you've been getting to bed routinely the night before), you often start to wake up every morning just before the alarm goes off. Your internal clock comes to know that it is time to wake up. Similarly (though less dramatically), with a regular sleep time your internal clock comes to know when it is time to go to sleep. Because disorganized sleep somehow can bring on mood symptoms, anything you can do to keep your sleep organized and predictable helps prevent repeat mood episodes.

The SRT researchers looked at many daily social rhythms. In most interpretations of their work, it seems that the most important rhythm they identified is *maintaining a regular pattern of sleep*—not just enough sleep, but regular sleep, because this seems to be such a strong organizer for a person's internal biological clock. An emphasis on this regularity appears in all three of the more comprehensive psychotherapies, which follow.

Psychoeducation

Researchers in Barcelona, Spain, developed a once-weekly therapy that they conducted in groups of eight to ten patients. This was a twenty-one-week program, in which each week a new topic would be presented and discussed within the group. Their program was very significantly superior to a twenty-one-session program in which the same two therapists sat with similar groups of patients in nonstructured meetings (in which they deliberately tried to avoid teaching about bipolar disorder—that must have been difficult). The topic list for the twenty-one-session Psychoeducation program included the following:

1. Introduction
2. What is bipolar illness?
3. Causal and triggering factors
4. Symptoms (I): mania and hypomania
5. Symptoms (II): depression and mixed episodes
6. Course and outcome
7. Treatment (I): mood stabilizers
8. Treatment (II): antimanic agents
9. Treatment (III): antidepressants
10. Serum levels: lithium, carbamazepine, valproate
11. Pregnancy and genetic counseling
12. Psychopharmacology versus alternative therapies
13. Risks associated with treatment withdrawal
14. Alcohol and street drugs: risks in bipolar illness
15. Early detection of manic and hypomanic episodes
16. Early detection of depressive and mixed episodes
17. What to do when a new phase is detected?
18. Regularity (presumably similar to SRT emphasis)
19. Stress-management techniques
20. Problem-solving techniques
21. Final session

As you can see, the first nine sessions present basic information about bipolar disorder and its treatment. Then come a series of sessions on special topics. Sessions 15 to 17 are very similar to prodrome detection, discussed earlier. Session 18 focuses on the importance of regularity, from SRT. Sessions 19 and 20 are short versions of techniques routinely used in CBT, discussed next. This is a very thorough program and very efficient because of the group approach they used. Interestingly, their results were no less strong than a more individualized approach—indeed, the group approach may actually strengthen this technique, through the social reinforcement many people experience in support groups, such as seeing others adopt the new strategies and do well. (Find more about this program and a link to their research on the Bipolar Psychotherapy page, linked from the Notes page on my website.)

Cognitive-Behavioral Therapy (CBT)

This technique has been around for decades now. Several very large studies have shown CBT to be as effective as antidepressant medications for the treatment of mild to moderate depression. (Read that sentence again, it's important. Most people don't know that therapy works as well as antidepressant medications. In the next chapter, you'll see evidence that exercise also has been shown to work as well as an antidepressant.) Recently, a *bipolar-specific variation of CBT*, when added to standard bipolar treatment consisting of medications and regular psychiatric follow-up, has been shown to be superior to standard treatment alone.

CBT is a fusion, as the name implies, of two previously separate approaches. The behavioral component focuses on concrete steps a person can take, such as scheduling pleasurable activities or using a relaxation technique. The cognitive component looks at a person's typical thoughts when in a mood episode and examines how those thoughts might perpetuate or deepen that episode; then it introduces alternative ways of thinking that are more likely to allow recovery. As its originators emphasize, this is not an emphasis on thinking positive, but on thinking about evidence. The approach teaches simple techniques for avoiding the highly irrational thinking that goes with mood episodes. The therapist is like a coach, helping you master both the cognitive and behavioral skills. Just as if you were learning to play soccer or the violin, great emphasis is placed on *practice*.

The bipolar-specific variations include several elements not typically found in standard CBT. These include an emphasis on

229

understanding the role of medications (just as in Psychoeducation) and habit-training to help stay regular in their use. Also included is a plan for early detection of returning symptoms, by writing out what one will watch for and how one will respond (just as in prodrome detection). Techniques for managing stress, such as problem-solving and communication skills, are emphasized. (These have long been a part of CBT, but when depression is the target, the focus often is more on thoughts.)

Family-Focused Therapy

The primary researcher behind this treatment is Dr. David Miklowitz, who has been studying this approach for many years. His work is a stunning achievement in patience and diligence, as one of his main results took over a decade to produce (refining the treatment, organizing the research team, collecting enough suitable patients and their families, conducting the treatment, and analyzing the results). He has described this method in *Bipolar Disorder: A Family-Focused Treatment Approach*, but that is a rather technical book. Many aspects of this therapy are also presented in his book for patients and families, entitled *The Bipolar Disorder Survival Guide*, which is an excellent resource presenting virtually all the psychotherapy approaches described here. If you cannot find a therapist familiar with one or several of these methods, his book is an excellent and important alternative.

Family-focused therapy assumes that bipolar disorder affects more than just the person with the symptoms. Other family members are directly affected by the symptoms. This therapy also assumes that family members can interact with a patient in ways that lower the likelihood of relapse—or increase it. Based on his years of research on how families express emotion, Dr. Miklowitz has assembled a program for families that emphasizes understanding the illness (just as in the Psychoeducation approach) and communication skills (as in CBT, but this time for the entire family).

In their most recent research, this research team has combined elements of SRT with the family-focused approach. An element of another psychotherapy, called *interpersonal therapy* (*IPT*), also is embedded in this most recent research and in all of his family-oriented work. IPT is a well-known treatment that has been shown to be as effective as antidepressants in mild to moderate depression. It focuses on a person's relationships and tries to improve the quality of the most important ones. You can see how this fits directly into family-focused work. When combined with Dr. Miklowitz's family-focused approach, these elements have produced strong long-term benefits.

If Several Are Available, How Do You Choose?

These therapies have not been tested against each other, so we don't know which is better. You can see they also overlap a great deal, so you may not really be making a choice. Moreover, few of these approaches are well-known, so it would be surprising if you found yourself in a position to choose from among them. Fortunately, CBT is one of the most common approaches and is used by *many* therapists. Even if they have not had training in bipolar-specific CBT, you can get much of what you need from a good therapist who knows CBT basics. Whether you work with a therapist, with your psychiatrist, or somehow on your own, you want to make sure you get the following elements of treatment.

First, if you have discrete episodes of mood symptoms separated by periods where you are your usual self (so-called well intervals), then some form of prodrome detection system is very important. Make sure your psychiatrist, therapist, or both have helped you prepare such a plan.

Second, a broad understanding of bipolarity and the role of medications is important. I hope this book may help in that respect. Its content is similar to that presented in the Psychoeducation approach, though mine obviously has not been tested and shown to be effective, as was the Barcelona group-education model. When their treatment manual becomes available in English, it might be a useful resource; going through it with your therapist or psychiatrist might be a close approximation of the original approach. In the interim, I hope my website may be an additional similar resource.

Third, regular daily rhythms are important, especially sleep, as discussed in Chapter 11. Note that maintaining such regularity, especially protecting regular sleep times, can be done entirely on your own, at no cost. But to actually *do* it, to maintain these rhythms, will require a commitment on your part. Many of my patients have to learn this the hard way because keeping regular hours and avoiding sleep deprivation can be a radical change from the way they have been living their lives. Remember, don't let the best be the enemy of the good.

Finally, one last important ingredient common to effective psychotherapies is to manage how much stress you take on. This, like maintaining a regular sleep pattern, may involve some sacrifices, such as saying no to late-night partying with friends. It may require saying no to a great job offer that calls for sixty-hour workweeks. Alternatively, you might try to accept the job but negotiate some understanding that the work cannot routinely interfere with sleep, in case it may jeopardize your health and thus your ability to do the work. The theme here is to be able to say no and keep your health needs in mind when making choices and explaining them. This calls for strong assertiveness and communication skills, which a good CBT therapist can help you learn, but which you can also work on by yourself. Among many resources for this are a couple of my favorites: *Winning Against Relapse* is almost a behavioral therapy manual; *Mind Over Mood* and *The Feeling Good Handbook* are good tools for teaching yourself cognitive techniques. But remember, *practice* is what makes it work, not reading about it! This is where a therapist can help: he or she can guide, fine-tune, and *motivate* your practice.

When Should You Start—and Stop?

Sometimes it seems best to wait to add a psychotherapy approach until after the severe symptoms are controlled. When you're extremely agitated, it is hard to concentrate or explain yourself. On the other hand, it's probably never too soon to start that process. Finding a good therapist can take a while. Also, good therapists often are booked well in advance, creating a natural delay in getting started. Starting too soon involves little risk, except that you might not be using your limited sessions in the most efficient manner (if your insurance or personal finances permit only a certain number of sessions per year).

Another reason to consider delaying the addition of psychotherapy is to clarify exactly what your targets for that treatment are.

- Are you looking for long-term relapse prevention?
- Do you need some help with specific skills, such as relaxation or assertiveness?
- Do you need more information about bipolar disorder and how it affects you?
- Does your family need help understanding what you're dealing with and how to help?

A brief delay before you begin therapy may help clarify what you're after and help you decide which kind of therapy to pursue.

Finally, if you add two treatments at the same time and then get better, this frequently will leave you wondering: "Which one is the basis for my improvement?" or, "Which one can I now taper off without relapsing?" This usually is an issue when two medications are started simultaneously, and it is a good reason for making only one change at a time. (However, sometimes symptoms are so bad that you might choose to be aggressive, using multiple medications at first, to get the symptoms under control.) Theoretically, this puzzle also can result if you start a psychotherapy at the same time as trying to find the right mood stabilizer(s). However, we usually can sort out later which change was the most important ingredient in your improvement, if only by carefully tapering one of the new approaches and watching closely for worsening. The same can be done by tapering off psychotherapy.

This leads to another question: how will you know when it is time to stop? This is a tricky issue. In years past, it was common for therapy to go on for years. Such treatments, often based on Freudian thinking, were difficult to test for effectiveness. By comparison, the bipolar-specific therapies described in this chapter, which all have been tested against medication-based treatment alone (or a comparable control therapy), are quite brief. Most cognitive-behavioral therapists start with the assumption that once you have learned and mastered the skills you need, therapy can come to an end. However, you may be surprised to hear that stopping can be difficult, as follows.

Most people develop a connection to the therapist that is oddly powerful, more so than you would expect. You may have experienced something like this before if you've ever worked closely with a teacher or coach. That person's role sometimes can become larger than life. His or her approval and satisfaction with your efforts can become very important to you. One branch of psychological research studies this phenomenon, called *attachment relationships*. We humans form deep attachments to our parents; that is part of normal human experience. But we also can form attachments with other people that can be similarly deep, in terms of the unusual power of those relationships. Think of the people you know whose illness, should they become very sick or die, would affect you greatly. These would include your parents, certainly, but also spouses, siblings, and significant others including close friends, teachers, or even close coworkers. In all these cases, you have an attachment to these people. The energy connected with such attachments can often seem oddly out of proportion: you are affected by shifts in the relationship itself, such as when these people become ill, get angry with you, or are absent for a long period of time.

This kind of attachment is common in psychotherapy. Shifts in the therapy relationship also can seem oddly out of proportion, especially when you are trying to bring the therapy to an end. When ending therapy, people can feel as though they are losing an important connection, even when they understand that the work they came to do is complete. This is a long-term risk, of sorts, for psychotherapy. Fortunately, it is one that most therapists are trained to handle carefully.

One more nonmedication approach, which technically would be part of behavioral therapy though I fear it is underemphasized, is exercise. Like the therapies described here, exercise also has strong evidence for being an effective mood treatment. Indeed, it is so effective, it should be part of every person's treatment program. Yet it is not widely used. The next chapter examines that paradox.

CHAPTER 13

Exercise: Not the Usual Rap

You've heard it before, exercise is great for your health, everyone should . . . , and so on. So let's face it, there must be something *very difficult* about getting exercise (at least in the American culture), because even though everybody knows it's a good thing, so few people actually do it. Thus we pay close attention in this chapter to what makes it hard to do.

Obviously exercise must be continued to maintain its benefits. The focus here is on how someone like you, probably pretty doubtful about this whole idea, can practice some sort of *sustainable* physical activity. After a brief review of some evidence, barriers, and benefits, we'll look at a simple program (no gym, no cost).

The Best Evidence You Ever Heard

Just in case you have any doubt whatsoever in your mind that exercise is the smartest mood treatment you could possibly adopt (can I get any more emphasis in this sentence?), here is the single research study that should quash any disbelief. It's even better than the exercise-versus-Zoloft (sertraline) study, in which exercise was as good as the antidepressant in the short run and better in the long run.

In the more recent study, with a group of nondepressed people in their sixties, a research team performed a series of tests showing that exercise improved mental skills on standardized tests of decision making, but then they took a huge step further. As you read in this book, we now know that mood symptoms, if not treated, often lead eventually to brain shrinkage, particularly in regions associated with decision making (frontal lobes) and memory (hippocampus). Effective antidepressants all seem to increase the brain's growth factors and reverse this shrinkage, at least in part. But no one had yet shown that exercise could also increase brain size, as the antidepressants do. So Drs. Stanley Colcombe, Arthur Kramer, and colleagues measured brain sizes in a second series of elders and found that sure enough, their brains were larger after the exercise program. A control group doing stretching exercises did not show this brain growth nor the improvement in decision-making ability. It looks like *aerobic* exercise is the key. How much aerobic exercise did they use?

The answer is one of the most important aspects of their study: the exercise program was *walking*. That's it. Walking three times a week, 45 minutes per day, for six months produced these changes. You can reverse the brain atrophy associated with mood problems by using antidepressants, as discussed in Chapter 7, and now it appears that a very attainable level of exercise might produce the same kind of changes. Perhaps you can see why I'd love to require everyone who wants an antidepressant to produce their pedometer results first. However, *knowing* the benefits is not enough to get people exercising. The results reported here are only the most recent. The mental and physical health benefits of exercise have been known for decades. (I published a summary of them as a medical student in 1987!) So what is keeping people from *doing* what they know will help them?

Why Don't More People Exercise?

We are fools, we humans. Just look at us. We use more trees than we plant, eat more fish than can reproduce, burn fuel as though it will last more than just the next thirty to forty years, and pretend the ice caps aren't melting. We ought to face it: we're not very good at looking at long-term risks. Instead, we look right in front of us and see our children's needs, the boss's expectations, or things that strike us as requiring attention right now (paying the bills, improving relationships with the neighbor, calling home to reassure Mom that the roof didn't fall in during last night's storm—doesn't that list just go on and on?).

We ought to face it. Exercise won't start happening regularly in our lives just from hearing another reason why it will be good for us weeks or months (or years) from now. Other priorities will win out nearly every time. For mothers, this is meeting someone else's needs. For good, responsible workers, it is pleasing the boss or the customer. For students, it is the upcoming exam. Benefits tomorrow or preventing a dam-burst today—guess which one wins? You have to have a system that can put exercise in front of almost everything, or it won't happen. That means lowering the barriers or raising the benefits, or both. Since I think the barriers are more of a problem in our society, let's start there.

Lowering the Barriers. Remember these three T's: time, tools, and traditions. Lack any one of them, and your exercise program is in trouble.

1. **Time:** Most people in the United States have tight schedules. Therefore, most people have to *change* their schedule to make room for regular exercise. Exercise is not the routine thing—it's an extra thing. That's a lost battle right there. If you can sit here and believe that exercise is important, you have to find a time for it. When I show you how easy the exercise program is, you may conclude that it might fit, after all.

2. **Tools:** Do you have what you need already at hand? If you think you need a gym membership and don't currently have one, there's a huge barrier. If you need a bicycle, and don't have one, same story. But you do have several pairs of shoes, right?

3. **Traditions:** I needed a *T* version of the word *habit, norm,* or *routine*. You don't decide to brush your teeth at night. You don't think, oh, I'm looking forward to brushing my teeth tonight. You just do it because you always do it. In our modern world, among readers of this book at least, you need to make exercise *routine*. If you have to *decide* to exercise, rather than just proceed with it as you always do, there are too many chances that you'll decide to do something else (putting out the burning fire du jour, most likely).

Raising the Benefits. Ideally, you'd be planning some kind of exercise that is actually fun. That's how kids do it, right? When did we stop using their approach, and why? When you look at what urban U.S. adults do for exercise, you'd think they aren't really interested in *fun* anymore. If you personally can figure out a way to get exercise while doing something you think is fun, what a bonus that would be—and how much more likely it is that you'd actually do it. Are we really that short of ideas on how to have fun while moving around? Just to jog your thinking, here's one I've found to be so much fun I have to tell myself to stop (which is a pretty good marker for what we're after). You know how many NordicTrack machines are out there for sale? They're everywhere in my little town. Try one with a pair of radio headphones on and go with the music. This ought to be the craze!

If you can't find something *fun*, better increase the benefits some other way. Here are two more: first, you can try charting your progress. Many people are motivated by seeing themselves make gains. Pick an outcome that is very likely to change, such as speed, endurance, strength, skill, or heart rate at a given level of exertion. (Don't pick weight. That might follow very slowly, which is what you want, since rapid loss is regained more than 90 percent of the time.) You can even chart the exercise itself—what you did and how long you did it—because that in itself is an achievement for many people. You can include your exercise on your mood charting (from Chapter 6). My website has a modified Harvard chart with exercise included, right there on the home page.

If you're going to increase your exercise to help treat mood symptoms, chart those symptoms themselves as well. Then when your exercise decreases, you might notice your mood symptoms are worse. (Trust me, it will decrease. A former Boston marathon winner said, "You're never in shape. You're either getting in shape or getting out of shape.") If your mood symptoms get better when you pick up your exercise again, then you have direct evidence that you personally do benefit from exercise. That's a great incentive.

Finally, if some significant others around you will benefit from your exercise program (because your mood will be better), you can measure their benefit as well as your own, and use that as an additional incentive. Are they acting nicer toward you? Are they less angry or crying less? It's probably best not to recruit them any more directly, however, such as allowing them to prod, coach, or remind you. This can undermine your sense that in the long run, you are working on getting more exercise for your own benefit, not for theirs. Too often their prodding may create additional resistance on your part, particularly if you can feel them blaming you somehow.

Are You Ready for a Simple Program?

If you just heard "no" inside your head, it must be coming from your head. What I mean is that the "no" really can't be coming from your body. You might have a bad knee or a weak leg, but for any physical limitation you can think of, someone somewhere has overcome that limitation somehow. Whatever you think is holding you back from some kind of regular physical activity is much more likely to be a mental thing than a physical thing. Almost always, the limiting factor is motivation (time, money, or other resource barriers are not far behind). Of course, motivation is not a depressed person's strength, right? If you have depression, you know that cooking dinner is hard enough. Look, even people who *aren't* depressed don't exercise regularly: most surveys indicate that at least half of all Americans get no regular physical activity. (And surely those who said they did exaggerated when asked. Wouldn't you?) So if *they* can't, or at least don't, why should we expect that *you* can? After all, you're the one with the mood problem, right?

Ah, but there's an irony here, one that you might be able to use to your advantage. *Motivation* may not be necessary! Motivation is a feeling, right? It's an inclination, a state of energy and willingness. Yet all the time, people act differently than they feel, right? I feel like yelling at my kid, but I *choose* to wait, calm down a little, and speak softly but firmly. So maybe you *don't need* to be motivated.

Maybe what you're looking for is the ability to do something different than what you feel like doing. That is a problem for a lot of people, and more so for people with mood problems! Being less impulsive and more deliberate about your choices can be very hard, especially when your emotions have too much hold on you. But how bad are things for you right now? Are they so bad that you're not in control of your behavior? For Mood Spectrum conditions, this would be very unusual. More likely, you probably are concluding that in reality, you *could* choose to get more exercise, but you are *choosing* not to do so. That's good news, because it means that at any point in time, perhaps today, you could choose otherwise. As you'll see, the exercise program I recommend is one that you really could do *today*.

For those of you who are very depressed, you might think that the depression itself is holding you back. You might think this whole exercise idea has to wait until you're feeling better. But that doesn't have to be the case. One depressed patient said to me, "I agree it is very difficult to walk when one is suffering depression, but I have forced myself out the door many times, knowing from experience I will feel better when I return home."

Here's Your Exercise Program

You may have answered, "Yes, I'm ready—but I don't *do* it!" You're in a big club there! You're like about half the U.S. population, as a matter of fact. All right then, let's try a different approach. Here we go. Please, stop right now, stop thinking about exercise in the way you've thought of it before. You didn't *do* it that way, so you may as well stop right now! Think of it in a different way. This way is called *sustainability*. If we're really serious about this exercise business as a health thing, we ought to be thinking very long term. So some exercise you might do for a while, but then completely abandon—nah, that's no good. Let's look for something so simple and easy you could almost put it in there with brushing your teeth.

Let's think about what kind of physical activity you could do repeatedly for a long time and not skip very often. In my view, the one that wins over everything else by a long shot is—brace yourself—going with a friend . . . nearly every day . . . for a short walk. Notice the friend part. That's *almost* as important as the walk part. Your friend will be out there when you're not really "feeling like it," but she or he will be waiting on you. That's a better motivator for most humans than their own health benefits.

Walking has the absolute best record for easy access. The director of the Bipolar Clinic associated with Harvard, Dr. Gary Sachs, says, "Here's your exercise program: go to the door, look at your watch. Walk 7.5 minutes in any direction, then turn around and walk home. Do that five days a week at least." And that's it. As I recall he calculated the average American would lose five pounds a year doing that. (There is the usual recommendation that people forty to forty-five years old or older have an evaluation by their doctor before starting an exercise program. So if you're going to do this today, then you might need to make an appointment with your doctor first. It seems a bit odd to me that I have to warn you about *walking*, but this is America.)

I often tell my patients that they don't have to tell anybody (except their walking buddy) about their exercise, because they don't need any additional pressure of family or friends' hopeful expectations. You know what I mean? Suppose you tell them you've started an exercise program and they watch to see if you're doing it. Then if you're not doing it, you're liable to get some comment or some look. Your resentment at being told what to do could come out by, whoops, not getting the walk in today. So try staying mum: just tell them you're going for a little walk and will be back in about fifteen minutes. That will do for today.

Pay Yourself First

There's a book series out there on how to be a rich businessman, entitled *Rich Dad, Poor Dad*. (I can't quite get the hang of it. Too bad the book doesn't pay a little more attention to the social consequences of everyone trying to be rich.) Anyway, there is a striking idea in these books: pay yourself first. The author says that you shouldn't put your money in savings *after* you've paid the electric bill, gas bill, insurance bill, and so on, but put the money in savings *first*! Wait a minute, you say, what if you're out of money at the end of the month and can't pay those basic bills? Ah, he says, doing it this way will show you: either you need to reduce your expenses or make more money—but either way, the most important step for your future has already been taken.

Interesting idea, don't you think? It sure made me think. It's so opposite from the usual, responsible way of handling money. Note that the key idea is to make your future such a priority that it gets *top position*. Assume that otherwise, the daily stuff is so much more obvious to you—after all, there's that bill from the gas company right there on the table—that you risk, every month, not being able to invest in your own future.

You can see how his idea applies in the context of your exercise: if everybody else's needs get taken care of before you take care of investing in your own future, then every day your long-term needs are pushed to the bottom of the list, behind that long list of more obvious, more immediate needs. Isn't that pretty close to your experience? What would happen if you paid yourself first? Aren't all of those other needs, even your kids', less important in the long run than *your* physical and emotional good health? After all, you can't really help them very well if your end of the boat is sinking.

Practicing and Preaching

You might be wondering if I really *do* what I'm recommending. Well, yes, although my life is probably much easier to structure than yours. Being one's own boss helps an awful lot. (Although someone told me, "Being your own boss allows you to choose *which* eighty hours a week you work.") In the last week, as I wrote this chapter, I did a different form of exercise every single day. In general, I start every day with a plan for where, how, and when the exercise is going to happen: bike to work, a quick paddle up the river, tap dance class—or perhaps today's schedule is such that I better grab some time on the NordicTrack machine before everything else gets going. Every day—have some fun. Now put the book down, walk to your front door, open it, and take one step outside.

CHAPTER 14

How Family and Friends
Can Help

Bipolar I, with the potential for full manic episodes and the patient's frequent complete lack of insight, presents major challenges for "significant others" (SOs) like family members, lovers, and friends. Dr. Miklowitz' book, *The Bipolar Disorder Survival Guide*, discussed in Chapter 12, is strongly oriented toward Bipolar I and its challenges. So is one of the best resources for friends and families, bpso.org (short for bipolar significant others), and many Internet resources. These resources can still be of great value for SOs of people whose symptoms lie in the middle of the Mood Spectrum, and I recommend them to you, particularly bpso.org. But how do the challenges differ when your loved one has a more subtle bipolar variation? As you've learned in this book, in people with Mood Spectrum variations, depression symptoms predominate, but other features are also present: recurrence, agitation and insomnia, or irritability, for example. How are you supposed to deal with all this?

In deference to readers who picked up this book because they have mood symptoms, I've only *outlined* here five important concepts (and a thought on dealing with doctors). For SOs, I recommend a much-expanded version of this chapter that would not fit in this book: just go to the Notes page on my website, psychedu cation.org/notes.htm, and take the Chapter 14 link to a full presentation of these principles, a chapter as long as most in this book.

From this point on in this chapter, I'll be speaking to the significant others. Of course, I fully expect that if *you* are the one with the symptoms, you'll want to know what I'm telling them! That's fine. Read along.

As a general strategy, nothing is better than learning *a lot* about what your loved one is dealing with, and thus what *you* are dealing with. I hope this book, and some of the links provided, have helped. Don't forget that. The most important step is to understand what's going on as best you can.

Now, let's take a look at my approach as a therapist and medication prescriber—because your role and your challenges are similar, in some significant ways. Moreover, most of these ideas are unusual, if not downright paradoxical, so you probably would not think them all up on your own. Experience might teach you—but maybe I can save you a few steps.

First, Do No Harm

They taught us this in medical school. In many cases, you may not be able to help much, they said; but at least, while you're trying, don't make things worse. How might you SOs be at risk for making things worse? One of the most common ways is judging. This is a normal, natural thing for humans to do; our brain is built for it. But acting on judgmental thoughts can damage relationships, which you need to preserve or you lose traction on everyday problems.

Don't Just Do Something, Sit There

You know the phrase "Don't just sit there, do something!" *Doing* is usually what happens when your loved one is feeling bad, and you want to make that stop: you try to calm them, tell them everything will be all right, point out the good side of things, help them shift their attention elsewhere. But as a therapist I learned that often it's best to let those feelings stay right there so we can see them better. Even more important, I do this so that my client sees that having these feelings is acceptable, understandable, and not as scary as it seems, and that while holding them right there, as bad as they are, they can become more manageable. It becomes more OK to just have them. This also helps avoid sending messages such as, "Don't have those feelings. Stop having them now. I can't handle it." Try sitting and listening well, rather than doing, and see how that goes.

Ask, Don't Tell: Collaborating

You want a certain behavior to increase or decrease, but every time you push, you just get a push back. A different approach emphasizes collaboration and begins with learning what your loved one is trying to achieve with these behaviors, and then comparing what you are hoping for. If some common ground can be found, it will be much easier to work together. For example, placing the emphasis on decreasing irritability, rather than on taking a particular medication, can put you on the same team.

Setting Boundaries

You want to stay in this relationship for the long haul. Therefore, you'd better make sure your approach is *sustainable*. Imagine doing what you're doing for years. Can you keep it up? Can you be the good listener for all that suffering? Can you be the first responder to every crisis? In the website chapter, we examine the "patchwork quilt model" where you are one square among many, so that if you occasionally are unavailable, your loved one is still warm. We also consider my mentor's maxim: "Never worry alone," and look at developing safety plans for those who need them—before they need them.

The Problem of Insight

This book is fine for people who know there's something wrong with their moods. What about those who don't? How are you supposed to cope with repeated episodes of irritability and destructive behavior that your SO does not recognize as such, or with someone who simply refuses to get help? Beyond a good book on this issue for severe mental illness, *I'm Not Sick, I Don't Need Help*, what else is there? Time to learn about "Stages of Change" and "Motivational Interviewing," both developed for substance use problems. The general idea is to recognize the person's willingness to change (everybody has at least a tiny, tiny bit) and tailor your strategies to that degree of readiness.

Finally, what do you do if your loved one's doctor does not encourage your involvement? At minimum, provide information (voice mail, e-mail, snail mail). Many people don't know that they can leave information for the doctor anytime. It's getting information that requires a release of information form, signed by the patient. So if you think your husband won't tell the doctor about problems he's been having, you can leave the doctor a voice mail or write a note. Be careful about how you do this. Remember Chapter 6 on working with the doctor: this, too, is a relationship that must be managed for the long term. If in doubt, ask to be told if you're doing something the doctor might not appreciate. Remember, make yourself useful, an efficient resource (lots of information the doctor can use, not much time or effort to get it), and you're more likely to find an open channel for communication.

Concluding Thoughts

You are probably quite ready to be done with this book. I hope it has not been overwhelming—so much seemed important to discuss. Remember, I've placed more detailed information, references, and links on the Notes page: psycheducation.org/notes .htm. Here we are about to finish. I have some thoughts for you, before you go. Among the many topics we've examined, we have one more to consider. (All right, there are at least twenty more, but I've got to stop somewhere, right? Many of those other topics are addressed on my website.) You should understand, if you haven't arrived there already, that coming to terms with an illness like a Mood Spectrum condition can be very slow and difficult. These illnesses can limit your freedom, require medications with significant side effects, and cause symptoms that are often hard to recognize as symptoms. All the while, you may be wondering: will this illness be with me for years?

I've put off this issue all the way through the book. Just trying to help you learn about bipolarity is much easier than the task of helping you learn to accept the illness. Yet at some point you must turn this mood problem from *the* illness into *your* illness. When I first saw that expression, I thought it was just the turn of phrase I needed for this chapter. But every time I wrote it down, I stumbled over it. Finally it occurred to me: as patients have shown me, this transformation of the illness from an abstract concept that you learn about, to something you recognize in yourself and accept, is extremely difficult. For most people it is more like a process, which often takes years and goes through different stages. People may deny for a time (sometimes forever) that they have a mood problem. They can be angry about having been given this illness, by their genes or their stresses (or more abstractly, God or their parents). They can feel overwhelmed or defeated by the task of getting their symptoms under control. They can go through phases of sadness or grief about being afflicted with this illness, even when they are not in a depressed phase.

For example, imagine that you just blew up at your spouse. Or you broke down into tears during a commercial. Or you found yourself worrying nonstop about a project that was basically complete, yet you couldn't leave it alone. People find themselves asking, "Is this me or is this my mood condition? Are these symptoms or is this just something anyone would do, or feel, or think?" The model presented in the first few chapters of this book may come to mind, in which you saw that there is no clear dividing line between normal and symptomatic. Yet obviously that's no answer to the question; indeed, it just makes the puzzle all the more difficult, right?

Treatment should help with this question. The easiest way to know for sure what's going on is to get your mood symptoms controlled. Ideally, you'll reach a point where you are no longer having *any cycling* of mood or energy. At that point, whatever you're seeing is more likely to be you. In the meantime, I tell patients who are having significant symptoms or obvious cycling to avoid making big plans, decisions, or arriving at any major judgments. For example, I hope that during this time people will avoid reaching conclusions such as, "My mother is hopeless, I just can't communicate with her" or "I hate my job." These should be put on hold as much as possible. This is especially important at the beginning of treatment when people often can improve substantially in a fairly short period of time and thus find themselves with a more stable, broader view of the questions and decisions they face.

In general, you should recognize that accepting the reality of a long-term mood condition takes time. Open expression of the frustrations and challenges this poses, with a diary, counselor from church, or therapist, as well as with your psychiatrist (if he or she can allow you the time for this), may help with this process.

Notice the absence in that sentence of family, friends, coworkers, whom you may find it wise to spare these frustrations. Use them for more positive support roles if there is any risk that you might burn them out with what might sound like frequent complaining to them.

Anyone writing a book hopes that someone will actually read the thing, all the way to the end. In writing the very last few sentences, the author likely imagines a reader, such as you, who has come all this way with her or him. So I am imagining you, whose time and effort in working through this book I appreciate.

In bringing this book to a close, I am imagining what I might want to say to you before you go. First, I want to convey my regret that you have had symptoms such that reading this book has been necessary. My patients have shown me how painful and difficult that can be. Second, you can understand my hope that the book has been useful to you somehow, or to those around you whose support you value. And last, here is my wish that your symptoms diminish, and that you find increasing capacity to tolerate and accept what does not seem to change.

Selected References

Remember, for more information see psycheducation.org/notes .htm, where you can find further explanations, links to useful resources, all of the following references and many more—all linked to their summaries (abstracts). A typical listing of published sources, however, is also necessary for a subset of references, thus the following.

Chapter 1: Understanding the Mood Spectrum and How It Can Help You

Akiskal, H. S., and G. Mallya. "Criteria for the 'Soft' Bipolar Spectrum: Treatment Implications." *Psychopharmacol Bull* 23, no. 1 (1987): 68–73.

Benazzi, F. "Bipolar II Disorder and Major Depressive Disorder: Continuity or Discontinuity?" *World J Biol Psychiatry* 4, no. 4 (Oct. 2003): 166–71.

Diagnostic and Statistical Manual of Mental Disorders, 4th ed. Washington, D.C.: American Psychiatric Association, 2000.

Chapter 2: Can You Be a Little Bipolar? Recognizing Hypomania

Benazzi, F. "Mixed States in Bipolar II Disorder: Should Full Hypomania Always Be Required?" *Psychiatry Res* 172, no. 3 (July 15, 2004): 247–57.

Judd, L. L., H. S. Akiskal, P. J. Schettler, W. Coryell, J. Endicott, J. D. Maser, D. A. Solomon, A.C. Leon, and M. B. Keller. "A Prospective Investigation of the Natural History of the Long-Term Weekly Symptomatic Status of Bipolar II Disorder." *Arch Gen Psychiatry* 60, no. 3 (March 2003): 261–69.

Chapter 3: No Mania or Hypomania? Understanding "Soft" Bipolar Disorder

Maskall, D. D, R. W. Lam, S. Misri, D. Carter, A. J. Kuan, L. N. Yatham, and A. P. Zis. "Seasonality of Symptoms in Women with Late Luteal Phase Dysphoric Disorder." *Am J Psychiatry* 154, no. 10 (October 1997): 1436–41.

Praschak-Rieder, N., M. Willeit, A. Neumeister, E. Hilger, J. Stastny, N. Thierry, E. Lenzinger, and S. Kasper. "Prevalence of Premenstrual Dysphoric Disorder in Female Patients with Seasonal Affective Disorder." *J Affect Disord* 63, no. 1–3 (March 2001): 239–42.

Chapter 4: Making *Your* Diagnosis

Geller, B., B. Zimerman, M. Williams, K. Bolhofner, and J. L. Craney. "Bipolar Disorder at Prospective Follow-up of Adults Who Had Prepubertal Major Depressive Disorder." *Am J Psychiatry* 158, no. 1 (January 2001): 125–27.

Ghaemi, S. Nassir, C. J. Miller, D. A. Berv, J. Klugman, K. J. Rosenquist, and R. W. Pies. "Sensitivity and Specificity of a New Bipolar Spectrum Diagnostic Scale." *J Affect Disord* 84, no. 2–3 (February 2005): 273–77.

Goldberg, J. F., M. Harrow, and J. E. Whiteside. "Risk for Bipolar Illness in Patients Initially Hospitalized for Unipolar Depression." *Am J Psychiatry* 158, no. 8 (August 2001): 1265–70.

Phelps, J. R. "Agitated Dysphoria After Late-Onset Loss of Response to Antidepressants: A Case Report." *J Affect Disord* 86, no. 2–3 (June 2005): 277–80.

Chapter 5: What Else Could It Be? Ruling Out Conditions That Mimic Bipolar Disorder

Barlow, D. H., J. M. Gorman, M. K. Shear, and S. W. Woods. "The Comorbidity of Bipolar and Anxiety Disorders: Prevalence, Psychobiology, and Treatment Issues." *J Affect Disord* 68 no. 1 (February 2002): 1–23.

Cole, D. P., M. E. Thase, A. G. Mallinger, J. C. Soares, J. F. Luther, D. J. Kupfer, and E. Frank. "Slower Treatment Response in Bipolar Depression Predicted by Lower Pretreatment Thyroid Function." *Am J Psychiatry* 159, no. 1 (January 2002): 116–21.

Freeman, M. P., S. A. Freeman, and S. L. McElroy. "The Comorbidity of Bipolar and Anxiety Disorders: Prevalence, Psychobiology, and Treatment Issues." *J Affect Disord* 68, no. 1 (February 2002): 1–23.

Geller, B., B. Zimerman, M. Williams, M. P. Delbello, J. Frazier, and L. Beringer. "Phenomenology of Prepubertal and Early Adolescent Bipolar Disorder: Examples of Elated Mood, Grandiose Behaviors, Decreased Need for Sleep, Racing Thoughts and Hypersexuality." *J Child Adolesc Psychopharmacol* 12, no. 1 (Spring 2002): 3–9.

Gitlin, M., L. L. Altshuler, M. A. Frye, R. Suri, E. L. Huynh, L. Fairbanks, M. Bauer, and S. Korenman. "Peripheral Thyroid Hormones and Response to Selective Serotonin Reuptake Inhibitors." *J Psychiatry Neurosci* 29, no. 5 (September 2004): 383–86.

Prior, J. C., Y. Vigna, D. Sciarretta, N. Alojado, and M. Schulzer. "Conditioning Exercise Decreases Premenstrual Symptoms: A Prospective, Controlled 6-Month Trial." *Fertil Steril* 47, no. 3 (March 1987): 402–8.

Scheffer, R. E., R. A. Kowatch, T. Carmody, and A. J. Rush. "Randomized, Placebo-Controlled Trial of Mixed Amphetamine Salts for Symptoms of Comorbid ADHD in Pediatric Bipolar Disorder After Mood Stabilization with Divalproex Sodium." *Am J Psychiatry* 162, no. 1 (January 2005): 58–64.

Steege, J. F., and J. A. Blumenthal. "The Effects of Aerobic Exercise on Premenstrual Symptoms in Middle-Aged Women: A Preliminary Study." *J Psychosom Res* 37, no. 2 (1993): 127–33.

Thys-Jacobs, S., P. Starkey, D. Bernstein, and J. Tian. "Calcium Carbonate and the Premenstrual Syndrome: Effects on Premenstrual and Menstrual Symptoms." *Am J Obstet Gynecol* 179, no. 2 (August 1998): 444–52.

Chapter 7: Where to Start: Guidelines for Choosing Treatment

Chlebowski, R. T., S. L. Hendrix, R. D. Langer, M. L. Stefanick, M. Gass, D. Lane, R. J. Rodabough, M. A. Gilligan, M. G. Cyr, C. A. Thomson, J. Khandekar, H. Petrovitch, and A. McTiernan; WHI Investigators. "Influence of Estrogen Plus Progestin on Breast Cancer and Mammography in Healthy Postmenopausal Women: The Women's Health Initiative Randomized Trial." *JAMA* 289, no. 24 (June 25, 2003): 3243–53.

Chapter 8: Mood Stabilizers: The Core Ingredient in Medication Treatment

Bauer, M. S., and L. Mitchner. "What Is a 'Mood Stabilizer'? An Evidence-Based Response." *Am J Psychiatry* 161, no. 1 (January 2004): 3–18.

Nemeroff, C. B., D. L. Evans, L. Gyulai, G. S. Sachs, C. L. Bowden, I. P. Gergel, R. Oakes, and C. D. Pitts. "Double-Blind, Placebo-Controlled Comparison of Imipramine and Paroxetine in the Treatment of Bipolar Depression." *Am J Psychiatry* 158, no. 6 (June 2001): 906–12.

Chapter 9: What You Need to Know When Considering Antidepressants

El-Mallakh, R. S., and A. Karippot. "Use of Antidepressants to Treat Depression in Bipolar Disorder." *Psychiatr Serv* 53, no. 5 (May 2002): 580–84.

Ghaemi, S. N., D. J. Hsu, F. Soldani, and F. K. Goodwin. "Anti-depressants in Bipolar Disorder: The Case for Caution." *Bipolar Disord* 5, no. 6 (December 2003): 421–33.

Ghaemi, S. N., M. S. Lenox, and R. J. Baldessarini. "Effectiveness and Safety of Long-Term Antidepressant Treatment in Bipolar Disorder." *J Clin Psychiatry* 62, no. 7 (July 2001): 565–69.

Gijsman, H. J., J. R. Geddes, R. M. Rendell, W. A. Nolen, and G. M. Goodwin. "Antidepressants for Bipolar Depression: A Systematic Review of Randomized, Controlled Trials." *Am J Psychiatry* 161, no. 9 (September 2004): 1537–47.

Goldberg, J. F., and C. J. Truman. "Antidepressant-Induced Mania: An Overview of Current Controversies." *Bipolar Disord* 5, no. 6 (December 2003): 407–20.

Wehr, T., and F. K. Goodwin. "Tricyclics Modulate Frequency of Mood Cycles." *Chronobiologia* 6, no. 4 (October–December 1979): 377–85.

Winsberg, M. E., S. G. DeGolia, C. M. Strong, and T. A. Ketter. "Divalproex Therapy in Medication-Naive and Mood-Stabilizer-Naive Bipolar II Depression." *J Affect Disord* 67, no. 1–3 (December 2001): 207–12.

Chapter 10: Managing Weight Gain from Medications or Other Causes

Hoeger, K. M., L. Kochman, N. Wixom, K. Craig, R. K. Miller, and D. S. Guzick. "A Randomized, 48-week, Placebo-Controlled Trial of Intensive Lifestyle Modification and/or Metformin Therapy in Overweight Women with Polycystic Ovary Syndrome: A Pilot Study." *Fertil Steril* 82, no. 2 (August 2004): 421–29.

Morrison, J. A., E. M. Cottingham, and B. A. Barton. "Metformin for Weight Loss in Pediatric Patients Taking Psychotropic Drugs." *Am J Psychiatry* 159, no. 4 (April 2002): 655–57.

Chapter 11: Simple Lifestyle Changes That Can Improve Symptoms

Barbini, B., F. Benedetti, C. Colombo, D. Dotoli, A. Bernasconi, M. Cigala-Fulgosi, M. Florita, and E. Smeraldi. "Dark Therapy for Mania: A Pilot Study." *Bipolar Disord* 7, no. 1 (February 2005): 98–101.

Frank, E., D. J. Kupfer, M. E. Thase, A. G. Mallinger, H. A. Swartz, A. M. Fagiolini, V. Grochocinski, P. Houck, J. Scott, W. Thompson, and T. Monk. "Two-Year Outcomes for Interpersonal and Social Rhythm Therapy in Individuals with Bipolar I Disorder." *Arch Gen Psychiatry* 62, no. 9 (September 2005): 996–1004.

Voderholzer, U., G. Weske, S. Ecker, D. Riemann, H. Gann, and M. Berger. "Neurobiological Findings Before and During Successful Lithium Therapy of a Patient with 48-Hour Rapid-Cycling Bipolar Disorder." *Neuropsychobiology* 45, Suppl. no. 1 (2002): 13–19.

Chapter 12: How to Use Psychotherapy Across the Mood Spectrum

Colom, F., E. Vieta, A. Martinez-Aran, M. Reinares, J. M. Goikolea, A. Benabarre, C. Torrent, M. Comes, B. Corbella, P. Parramon, and J. Corominas. "A Randomized Trial on the Efficacy of Group Psychoeducation in the Prophylaxis of Recurrences in Bipolar Patients Whose Disease Is in Remission." *Arch Gen Psychiatry* 60, no. 4 (April 2003): 402–07.

Perry, A., N. Tarrier, R. Morriss, E. McCarthy, and K. Limb. "Randomised Controlled Trial of Efficacy of Teaching Patients with Bipolar Disorder to Identify Early Symptoms of Relapse and Obtain Treatment." *BMJ* 318, no. 7177 (January 16, 1999): 149–53.

Rea, M. M., M. C. Tompson, D. J. Miklowitz, M. J. Goldstein, S. Hwang, and J. Mintz. "Family-Focused Treatment Versus

Individual Treatment for Bipolar Disorder: Results of a Randomized Clinical Trial." *J Affect Disord* 82, no. 3 (November 1, 2004): 343–52.

Chapter 13: Exercise: Not the Usual Rap

Babyak, M., J. A. Blumenthal, S. Herman, P. Khatri, M. Doraiswamy, K. Moore, W. E. Craighead, T. T. Baldewicz, and K. R. Krishnan. "Exercise Treatment for Major Depression: Maintenance of Therapeutic Benefit at 10 Months." *Psychosom Med* 62, no. 5 (September–October, 2000): 633–38.

Colcombe, S. J., A. F. Kramer, K. I. Erickson, P. Scalf, E. McAuley, N. J. Cohen, A. Webb, G. J. Jerome, D. X. Marquez, and S. Elavsky. "Cardiovascular Fitness, Cortical Plasticity, and Aging." *Proc Natl Acad Sci* U.S.A. 101, no. 9 (March 2, 2004): 3316–21.

Index

Monoamine oxidase
inhibitor (MAOI)
antidepressants,
weight gain and, 197
Mood, metabolic syndrome
and, 195–96
Mood Disorder
Questionnaire
(MDQ), 75–76
Mood disorders
atrophic factors of,
133–34
causes of, 130–34
guidelines for managing
variations of,
134–41
strategies for treating
complex, 141–46
trophic factors of,
131–33
Mood instability,
antidepressants and,
172–84
Mood problems
reproductive hormones
and, 85
thyroid status and,
83–85
Mood Spectrum, 3
for diagnosing bipolar
variations, 10
vs. *Diagnostic and
Statistical Manual of
Mental Disorders
(DSM)*, 7–9
hypomania and, 29–30

Mood Stabilizer Spectrum,
149–50
Mood stabilizers, 43, 48,
142–43, 147–48
antidepressants and
preventing
response to
treatment with,
178–79
balancing hope and
realism when
using, 165–66
carbamazeine (cbz),
152
choosing most
important qualities
of, 159–61
comparative studies of,
164–65
considerations for
choosing, 157–58
expert opinions and,
163–65
FDA approval for,
161–62
length of time required
for taking, 166–67
lithium, 142, 150–51
oxcarbazepine (oxc),
152
pharmaceutical
companies and,
163–65
resources for, 148–49
risks of taking, 167–68
side effects of, 168

About the Author

Jim Phelps, M.D., has been practicing psychiatry for two decades and specializing in treating bipolar disorder for the past ten years. He is currently collaborating with Dr. Nassir Ghaemi (associate professor of psychiatry and director of the Bipolar Disorder Research Program at Emory University) on helping develop bipolar diagnostic guidelines for clinicians to use in primary care, and on a position statement for the International Society for Bipolar Disorders (ISBD) on the diagnosis of bipolar variations, to be published in 2006. Dr. Phelps heads the Bipolar Spectrum subgroup for the ISBD.

Following a residency in psychiatry at the University of New Mexico, he spent a year there in a fellowship position in medical education, then worked for the family practice and psychiatry departments, earning the Teacher of the Year award in both departments.

He moved to Corvallis, Oregon, in 1994 to raise his family in a small town. Once there he began to focus on complex mood disorders, in both an inpatient setting and a consultation role with local primary care doctors. He is a member of the American Psychiatric Association, the International Society for Affective Disorders, and the ISBD. He presented his website, PsychEducation .org, which discusses bipolar variations, the possible risks of antidepressants, and many other aspects of mood disorder care, at the 2004 ISBD meeting in Sydney. The website has been number one on the Google search engine for years when searching *Bipolar II* and several other topics.

Dr. Phelps maintains a private practice of psychiatry in Corvallis, while expanding his teaching and writing. He continues to add to PsychEducation.org with the goal of providing patients, families, and primary care physicians with user-friendly information about complex mood disorders, promoting routine use of evidence for health-related claims, and fostering collaboration between patients and their doctors through education. He has authored journal articles for *American Journal of Medicine, Academic Psychiatry, Academic Medicine,* and the *Journal of Affective Disorders* and speaks on bipolar disorder throughout the Pacific Northwest.